RENCONTRES
536

Mentoring through the Centuries

This volume was published with the support
of the University of Melbourne and La Trobe University

Mentoring through the Centuries

On the Dynamics of Personal and Professional Growth

Edited by Véronique Duché and Gregoria Manzin

PARIS
CLASSIQUES GARNIER
2022

Véronique Duché is A.R. Chisholm chair of French at the University of Melbourne. A specialist in early modern French literature, she is particularly interested in the history of translation.

Gregoria Manzin is Lecturer in Italian Studies at La Trobe University. She specialises in the study of contemporary Italian literature, with a specific interest in women – both as writers and characters.

ISBN 978-2-406-12919-6 (livre broché)
ISBN 978-2-406-12920-2 (livre relié)
ISSN 2103-5636

PREFACE

Many of us are or have been mentors. Many of us are or have been mentees. And in a context of peer or reverse mentoring, many of us – at whatever career stage we might be – fall into both categories simultaneously, with the self-reflexivity this situation affords us serving more broadly to enhance our understandings of the practice of mentorship. Although present in multiple forms and across most areas of human activity, mentoring is increasingly part of the set of professional responsibilities expected, in particular of more senior staff, across a wide variety of sectors. It manifests itself formally and informally within most organisations. It can be a voluntary activity outside fixed structures, offered for example by professional associations to those aspiring to success in a particular career path. Mentoring can also be an invaluable means of enhancing the presence of those in underrepresented groups in a specific profession or organisation, and may address perennial issues of under-recognition associated with promotion either delayed or denied. In short, mentoring takes multiple forms, is conducted in multiple contexts, responds to multiple motivations and lends itself to multiple outcomes.

For some, to act as a mentor is an ethical responsibility as they attempt to ensure that the profession they eventually leave is more equitable and representative than the one they initially entered; in this way, it can be a means of indirectly repaying a debt to those who previously mentored them; but for others, the task becomes a chore, an undervalued activity that prevents them from focusing on aspects of their work that they consider more visible and more valuable. Any such scepticism can additionally be increased by the advent of a mentoring industry, associated with training programmes, jargon, formal accreditation, the apparatus of consultancy – and a sense that mentoring risks on occasion being a fundamentally corporate and even conservative practice, a cloning model aimed at compliance and perpetuation of a status quo rather than at the forms of creative and (on occasion) disruptive questioning associated with genuine personal and professional growth. At its best, however, mentoring still involves a transfer of knowledge and experience from which both mentor and mentee can learn reciprocally. It is more open-ended than goal-oriented coaching in its creation of a supportive environment in which a mentee can test ideas and explore options in ways that may not be feasible in more formal supervision. Moreover, mentoring as a practice continues to evolve beyond its first historical manifestations. The traditional one-to-one model has given way to other configurations, such as mentoring in groups, and any insistence on the value of face-to-face meetings has been challenged by the new possibilities afforded by digital technologies. And the transgenerational logic of a hierarchical apprenticeship approach, whereby an established practitioner shares their insight with a newer recruit, is deliberately disrupted by the new dynamics of processes such as reverse mentoring, which encourage an ostensibly more experienced mentee to be guided by a more junior mentor in order to see the world (or at the very least the workplace) through fresh eyes.

Just as definitions of mentoring are capacious, covering a variety of understandings of the practice outlined already, so its historical roots may be seen as equally expansive. The origins of the term and practice are well rehearsed, associated with precedents in ancient history and classical literature that have been persistently instrumental in shaping understandings of the role of mentor and mentee and the processes in which they engage. The roots of mentoring are often seen to derive from Greek myth, specifically from the character Mentor, son of Alcimus, who became in later life a friend of and counsellor to Odysseus. On Odysseus's departure for the Trojan War, he passed to Mentor responsibility for his son Telemachus, reflecting in the process the transgenerational transfer of knowledge and experience with which mentoring is now often associated. It is striking, however, that Mentor's influence remains largely ineffective, with more valuable advice being provided at the point when the Goddess Athene, whose influence is evident throughout Homer's *Odyssey*, takes on his appearance to offer more targeted guidance to Telemachus. She urges the young man to visit his father's former comrades, whose stories encourage him to undertake a journey of his own in search of Odysseus. This is the process that allows him to develop qualities associated with masculinity and adulthood.

The literary genealogy that begins with Homer extends to Mentor's reappearance in the late seventeenth-century didactic novel by Fénelon, *Les Aventures de Télémaque, fils d'Ulysse*, a critique of the reign of Louis XIV and an advocacy of political and economic models based on cooperation rather than competition. This text fills a gap in the narrative of the *Odyssey*: Mentor accompanies the eponymous Telemachus on his journey through countries such as Egypt, Tyre, Cyprus, Betica and Salentum, dispensing wisdom along the way, but he is again revealed to be both divine and female (on this occasion Minerva, goddess of wisdom, in disguise). The text's influence in eighteenth-century culture, politics and economics, both in France and more broadly, was extensive. The book's reputation was cemented in the 1760s by its inclusion by Rousseau in *Émile, ou De l'éducation*. Here, it is one of only two novels that the protagonist receives during his education, a process completed by a journey during which *Les Aventures de Télémaque* serves in many ways as a guide. Rousseau not only underlines the place of mentoring in a formal educational context, but also provides in his book the frame for a series of key questions posed and answered more broadly in the chapters that follow: in taxonomic terms, how does the mentor differ from the teacher or guide? What are the dynamics linking this mentor and mentee? Is mentoring part of broader processes of social conforming or rather of existential questioning? And how is mentoring different from other, more formal pedagogical processes?

These literary origins serve to underline the ambiguities of mentoring as a practice, and highlight the ways in which cultural and historical representations can help us better explore the lived dynamics that often diverge from conventional understandings of the phenomenon. In this sense, literature has the potential to prize open our understandings of mentorship. It can illustrate what successful (or unsuccessful) mentoring might look like, can set out the multiple contexts (formal and informal, professional and familial) in which mentoring takes place, but also challenges and regularly disrupts our understanding of its functioning. Literary texts can also illuminate those intersections of mentoring with other relational and developmental practices that are often difficult to unpick. Although a gendered and transgenerational form of mentoring is at first implied in the *Odyssey*, in the relationship between Mentor and Telemachus, the advice of the older man, as noted already, proves largely ineffective, and it is Athene's interventions – in the guise of Mentor, and in that sense as the original 'mentor' – that prove definitive in the younger man's development. In Fénelon's novel (as well as in its adoption by Rousseau), the contestatory potential of the mentor's intervention – challenging the status quo and encouraging her mentee to imagine other possible futures – is brought to the fore.

The contributors to the present volume continue this work of attenuation, drawing on a broad corpus of literary representations and historical precedents that go far beyond the now largely predictable origin story associated with Mentor and Telemachus and their various literary re-figurings. The chapters are a reminder of the complex, multidirectional and relational dimensions of mentoring. They provide a framework for considerations of some of the key aspects associated with being human, including the accumulation of wisdom, engaging with the machinations of power, the experience of ageing. Pauline Eaton's study of (quasi-)mentoring relationships with varying degrees of success in two novels by Marie NDiaye is exemplary in this respect, in that it asserts the need for a clearly shared ethical framework for the practice and highlights the perils of entering into such a process without this framework in place. In her work, NDiaye foregrounds issues of equality and power, and focuses on the often unspoken motivations of the mentor and mentee. Her bleak conclusions suggest that the nature of the mentoring dynamic often leads to inequalities between mentor and mentee. At the same time, however, cultural representations can suggest the extent to which the clear taxonomies and responsibilities inherent in this polarised view of mentoring fail to tell the full story. In Fatou Diome's *Celles qui attendent*, for instance, analysed in this volume by Charlotte Mackay, there is a blurring of boundaries in mentoring, with characters acting as neither fully mentor nor mentee, drawn into the process that Umberto Eco described as one based in "love, reciprocal trust and exchange". Several contributors in the chapters that follow focus on similar interrelationship of friendship and mentorship, terms that can become, in often enabling ways, semi-synonymous, although the overlaps between the two may bring with them certain perils in terms of the effectiveness of the mentoring relationship.

In all of these aspects, literature also affords us the potential to help us fathom the affective dimensions of mentoring. In NDiaye, for instance, we seen an almost anthropological interest in dynamics of mentoring, beginning with the initial mutual disclosure that the process requires, passing via the negotiation of a bilateral relationship, and ending in the outcome of the process, expected or unanticipated, positive or negative (or often, more ambiguously, in-between). It is this reciprocity that leads to a focus on issues of emotional detachment and attachment, with an emphasis on the latter leading to the intensity of the experience of mentoring. In the case of Pietro Giordani and Giacomo Leopardi, studied in this volume by Luigi Gussago, a brilliant mentee ultimately outshines his established mentor, leading to the deterioration of their relationship. In another chapter, Mark Nicholls detects a very different relationship between Sergei Diaghilev and Vaslav Nijinsky, one in which friendship tips into eroticism as mentor and mentee become lovers, interdependent in each other's lives. The collaborative potential of the mentoring relationship can be compromised by personal passions or by the narcissism of a mentor for whom only one pathway to development (their own) is feasible. Yet alternative models, with long pedigrees, persist, as Clément Marot and Nicolas Gueudeville's collaborations around the work of Erasmus (explored in this volume by Anne-Laure Metzger-Rambach) make clear. The hallmark of successful mentorship may be seen as the progressive empowerment of the mentee, the creation of a context in which self-reflection can occur, and the ultimate acquisition of independence.

Finally, this collection is a reminder that, while literary and historical sources can assist in the interrogation of mentoring as a practice in the present, a focus on the relationship of mentor and mentee can also allow us to read literature in new ways. Each representation of a mentor-mentee relationship is *sui generis*, a case study in the dynamics of the exchange of knowledge and experience. Foregrounding mentoring permits the reader to consider the distinctiveness of those relationships and to tease out the vectors on which they depend: conventional understandings of mentorship often imply a unilateral process, whereas the chapters in this volume all reveal its more complex bilateral and even multidirectional nature. The focus on the interrelationships between what is customarily a pair of protagonists lends itself to broader considerations of personal motivation, of forms of communication and of the types of longitudinal development that accompanies ageing. At the same time, each instance of mentorship emerges in a particular socio-cultural niche. Carefully contextualised and historicised attention to the practice allows us to understand the changing dynamics – intergenerational and other – of mentorship. Certain texts – such as the *Odyssey* – place mentoring as one of their central considerations, while others benefit more unexpectedly, in often unanticipated ways, from being read through this prism. Charlotte Mackay's analysis of Fatou Diome's work from this perspective suggests fresh and previously unimagined readings, for instance: it reveals how attention to non-traditional mentoring outside a conventional mentorship frame highlights the (a)symmetries of knowledge transfer as well as the ways in which the mentor-mentee relationship can be a means of re-interrogating literary representations of friendship.

As the chapters that follow make clear, the dynamics of the mentoring relationship, with the differing and often divergent motivations of mentor and mentee, are all aspects that lend themselves to creative and often narratological development, the latter in terms of plot, character and mode of focalisation. Mentoring thus supplements more conventional ways of understanding relationships between characters – in terms of friendship, of homosociality, of eroticism – and allows an intense focus on the questions of mutuality, reciprocity and relationality inherent in human and social interaction. The volume is highly suggestive in terms of showing how literary sources and historical examples, beyond those very obvious ones which I too discussed at the opening of this preface, might enhance the ways we conceive of mentorship and improve the means by which we prepare both mentor and mentee for the challenges of the process. At the same time, as Kirk Weeden's study of adapting Molière in contemporary Australia makes clear, it is important to recall that the core activities of the Humanities – reading literature, analysing history, studying human interactions in their multiple forms – are themselves an invaluable form of mentorship in their own right.

Charles Forsdick
University of Liverpool
United Kingdom

MENTORING PARTNERSHIPS AS AVENUES FOR GROWTH

The transmission of knowledge is at the core of any society. Nowadays mentoring programs are thriving in the academic sector as well as in the professional one. The abundance of such programs highlights the interest and the undisputable value attributed to mentoring partnerships. Our contemporary society views them as promising accelerated pathways into knowledge transmission, social change and the fostering of leadership potential. Institutions, multinationals, and governments alike seek to build on the added value we recognise in mentoring. They do so by fashioning formalised mentoring programs which match mentees' expectations with mentors' expertise. Mentoring programs are thus programmatically designed to maximise benefits and ideally limit risk, the latter a crucial component of personal and professional growth. The results can be beneficial, but the ultimate goal is that of creating transactional relationships on the path towards one's professional success.

The thriving of modern formalised mentoring programs is linked, we believe, to contemporary society's emphasis on personal/professional success to the detriment of collegiality. Yet collegiality is an investment into the future; it implies the recognition that experts need to contribute to the field by nurturing the future generations that will take up the role they now perform. In this sense, mentoring is seen as a tool to foster the growth of the generations to come.

FOSTERING GROWTH AND ENHANCING POSITIVE OUTCOMES IN THE EDUCATION SECTOR

In the academic world, structured mentoring programs are now a common encounter. Yet, in this move towards more formalised and organisation-based settings, roles and expectations of mentors and mentees might remain misaligned. Grogan, Eviner and Hobbie, for instance, have recently highlighted how "[m]entoring is a core activity for many scientists, and yet few of us have had any formal training in how to do it well"[1]. Similarly, Gaston Gayles and Kelly Turner point out that "[t]he lack of shared understanding about mentoring leads to unevenness in terms of the extent to which people's needs are met, particularly those new to the academy"[2]. Recognising and addressing this issue, Fountain and Newcomer examined the practice of mentoring in a selection of US universities which form future public servants. They propose several recommendations for effective and sustainable mentoring, among which the necessity to appropriately train mentors in "both hard and soft mentoring knowledge and skills"[3]. They also single out the importance of recognising and rewarding effective mentoring. The relevance of mentoring is also acknowledged by Curtin, Malley, and Stewart who focus on the mentoring of doctoral students and the impact that such activity may have for this cohort's future career decisions and outcomes[4].

Still within the realm of academia, scholars are now increasingly emphasising the need for accessible, effective, and collaborative mentoring

1 Paul Grogan, Valerie Eviner and Sarah Hobbie, « Keeping up with the Times: Equity Issue Is Now Added to Our Self-Reflection Worksheet for Improving Scientific Mentoring », *Bulletin of the Ecological Society of America* (ESA), 2021, vol. 102, n° 2, p. 1.

2 Joy Gaston Gayles and Bridget Kelly Turner, « Mentoring for Success across the Academic Spectrum », Lori A. Flores and Jocelyn H. Olcott (eds), *The Academic's Handbook 4th Edition. Revised and Expanded*, Durham NC, Duke University Press, 2020, p. 232.

3 Fountain, Joselynn, and Newcomer, Kathryn E., « Developing and Sustaining Effective Faculty Mentoring Programs », *Journal of Public Affairs Education*, 2016, vol. 22, n° 4, p. 500.

4 Nicola Curtin, Janet Malley and Abigail J. Stewart, « Mentoring the Next Generation of Faculty: Supporting Academic Career Aspirations Among Doctoral Students », *Research in Higher Education*, 2016, vol. 57, n° 6, p. 714-738.

in order to overcome various equity barriers whose existence is widespread across institutions and countries. Lisa Costello, for instance, zooms in on the challenges faced by women who pursue an academic career. Costello highlights that

> [m]any mentorship programs exist, especially in the last ten years, but these kinds of resources need to be accessible to all women and valued as promotion criteria at institutions across the country. This study furthers the call made by Misra et al. for a more comprehensive approach to mentoring for women and also expands on the idea of mentoring as a collaborative effort that must be formalized at every institution[5].

Along similar lines, Phruksachart delves into the tricky situations faced by students from underrepresented minority groups, such as women and queer of colour. Interestingly, she notes how the old-school 'charismatic model' of mentoring (i.e. based on the master-disciple or apprentice paradigm) is particularly problematic in this context. For instance, she cites a study that suggests that positive outcomes are skewed towards specific categories along the race/gender axe[6]. In her article, Phruksachart explains how she came to be a co-organiser of the Mentoring Future Faculty of Color (MFFC) project, a community of scholars committed to introduce and foster diversity within the world of academia.

Campbell *et al.* explore further this limitation by looking at the obstacles faced by US-based medicine students from underrepresented groups (e.g. Blacks, Latinx, American Indians, Alaska Natives, Pacific Islanders)[7]. While enhanced mentoring is seen as a viable tool to rectify the structural asymmetry related to power and opportunity, the issue of finding suitable mentors remains compelling, as senior staff members with a comparable background – hence pry to the specific difficulties individuals have to face – are, most obviously, also scarce. This paper puts forward a novel strategy, which capsizes the traditional hierarchical model at the basis of mentoring. Through the scheme of 'reverse mentoring', junior staff members mentor a senior member within the same institution

5 Lisa A. Costello, « Standing Up and Standing Together: Feminist Teaching and Collaborative Mentoring », *Feminist Teacher*, 2015, vol. 26, n° 1, p. 2.

6 Melissa Phruksachart, « On Mentoring Future Faculty of Color », *Feminist Teacher*, 2017, vol. 27, n° 2-3, p. 118.

7 Kendall M. Campbell, Michaela M. Braxton, Dmitry Tumin, and José E. Rodríguez, « Reverse Mentoring between Minority Students and Faculty », *Journal of Best Practices in Health Professions Diversity*, 2020, vol. 13, n° 2, p. 184-188.

in order to shape a renewed knowledge base and sharing system. Loue and Loff also point out the benefits that mentoring may provide for both parties involved, mentors and mentees. While in the past the relationship was viewed as destined to benefit the junior participant only, namely the mentee, nowadays it is recognised that mentors may gain new insights too. The authors also highlight how this alliance can help establish the basis for a mutually fruitful professional collaboration[8].

While we now recognise mentoring as a crucial factor in the professional growth of future scholars, mentoring is also viewed as a fundamental stepping-stone in the successful development of children. Kearney and Levine highlight how both role models and mentors can help shape a child's life trajectory. Through a large-scale analysis, and focusing particularly on children from a disadvantaged background, the authors suggest that "[c]hildren who participate in formal mentoring programs see improvements in their school performance and are more likely to avoid the criminal justice system"[9]. Van Dam *et al.* present an interesting perspective and explore the potential benefits associated with the presence of a 'natural mentor' in the life of adolescents. The scholars define a 'natural mentor' as an adult who provides support to the younger person without relying on a structured program that matches youth with adults. Natural mentors are "companion[s] to youth and provid[e] reliable support, [...] [they] help to foster a range of positive developmental outcomes and resilience"[10]. Continuing with the area of children's education, mentoring for teachers has also been identified as a useful tool to support the professional development of this category. Reinforcing the claims of other studies, Polikoff *et al.* also suggest there is a paucity of evidence which affects our capacity to design effective mentoring programs[11]. The authors highlight how "recent evidence

8 Sana Loue and Bebe Loff, « Mentoring International Research Ethics Trainees: Identifying Best Practices », *Journal of Empirical Research on Human Research Ethics: An International Journal*, 2013, vol. 8, n° 5, p. 52.

9 Melissa S. Kearney and Phillip B. Levine, « Role Models, Mentors, and Media Influences », *The Future of Children*, 2020, vol. 30, n° 1, p. 83.

10 L. Van Dam, D. Smit, B. Wildschut, S. J. T. Branje, J. E. Rhodes, M. Assink, and G. J. J. M. Stams, « Does Natural Mentoring Matter? A Multilevel Meta-analysis on the Association Between Natural Mentoring and Youth Outcomes », *American Journal of Community Psychology*, 2018, vol. 62, n° 1-2, p. 204.

11 Morgan S. Polikoff, Laura M. Desimone, Andrew C. Porter, and Eric D. Hochberg, « Mentor Policy and the Quality of Mentoring », *The Elementary School Journal*, 2015, vol. 116, n° 1, p. 76.

suggests that mentoring effects depend on the nature of mentoring policies, the quality of their implementation, and the interactions between teachers and mentors that ensue as a result." (*Ibid.*, p. 77)

This brief survey of recent studies on mentoring in education, albeit not comprehensive, offers nevertheless a clear sense of the relevance mentoring has gained in the last few decades. Of particular importance to us is the fact that scholars agree in identifying the human relationship between mentors and mentees as a core factor for the success of this enterprise.

ORIGINS AND TRADITIONS

The conception and practices of mentoring have shifted over time and across cultures. Historically, the mentor character dates to ancient Greece. In Homer's *Odyssey*, Mentor is "Ulysses old friend [...] with whom Ulysses left his house in trust", in particular his son Telemachus[12]. This wise counsellor is in reality the goddess Athena in disguise, who goes to Ithaca and guides the young boy, teaching him how to avoid the traps of the suitors.

If Homer has created the prototype of a good mentor, it is Socrates who embodies its perfect incarnation. According to Françoise Waquet, Socrates epitomises

> the master who does not impose his knowledge, [...] who, in his unawareness, questions without asserting and who, by practicing, through dialogue, a kind of midwifery, leads the disciple to find the knowledge that he has within himself[13].

The complex relationship between master and disciple is the subject of a long tradition of research, in particular in the humanities. For instance, four collective volumes in French – *De l'un à l'autre. Maîtres et disciples* (2013), *Figures du maître. De l'autorité à l'autonomie* (2013), *Maître-disciple:*

12 Homer, *Odyssey*, 2, 220-221, trans. Thomas Hobbes, *Clarendon Editions of Works of Thomas Hobbes: Translations of Homer*, Volume XXV, Clarendon Press, 2008, p. 24.

13 Françoise Waquet, *Les enfants de Socrate. Filiation intellectuelle et transmission du savoir XVIIe-XXIe siècle*, Paris: Albin Michel, 2008, p. 75-76, (our translation).

une relation topique (2018) and *Maître(s) et disciple(s)* (2019)[14] – have recently revived interest in this field, where George Steiner appears as the major contemporary reference for studies on the matter[15].

Focusing on the transmission of knowledge, Steiner identifies three kinds of mentoring relationships. While the first two lead to the destruction of the disciple ("the master's power to exploit his student's dependence and vulnerability; the complementary threat of subversion and betrayal of the mentor by his pupil")[16], the third one, "the reciprocal exchange of trust and love of learning and instruction between teacher and disciple" (*ibid.*) delineates the ideal mentoring process.

However, a mentor is not always a master, and the mentee not always a disciple. The mentoring relationship could be approached through terms such as advisor, father (the masculine figure dominates the traditional model, nowadays revised and challenged), guide, tutor, trainer, initiator, coach or role model – *imitatio* appears as a key concept in defining this relationship. And a potentially hierarchical relation can develop in friendship. But the mentoring process is not without danger, as stressed by Steiner. The failure of the mentoring relationship can come from the mentor, who takes advantage of his posture of authority; or from the mentee, by resisting the mentor's lessons. In addition, the protégé can also have not just one mentor, but a constellation of different mentors, the dyadic relation shifting to team- and network-based mentoring.

The relationship between mentor and protégé (in particular between master and disciple) has been extensively explored by writers and novelists since Homer. As demonstrated by Charles Forsdick in the Preface, literature in itself is a powerful mentoring tool. The volume encompasses reflections on the relationship forged by mentors and mentees which arise from a thematically broad range of case studies. The overall aim is that of showcasing the meaning of mentoring in the humanities and performing arts. Contributors do so by engaging with fictional

14 Cristina Noacco, Corinne Bonnet, Patrick Marot *et al.* (eds), *Figures du maître. De l'autorité à l'autonomie*, Rennes, Presses Universitaires de Rennes, coll. « Interférence », 2013; Aurélie Névot (ed.), *De l'un à l'autre. Maîtres et disciples*, Paris: CNRS éditions, 2013; Véronique Duché, Madeleine Jeay and Yen-Maï Tran-Gervat (eds), *Maître-disciple: une relation topique, Topiques, études satoriennes*, n° 5, 2018, https://www.erudit.org/en/journals/topiques/2018-v4-topiques05785/; Edyta Kociubińska and Judyta Niedokos (ed.), *Maître(s) et disciple(s), Quêtes littéraires*, n° 9, 2019.

15 George Steiner, *Lessons of the Masters*, Cambridge MA, Harvard University Press, 2003.

16 *Ibidem*, book jacket.

mentoring relationships, as well as real mentor-mentee partnerships from the academic and artistic world, including everyday life.

These essays examine the various shapes of mentoring, its power dynamics (gains and losses, benefits and risks), as well as the reciprocal process of change the mentoring relationship can instigate. These chapters also highlight how such relationships come about in an organic fashion: a meeting of minds and personalities often facilitated by key interactions within one's specific milieu. In doing so, the authors outline the intrinsically individual and organic nature of the mentoring partnership.

Readers will delve into an exploration of notable figures of mentors, consider their role and relevance, and reflect on the literary representations of the relationship between mentors and mentees with its many nuances. Whether fictional examples, scholarly influential relationships, or real artistic partnerships, these essays outline how the human process of intellectual and emotional growth is often spurred and accompanied by a mentoring relationship. By highlighting the multifaceted shapes that this relationship can take, these chapters reveal the blurred margins of the relationship between mentors and mentees, as well as the benefits and risks generated by this partnership.

THE ESSAYS

The volume is divided into three parts which follow a chronological sequence. Part I 'Medieval and early modern mentors' consists of four chapters. Madeleine Jeay examines the *Chevalier errant* (The Wandering Knight), a prosimeter written in French at the end of the 14th century by Thomas III of Saluces (*ca* 1356-1416). This autobiographical text describes the wanderings of the author's allegorical double, visiting successively the god of Love, Fortune and Knowledge in a meditation on the meaning of human life. Jeay firstly identifies the several mentor figures which the knight meets on his voyage, such as *Espérance*, *Foi*, and *Connaissance* (Hope, Faith, and Knowledge). She then anatomises the failure of this mentoring process.

Anne-Laure Metzger-Rambach investigates the work of one of the most famous humanists, Desiderius Erasmus (1466-1536). The *Colloquia*

(Colloquies) are a collection of dialogues conceived by the author as informal Latin exercises. These texts have quickly been translated into French by the famous poet Clément Marot (1496-1544) and pamphleteer Nicolas Gueudeville (1562-1721) among others. Focusing on three conversations by each translator, Metzger-Rambach explores the relationship between mentor and mentee. She demonstrates that both Marot and Gueudeville reduplicate the Erasmian pattern: while in the *Colloquies* the transmission of knowledge by the mentor relies strongly on the pleasure of the mentee, the translators redefine accordingly the relationship between the reader and the author.

Gianluca Caputo analyses a work by Italian geographer and diplomat Giovan Battista Ramusio (1485-1557), *Navigationi et Viaggi* (Navigations and Travels), a collection of explorers' accounts of their travels. By investigating the cultural and philosophical background and identifying the importance of Cicero's discourse on friendship as well as Venetian Neoplatonism, Caputo shows how past and present mentors are staged on the global theatre of printed knowledge.

Kirk Weeden dissects *Les Femmes savantes* (The Learned Ladies), a comedy by famous French playwright Molière (1622-1673), and its adaptation, *The Literati*, by Australian playwright Justin Fleming. A satire on academic pretentiousness and on female education, *Les Femmes savantes* is updated for an Australian contemporary audience. Weeden argues that Molière is "a timeless moral and social commentator and mentor", and that *The Literati* offers portraits of mentors in action. In particular, the reconfiguration of Vadius, a 'learned gentleman', as Athénaïs Vadius, a new world feminist, adds a mentoring dimension to the character.

In Part II 'Mentoring in the 19th and 20th century', the at times tumultuous relationship between mentor and protégé is acknowledged in three artistic disciplines: poetry, dance, and theatre. Luigi Gussago examines the legendary epistolary exchange between Italian writer Pietro Giordani (1774-1848) and famous poet and philosopher Giacomo Leopardi (1798-1837). Gussago demonstrates that, although Giordani was very reluctant to take on the role of intellectual guide for 'the fabulous young man', the classicist had a profound influence on the young and sick poet. Specifically, Gussago shows that Leopardi's poetic program, his 'theory of the *pellegrino*', finds its roots in Giordani's philosophical, time-transcending conception of poetry.

Mark Nicholls focuses on the Ballets Russes, the glamourous and influential ballet company (1909-1929) founded by Sergei Diaghilev (1872-1929). Specifically, Nicholls examines the relationship between Diaghilev and his premier dancer, Vaslav Nijinsky (1890-1953). Although emotional and personal factors were a strong component of this partnership, Nicholls demonstrates that the mentoring relationship was primarily professional.

Amanda Cole delves further into the field of performing arts. She focuses on Marjorie Barstow (1899-1995), a dancer and dance teacher who was the first to graduate from Australian Frederick Matthias Alexander's (1869-1955) method of training. Cole examines what she calls 'the constellation mentorship' from which Barstow benefited, and details the contributions of each mentor. Cole's study shows how, in Barstow's case, the Alexander technique has been tinged with philosophical pragmatism.

In Part III 'Mentors in contemporary novels', recent works of fiction offer a further opportunity to discuss portraits of mentors and the relationship with their mentees. Pauline Eaton focuses on two novels by French author Marie NDiaye, the winner of the prestigious Goncourt Prize in 2009. *Mon cœur à l'étroit* (My Heart Hemmed In) and *Trois Femmes Puissantes* (Three Strong Women) present interesting portraits of mentors. In the first novel, an experienced Noget mentors the main character Nadia; in the second one, a young Lamine performs this role for Khady on her migration journey. Eaton examines the unequal nature of these mentoring relationships and shows that the real power does not always lie where one thinks.

Charlotte Mackay scrutinises *Celles qui attendent* (Women Who Wait), the fourth novel of Franco-Senegalese author Fatou Diome, where "no clear-cut (nor masculinised) master-mentor figure" can be identified. Thus, Mackay examines female and non-Western mentoring relationships. She first explores the concept of 'multidirectional and symmetrical mentor-friendship between women' by looking at the main characters Arame and Bougna. She later moves on to discuss intergenerational mentorship.

Lastly, Gregoria Manzin turns to Sardinian novelist and activist Michela Murgia. She explores the award winning novel *Accabadora* (2009) and analyses a specific type of informal adoption, by which a young girl is taken up as a soul-child (*fill'e anima*) by an old woman who lives in the same village. Manzin's chapter looks at the relationship between the girl and the old woman, Maria and Bonaria, through a theoretical framework grounded in the ethics of care. Relying on Adriana Cavarero's conceptualisation of 'inclination', Manzin frames this relationship as originating in Bonaria's response to a silent call for care. The old woman recognises in Maria a vulnerable and helpless subject and embraces an unspoken request for nurturing. In this essay the traditional mentoring paradigm is capsized. Firstly, both mentor and mentee are women and, secondly, their empathetic bond is sealed through the recognition of their own limitations.

The ten chapters, and the accompanying Preface by Charles Forsdick, highlight the complexity of the relationship between mentor and mentee, its breadth and depth, its power dynamics, the potential for success, as well as the intrinsic risk of failure entailed in this partnership.

Véronique DUCHÉ
The University of Melbourne
Australia

Gregoria MANZIN
La Trobe University
Australia

FIRST PART

MEDIEVAL AND EARLY MODERN MENTORS

A WANDERING KNIGHT'S QUEST FOR A MENTOR

Thomas de Saluces's *Le Chevalier errant*

The *Chevalier Errant* (*Wandering Knight*) is an allegorical prosimeter written by Thomas de Saluces, the Marquess Thomas of Saluzzo, during his captivity in Turin between 1394 and 1396[1]. It takes the form of a learning journey told in the first person, punctuated by successive meetings that the Knight makes during an itinerary that leads him from the Court of Love to the estate of Fortune, then to an encounter with Knowledge. Thomas de Saluces's novel can be related to the genre of pilgrimages of human life, the edifying allegorical narratives that flourish in the 13th and 14th centuries, following the tradition of the *Roman of the Rose* and of the genre of *Paths of Hell and Paradise*[2]. In this allegorical autobiography, personal allusions are intertwined with didactic aims, political actuality with literary reminiscences.

The three stages of the *Wandering Knight* seem to relate to the different periods of life, with the transition from youth to maturity, from the search for pleasure to the quest of wisdom. The first experiences of youth correspond to the discovery of love, its pleasures and its sorrows: the Knight falls in love with a lady, a love that will be lived at the court of the god of Love after having met several obstacles. The relationship is interrupted, the Knight pursues his route and arrives at the castle of Fortune, a metaphor for the active life proper to the achievements of adulthood, where he discovers their volatility. He ends his peregrination with the encounter of Knowledge whose teaching corresponds to the aspiration to wisdom proper to old age. In each of these stages, he is

1 This captivity is a consequence of the tension between the Marquesses of Saluzzo and the hegemonic threat of the Counts of Savoy.

2 Jean-Claude Mühlethaler, « Entre la France et l'Italie: Jules César chez Thomas III de Saluces et Eustache Deschamps », *Cahiers de recherches médiévales et humanistes*, n° 14 spécial: *La Figure de Jules César au Moyen Âge et à la Renaissance (II)*, 2007, p. 192.

accompanied and supported by allegorical figures of mentors, personifications whose meaning will evolve during his journey. Faith, which in the first section refers to the loyalty of courtly lovers, takes on a religious connotation in the last one; Hope, representing at the beginning the expectation that love is mutual and fulfilled, is identified at the end as the daughter of Knowledge, and becomes a theological virtue[3].

At a first level, the *Wandering Knight* can be seen as an edifying story, that of a spiritual progression which, after the search for the *Vita voluptuosa* at Love's court, is an evocation of the *Vita activa* at Fortune's castle, leading to the catechetical teaching of Knowledge which culminates with an *ars moriendi*[4]. We will see, however, that this interpretation, which is supposed to represent the stages of a personal development, needs to be qualified. As Richard Trachsler has observed, the *Wandering Knight* is not so much the account of a process of maturation than an accumulation of lessons[5]. In this perspective, we must regard the work as a sum of references, literary in the first section, historical and intellectual in the second and theological in the third. Putting them in perspective contradicts the edifying interpretation suggested by the three stages of the Knight's journey, and opens it to ambivalence.

Our analysis of mentoring relationships in the *Wandering Knight* will take the form of a diptych. We will first concentrate on the mentor figures that guide the Knight in that journey, allegorical personifications such as Hope, Faith and Knowledge – *Espérance*, *Foi* and *Connaissance* –, and characters who provide advice to the Knight on several occasions. Then we will focus on the obstacles that can make the pedagogical process unsuccessful, whether from the teacher, or the student or both partners.

---

3 Florence Bouchet, postface to the translation of the *Wandering Knight* in modern French: Thomas D'Aleran, *Le chevalier errant*, ed. Daniel Chaubet, Moncalieri, Centro interuniversitario di ricerche sul viaggio in Italia, 2001, p. 397.

4 Richard Trachsler, *Disjointures – Conjointures. Étude sur l'interférence des matières narratives dans la littérature française du Moyen Âge*, Tübingen and Basel, A. Francke, 2000, p. 346.

5 *Ibid.*, p. 347.

MENTOR FIGURES IN THE *WANDERING KNIGHT*

The Knight's journey – and the text itself – is framed by his two meetings with Knowledge. She is the first figure of mentor the Knight meets, at the very beginning of the text. Described as a lady riding a palfrey, she approaches him because she wants to advise him so that he does not behave anymore like a child but as a wise man. She will show him the right way. Her dialogue with the Knight evokes the exchange between Virgil and Dante in the first *Canto* of *Hell*: she will show him the right way and he agrees to follow her[6].

The lesson she gives him is both social and moral in nature: he must seek honor and in that quest, accept the difficulties and sufferings he may encounter. But the Knight is not ready to receive it, he does not yet have the discernment that would allow him to truly understand what honor is. This is precisely what is shown by the narrative motif of the arrival of the traveler at a crossroads and the choice he has to make of the right direction which is, as tradition dictates, on the right-hand side. The Knight's decision to choose the left side demonstrates his misunderstanding of the essence of what honor is, that he confuses with pride and vain glory.

He will meet Knowledge again at the end of his travels. He assures her that he finds himself, after the experiences he has lived and the teachings he has received, in a disposition of mind that allows him to follow her advice. He is now ready to avoid the wrong path he took at the beginning of his adventure. This has not always been the case, as we will see with his reaction to the moral injunctions of Reason. This third part, the only one which is openly edifying in the work, is centered on a series of lectures by Knowledge to the Knight. Her teaching takes the form of a dialogue between the teacher and the disciple, a dialogue in which she addresses him with the apostrophe of "son". It is actually a succession of presentations punctuated by questions from the

6 The edition used is Tommaso III di Saluzzo, *Il Libro del Cavaliere Errante* (BnF ms. fr. 12559), ed. Marco Piccat and Laura Ramello, Boves, Araba Fenice, 2008; Dante, *The Inferno*, trans. Robert Pinsky, *A New Verse Translation, Bilingual Edition*, Farrar, Straus and Giroux, New York, 2014, Canto I, v. 88-89.

Knight. Knowledge begins her teaching with explanations about the various vicissitudes of his journey. The abbey where he was led when he took the wrong way at the beginning of his voyage is a reflection of his vanity. The so-called monks he met there are actually Lucifer's henchmen, that is, the seven deadly sins. As for Fortune's instability, it is not arbitrary, but a consequence of the excess of pride and vanity of those who wish to rise too high.

These moral considerations lead to explanations about the nature of Vain Glory, followed by a lengthy commentary on each of the seven deadly sins: pride, envy, anger, laziness, greed, gluttony, and lust; followed itself by remarks about hell and purgatory. Then Knowledge addresses the issue of the responsibilities of princes, notably to uphold justice and protect their subjects, and to achieve that, to surround themselves with good advisers. She continues with the duties of knights, especially with respect to the prince whose honor they must protect. If chivalry respected its duties, she insists, the world would not be in trouble, an affirmation which is logically followed by the presentation of the seven virtues: Faith, Hope, Charity, Justice, Prudence, Fortitude and Moderation. Knowledge's moral and theological lecture leads to a lesson on the good death with an evocation of the sufferings of Hell to which responds the vision of the enjoyments of Paradise.

Knowledge can be considered the most significant mentor figure in the *Wandering Knight*, as she plays for the Knight the role of a counselor attached to his moral and spiritual development. Hope and Faith who accompany him in his various adventures and lead him to his final encounter with her, represent various facets of mentoring. The encounter with Hope happens in the courtly context of the lover's aspiration for his lady's love. She is introduced to the Knight by allegorical personifications inspired by the *Romance of the Rose*, *Beau Regard* (Fair Gaze) and *Bel Accueil* (Fair Welcoming).

First, Hope acts as his guide, helping him to cross the thick metaphorical forest towards the lady and showing him the way to the tower where she is held captive. As he must give up trying to get in this dungeon, Faith approaches, described as a knight, who will also be a guide for him. He asks the Knight to follow him, an invitation that again evokes that of Virgil to Dante[7]. Both, Hope and Faith, lead him

7 *Le Chevalier Errant*, ed. cit., p. 65, v. 705-706.

to Reason, who will advise him on his quest for love. As he is not happy with the teachings of the latter, they will take him to Fortune who may be able to assist him. Then they lead him to the philosopher and historian Orose who will explain the reasons for the rise and fall of heroes and civilizations. Finally Hope who is no longer the representation of courtly desire, but the theological virtue, will introduce him to her mother Knowledge.

Beside this function of guidance during the Knight's travel, Hope and Faith also play the role of advising, helping and comforting him. These aspects of the mentoring relationship, accompaniment and support, are located in the first part of the text, concerning the Knight's quest for love and his love affair with the lady hindered by various obstacles. His counsellor in matters of love is Hope. She begins by urging him to pray to the God of Love, then she insists on the value of suffering. She reassures him by pointing out that one can find happiness after experiencing adversity. But above all, she warns him against lust that makes one forget one's duty, while pain is a source of wisdom. In the role of adjuvant, it is mainly Faith who intervenes, either acting as an intermediary between the Knight and his lady or seeking help at King Arthur's court to release the Knight held prisoner of Morgane le Fay's enchantments. For his part, Hope speaks for him to the god of Love and brings to Fortune a letter from him that receives an answer full of wisdom on the fact that all human beings experience rises and falls, a thought-provoking answer preparing him to meet her in the second part of his journey. Of course, it is Hope, according to the significance of her name, which brings comfort: she gives the Knight hope that he will be well received by his lady and that Love will come to his rescue; also she assures him that his happiness will be more intense after his torments. The limit to the authority of Hope and Faith is revealed in the third part of the text, when the travelers meet a weeping lady on the seashore who is lamenting her fate. They are unable to explain the cause of her complaints. Knowledge will tell later that this figure is the allegory of the city of Genoa whose power on land and sea is shaken by the revolt of its citizens. In this case, it is not an emotional accompaniment that the Knight needs, but intellectual and political information.

A third guide appears at the Knight's side with Hope and Faith. It is Labour (*Travail*) whose role evolves as well over the course of the text.

He is first introduced as the valet of Hope and as such, he is present with her and sometimes with Faith for the tasks to be performed in favour of the Knight, for example delivering letters to the lady. After having been the servant of Hope, he will become that of the Knight. Labour's last incarnation reverses their positions, because from then on he acts for him as a teacher who provides explanations on Italian politics. He sets out for him the elements of the conflict between the Guelphs and the Ghibellines, a presentation which leads to wider considerations concerning tyranny.

The Knight's stay at Fortune's Court generates several lessons of an intellectual nature. First, she offers a long development on the advent of the Antichrist and the Last Judgment, which allows her to present a review of the seven ages of the world. Questioned by the Knight, one of the listeners of her speech makes a formal lesson on the origin of the papacy and its history since Peter. Then the historian Orose addresses the question of temporal power since the Babylonian kingdom, with most of the talk devoted to Rome. When he learns the identity of his interlocutor, Thomas de Saluces, Orose interrupts his presentation to tell him the famous story of the Marquess's ancestor Griselidis, exemplary because of her patience with the inordinate demands of her husband. In order to test her patience and her loyalty, he abducted her two children for some time and pretended to marry another woman. The extreme nature of the anecdote leads Orose to specify how to interpret it so that his listener – and the reader – do not draw an erroneous conclusion. This story must be understood as any exemplary narrative, that is to say, allegorically and not in the first degree. It is not meant to show how women should behave with their husbands, but how each of us should act towards God when He puts us to the test.

The Knight receives other lessons of a social and political nature in the transition period between the second and the third part of the text, between his stays with Fortune and his meeting with Knowledge. He meets two hermits who will nurture his understanding of society by showing him the importance of moral values. The first hermit, to whom he confides his suffering due to the loss of his Lady, does not find him in the appropriate attitude to be receptive to his advice. For that, he would have to come back to him with the inner knowledge of good and evil, that consciousness which barons and prelates do not possess themselves, harming the Church because of their lack of devotion and their bad morals.

The Knight then searches for barons and other temporal authorities to find moral consciousness among them, but his quest is unsuccessful. Having returned to the hermit to tell him that he has not found any, he asks if some can be found among the representatives of religious power.

To his question, the hermit can only complain about the tribulations which they make the Church suffer by their lack of devotion and their corruption. Pursuing his route, the Knight arrives at another hermit's house with whom he shares what he has just learned about the behavior of the princes of the Church. This second hermit confirms the opinion of the first one and criticizes their attitude towards the poor whereas they could not survive without their work. He continues with a speech on the organization of society in different orders and the responsibility of the prince to enforce a balance between them so that no one is crushed because of the greed of the powerful[8]. Following an explanation he gives to the Knight on the reasons for being insatiable and not content with what God gives, he embarks on a development of the four humours and the perverse effects on the excess of melancholy that drives men to be deceitful.

In the mentoring relationship established between the Knight and the allegorical figures or the characters who assume the role of guide in the *Wandering Knight*, whether their teaching is emotional, moral or intellectual, we have noticed several indications showing the limits and obstacles to its success. We will see now how the text articulates these limitations.

FALSE MENTORS AND BAD STUDENTS

The obstacles to a teaching relationship may be due to the mentor's deficiencies or the student's shortcomings, the failure sometimes resulting from the combination of the two. This is precisely what happens during the episode of the Knight's stay in the abbey where he arrived

8 As we have seen, Knowledge will resume these explanations about the responsibilities of princes that arise from the two major obligations of upholding justice and relying on good advisers.

after taking the left path, despite the warning written on the cross planted in the middle of the crossroads: he should not take the road to the left, but follow the one on the right because it will be good for him. In the ardor of his youth, as we have seen, the Knight proceeds to the left, driven by a false conception of honor. He believes that he will find there greater challenges, but in fact he is abused by his temerity and his vanity. He arrives at an abbey where he lets himself be deceived about the true nature of the monks who welcome him. The readers are informed of the meaning to be given to the episode by a remark by the narrator in the form of a proverb, to the effect that it often happens that one thinks to be well received while one is badly hosted[9]. They will therefore be conscious of the contradictory behavior of the monks. While their appearance is that of hermits living in asceticism, the Knight is welcomed with all the pleasures that one can have in this world. Just as questionable is their refusal to let him hear Mass the morning of his departure.

But inadequate masters can only abuse disciples who have not yet developed a capacity for discernment that would allow them to unmask their duplicity. When the Knight finds Knowledge again at the end of his journey, he is now ready to understand the meaning of his mistake in choosing the left path that led him among these deceitful monks. The cross planted in the middle of the crossroads evoked that of the Savior. But the Knight took a decision dictated by the devil who made him commit the same sin, false pride, as the one he committed himself. That's how he came to an abbey under the governance of an abbot who was a disciple of Lucifer. A successful mentoring relationship is the result of shared responsibility. This is also shown by the topos of the good advisors with whom the prince must surround himself. Unfortunately, many powerful people are too sensitive to flattery to be able to choose the right counselors. The model of the good mentor for the prince, conveyed by the literary tradition and taken up by the *Wandering Knight*, is that of Aristotle for the Emperor Alexander.

Apart from these examples of the ways in which the shortcomings of both partners affect mentoring, Thomas de Saluces presents a situation where the student is the only one responsible for its failure. In search of advice about love, the Knight meets Reason, an allegorical

9 « *Tel cuide bien estre hostellés / Qui est mauvaisement herbergiés* », p. 56, v. 297-298.

figure that Thomas de Saluces borrows from Jean de Meun's *Romance of the Rose*. In the sequel he has written to Guillaume de Lorris's story, De Meun stages a succession of interviews between the young lover in search of the rose, metaphor of the beloved lady, and allegorical personifications that gives him a teaching compliant to the reality they represent. Reason details the different forms of love; after her, Friend plays the role of the experienced confidant who gives him instructions to seduce the rose, for example to avoid concealing his intentions and make modest gifts. Wealth insists on this last point by explaining that too much generosity leads to poverty. After that, the Jealous Husband warns the Lover against marriage, because it leads to the domination of the husband over his wife, which destroys love. The last lesson on love is that of la *Vieille*, the Old Lady, the former prostitute who acts now as procuress, who claims that it must be sold to the highest bidder. At no time during their speeches will the Lover or the reader of the *Romance of the Rose* receive from the narrator any indication about the lesson to be drawn from the diversity of these presentations. It is up to them to develop their own interpretation, and their own conduct from the diversity of situations and messages that have been presented.

In the *Wandering Knight*, Reason's considerations about love, set forth in terms of values and moral choices to make, are violently rejected by the Knight. She warns him against amorous intoxication and asks him to control his heart so that he does not abandon himself to this madness. Although she realizes that her guidance is useless, she insists on the need to heal oneself of love when it means just a search for pleasure. However, it is no use acting as a good mentor if the student is not ready to hear the lesson. Reason gets from the Knight an unequivocal reply: "You lecture me for nothing, for I do not care about your speeches; I'd rather die than believe them, and I'd be really stupid and pathetic if I listened to them."[10] She nevertheless continues her teaching with a statement consistent with the conception of society erected by the Gregorian reform that established a strict division between the clergy committed to chastity and the laity destined for marriage and procreation, between spouses of good morals, equal in age and nobility. The Knight's reaction is once more categorical: he does not want to take Reason's advice into account. He replies that he

10 *Le Chevalier Errant*, ed. cit., p. 338.

does not wish to give up looking for love and concludes with an insult, calling her "miserable oldster"[11]. It must be said that according to the figure of the cleric that Reason incarnates in this sermon, her negative vision of love goes with a derogatory view of women to which the Knight reacts by putting forward a list of exemplary women. Among these women is Griselidis, whose adventure, as we have seen, is told in the narration of the history of Rome by Orose.

We can see in the Knight's attitude that he does not behave like a passive listener to the lessons that have been provided to him along the way. He may not have always reached the level of maturity that will allow him to benefit from them, but it is precisely to this learning process that the *Wandering Knight* invites us. For that reason, reading the text also works as the reader's education. Like the Knight himself, we are confronted with a diversity of experiences that correspond to the different stages of life. The pedagogy that emerges from the text is truly maieutic. Quite a few references in the text permit the identification of the hero of the story with Thomas III of Saluces, descendant of the patient Griselidis and defeated rival of a vassal of the Duke of Savoie, who found, during his years in prison, a salutary comfort in study and writing. However, the fact that the main actants of the story are allegories of the knight taken to a level of generalization that gives him a general scope, allows the transposition to each reader of the vicissitudes of the journey and the lessons that are proposed. From the presentation of situations and instructions to all levels of personal and collective human reality, be it emotional, moral, intellectual, political and theological, readers as well as the Knight are led to draw their own conclusions. The *Wandering Knight* does not therefore offer a prescriptive discourse intended for conversion[12]. The options presented to meditation are all the more open as an important part of the text, especially in the courts of Love and Fortune, is made up of literary reminiscences. Thomas de Saluces draws on numerous ancient and biblical references and borrows from the entire medieval literary corpus: the *Roman de la Rose*, as we have seen, poetry, antique and Arthurian romance, chanson de geste, and fabliau[13]. All this wealth of

11 *Ibid.*, p. 352.

12 In this, Thomas de Saluces is faithful to Jean de Meun's *Romance of the Rose*.

13 About these references, see: Madeleine Jeay, « Le narrateur "désinvolte" ou l'écriture en trompe l'œil », Memini, *Construire le sens par la disparité : lectures croisées du Chevalier Errant de Thomas de Saluces (1394-1396)*, 27, 2021. http://journals.openedition.org/memini/1842;

texts and knowledge referred to by the *Wandering Knight* gives the work an encyclopaedic scope. Their diversity and the possible discrepancies in the messages they propose prohibit, however, the closure of meaning, maintaining instead the ambiguity that is the very essence of literature.

Madeleine JEAY
McMaster University
Canada

---

id., « L'emprise du narrateur : la manipulation des discours et des récits enchâssés dans le Chevalier errant de Thomas de Saluces », *Nouvelles en mouvement (XIIIe-XVIe siècles). Novelle in movimento (XIII-XVI secolo)*, ed. Margherita Lecco and Jean-Claude Mühlethaler, Alessandria, Edizioni dell'Orso, 2021, p. 81-108.

THE RELATIONSHIP BETWEEN MENTOR AND MENTEE IN THE FRENCH VERSIONS OF ERASMUS' *COLLOQUIA*

Clément Marot and Nicolas Gueudeville

When Erasmus' *Colloquia* were first published, in 1518, in Latin, Erasmus was unaware that his work was being sent to print. Later, he revealed that the texts were his own and consequently added new sections to the early 1518 version. The last publication of the *Colloquia* in Erasmus' lifetime dates from 1533. In France, the *Colloquia* were translated into French by Barthélémy Aneau[1], Louis de Berquin[2], Clément Marot and later by Nicolas Gueudeville[3]. In this paper, six Conversations, translated by Clément Marot and Nicolas Gueudeville, will be discussed.

The texts by Marot[4] are *Colloque de l'Abbé et de la femme sçavante* [Conversation between the Abbot and the wise lady][5], the diptych *Colloque de la Vierge mesprisant mariage* [Conversation with the maiden who despised marriage] and *La Vierge repentie* [The repentant Maiden] which Jean Céard[6]

1 *Comédie ou dialogue matriomonial exemplaire de paix en mariage, extraict du devis d'Érasme, translaté de latin en françois, duquel est le titre Uxor memphigamos, c'est-à-dire la femme mary plaignant* was composed in 1536 (see V. Zaercher-Keck, p. 1112).

2 *Le Symbole des Apostres (quon dict vulgairement le Credo contenant les articles de la foy: par maniere de dialogue: par demande et response. La plupart extraict dung traicté d'Érasme de Roterdam intitulé Devises familieres.* On this text see Mann, p. 316-322.

3 Rosenberg, Aubrey. *Nicolas Gueudeville and his work (1562-172?).* Martinus Nijhoff Publishers, 1982.

4 All quotations from *Œuvres complètes de Clément Marot.* ed. C.A. Mayer. Tome VI: Les traductions. Slatkine, 1980.

5 All translation from the French into English are mine. For the English version of the Latin *Colloquies*, see *Collected works of Erasmus.* Translated and annotated by Craig Thompson, University of Toronto Press, 1997: "The whole duty of youth", p. 88-108, "The girl with no interest in marriage", p. 289-301, "The repentant girl", p. 302-305, "Marriage", p. 306-327, "The Abbot and the learned Lady", p. 499-519.

6 Jean Céard, « Marot traducteur d'Érasme », *Clément Marot, « Prince des poètes françois » 1496-1996*, ed. G. Defaux and M. Simonin, Paris, Champion, 1997, p. 107-120.

suggests was written in 1536. These last two texts are Conversations between Catherine and Clement, which come before and after Catherine's attempt to become a convent nun. As for Nicolas Gueudeville, he translated all of Erasmus' *Colloquies* and published his translation in Leyde, in 1720, under the title: *Les Colloques d'Érasme, ouvrage très interessant, par la diversité des sujets, par l'Enjoûment, et pour l'Utilité morale* [Erasmus' Conversations, a very interesting work, for the diversity of its subjects, for its Mirth, and for its moral Utility]. Three particular Conversations[7] from Gueudeville's text will be analyzed in detail here: « Dialogue d'un gros abbé avec une savante » [Dialogue between a fat abbot and a wise lady, Tome 1 Les Femmes, p. 152-166], « La femme qui se plaint de son époux, ou le mariage » [The wife complaining about her husband, or marriage, Tome 1, Les Femmes p. 59-107], « Le jeune dévot ou la piété puérile » [The devout youth or young piety, Tome 5 Les trois principaux mobiles de l'homme. Le Culte, la Nature et l'Art, p. 34-62].

The particularity of these specific texts is that they are directly related to Erasmus' very limited teaching experience. At the time, Erasmus was a private tutor in Paris, teaching to students eager to learn Latin. The content of his work, however, is not that of a tutor nor even of a teacher, but that of a mentor[8]. This comes as no surprise since Erasmus avoided classroom situations and would never have wanted to be caught in one. Indeed, he declined to teach at Saint Paul School in London, even though the institution had recently been refounded by John Colet and Erasmus had only helped to recruit the first teachers of the *Collegium Trium Lingarum*, but declined again to be recruited.

Beyond these historical aspects and the fact that the linguistic aim of the first Colloquies was to teach Latin, Erasmus' *Colloquia* have the added interest that they inform on what the Silenic conception of knowledge transmission was. Indeed, Erasmus' *Colloquia* are conversations between two or more parties that shroud the author's own thoughts during discussions on highly controversial matters such as the monastic vocation, the necessity to condemn Luther, military action, or marital relationships. In a very convenient strategy of dissimulation, the point of view of the

7 *Les Colloques d'Érasme. Ouvrage très interessant par la diversité des Sujets, par l'Enjoûment, et pour l'Utilité Morale. Avec des Notes et des Figures très ingénieuses.* 6 Tomes. Leiden, Vander Aa, 1720.

8 Bierlaire, Franz, *Les Colloques d'Érasme: réforme des études, réforme des mœurs et réforme de l'Eglise au XVIe siècle.* New online edition PU Liège, http://books.openedition.org/pulg/290.

personna do not necessarily echo the author's view. This deceptive approach to teaching led Erasmus to be called an eel by his exasperated detractors but also reveal the originality of his pedagogical approach.

As in *The Praise of folly*, in which Erasmus' *nugae* [trifles] were used to depict far more serious matters than first meet the eye, these texts of his *Colloquia* combine pleasure and earnestness to shape the minds of individuals not very prone to effort. In Marot and Gueudeville's translations, transmission of knowledge relies strongly on the pleasure of the mentee. Learning, however, also requires some effort. Indeed, the voices of the mentor and the author do not necessarily superimpose and must be unraveled. This is especially the case of the Colloquies of conversion, in which a dialog between two characters leads to a change of mind. By reduplicating the pattern existing at the characters' level, the specific ties existing between a mentor and a mentee redefine the relationship between the reader and the author. What could be considered as an education based on power and authority turns out to be an experience where reverence is totally absent. In doing so, the situation depicted gives the mentee full responsibility for his or her final decision: the mentor is but a witness and a warden instigating effective change.

MIRTH AND GRAVITY INTERMINGLED
The core of the mentor/mentor relationship

Erasmian translators into French had a taste for *festivitas*[9] (fun), as becomes obvious when exploring the implicit meaning of their translations. The subtle implications of apparently neutral or innocent remarks become part and parcel of a learning process in which the pupil is tricked. From this angle, the *Dialogue d'un gros abbé avec une savante* [Dialogue between a fat abbot and a wise lady] is a far reaching text, as in this Discussion, Antrone – whose name derives from a city famous for its donkeys[10]– blames Magdalie for the books present in

9 Daniel Ménager, « Ironie ». Érasme, *Éloge de la folie*, ed. by Claude Blum, André Godin, Jean-Claude Margolin, Daniel Ménager, Laffont, 1992, p. CXLI.

10 See *Antronius asinus*, *Adagia*, II, v. 68. Donkeys are famous for being all the more stupid than they are fat. The Latin title of this *Colloquie* « Abbatis et erudita » makes no mention

her room. He believes it is good to be proud of one's ignorance and claims a right to a life of pleasure. Composed of hunting, fine dinners and other distractions (the exact nature of which he refuses to disclose) the abbot's life is that of obvious contempt for wisdom. The abbot's immoderate taste for power, however, turns his example into that of a counter example. Ultimately, he embodies a misguided authority whose legitimacy is based neither on wisdom nor on virtue.

Indeed, Antrone considers wisdom to be a flaw, especially when it comes to women, and believes all should be rid of it. In this respect, he is, in many ways, like the fool of the first chapter of the *Ship of fools* by Brant[11], the abbot is so proud of his ignorance that he can't be viewed as a master nor as a pupil: his *philautia* is too deeply embedded in him.

> Antrone: To Hell with such foolish Wisdom! Don't speak of it to me: I neither want nor understand it, and would be a sorry for it.
>
> Magdalie: But if I were to draw more pleasure in reading a good Author, than you in hunting, in Wine, Cards, etc. would you consider me as an unfortunate person, unable to taste the pleasures of Life?
>
> A: I will not say how I would consider you, but I know that if I were to be so flawed, I would be very sorry and would feel extremely unhappy: therefore I would not linger to make amends.
>
> M: Pray, pay attention to the form and content of my question: I do not ask you what you prefer most in life, but which should please you more. What best deserves your liking and your affection?
>
> A: I would be very displeased if my Monks were to be big *Readers*.
>
> M: My husband has opposite feelings: for he approves of my inclination for reading. But again, Reverend Father in God, why do you think it bad for your Monks to like books and study them?
>
> A. Because the wiser they become, the less obedient and submissive they are: this is what I have learnt from experience on more than one occasion. When I require something from studious monks, when my intention is to give them an order, they baulk like recalcitrant horses: they oppose me with decrees, decretals, Epistles from Saint Peter and Saint Paul, and other similar trifles which they believe allow them to shun my authority. But I don't care. There are no such things as sacred or canonical Authors. The Despotism of my Crosier must prevail[12].

---

of the abbot's corpulence, but his weight can be inferred from the saying that the fatter the donkey, the more stupid it is.

11 Sebastian Brant, *Das Narrenschiff*, ed. Manfred Lemmer, Max Niemeyer, 1986, p. 8, v. 18-24.

12 « *Antrone. Fi! Au Diable, une si sotte Sagesse! Ne m'en parlez point: je ne la comprends, ni ne veux la comprendre, j'en serois bien fâché. – Magdalie. Si je prens plus de plaisir à lire un bon Auteur, que*

As a partisan of ignorance, the abbot readily admits that the Monks under his responsibility are more learned than he and he begrudges them this. Antrone is the very embodiment of error insofar as the intellectual and moral superiority of the everyday monk doesn't bring him satisfaction but, on the contrary, is felt as a threat to his own power, a power he wishes to wield even though it has no legitimacy. Because Magdalie argues in favor of knowledge – including that of women – she becomes the reader's true mentor. When the abbot has made it quite clear that the monks within his convent should not be learned and therefore not think independently and that he himself should not get any wiser, the argument shifts from the education of women to the more general issue of wisdom. What is ultimately at stake is knowledge for all and goes beyond the apparent immediate question concerning the education of women. The reader therefore becomes the real disciple who is expected to enjoy noticing Antrone's mistake, when the fat abbot assumes Virgin Mother spent her time reading her owns hours.

> Magdalie: What do you believe, concerning the Virgin Mother?
> Antrone: In everything the Faith orders me to believe.
> M.: Well, wasn't this blessed among all women, very keen to read?
> A.: I do think Our Lady read, but not that sort of book.
> M.: What, according to you then, was the object of the Holy Virgin's study?
> A.: She read the Canonical hours, or she recited her Rosary, or her Chaplet.
> M.: Your answer is worthy of Your learned and clever Reverence. But, pray, to which use did this blessed maid and woman read the Hours?
> A.: To the use of the Order of Saint Benedict[13].

vous n'en prenez à la chasse, au Vin, au Jeu, etc. me regarderez vous, pour cela, comme une infortunée qui ne goute point les plaisirs de la Vie? – A. Je ne dis point comment je vous regarderois: mais je sais bien que si j'avois un si grand défaut, je m'en voudrois du mal, et m'estimerois fort malheureux: aussi ne tarderois je guere à m'en corriger. – M. Prenez garde, s'il vous plait, au fond et à la nature de ma question: je ne vous demande pas ce qui vous plait le plus dans la vie, je vous demande ce qui devroit vous plaire davantage; quelles sont les choses qui meritent le mieux votre penchant et vôtre attachement? – A. Je serois très faché que mes Moines fussent de grans Liseurs. – M. Mon Mari est d'un sentiment bien opposé: car il approuve fort mon inclination pour la lecture. Mais encore, Révérend Pere en Dieu, pourquoi trouvez vous mauvais que vos religieux soient amateurs de livres et qu'ils s'appliquent à l'étude? A. Parce que plus ils sont savans, moins ils sont disciplinables et soumis: c'est ce que l'experience m'a fait voir plus d'une fois. Quand je veux exiger quelque chose de ces Moines studieux, quand je prétens leur faire un commandement, je trouve des Chevaux qui se cabrent et qui sont rétifs: ils m'opposent les Decrets, les Decretales, les Epitres de Saint Pierre et de Saint Paul; et d'autres bagatelles semblables avec quoi ils s'imaginent pouvoir éluder mon autorité de Supérieur: mais je m'en moque: il n'y a Auteurs ni sacrés ni canoniques qui tiennent: il faut que le Despotisme de ma Crosse aille son train. » (p. 156-157).

13 « *Magdalie. Que croyez vous de la Vierge Mere? – Antrone. Tout ce que la Foi m'ordonne d'en croire. – M. Hé bien cette bénite entre toutes les Femmes, n'étoit elle pas amatrice de la lecture? – A. Je*

Madgalie's sarcasm is all the more impertinent as it lets Antrone display his ignorance further still. In Marot's version of this passage, just as it is in the Latin original, Ysabeau replaces Magdalie, and the abbot's error is even sillier:

> Ysabeau: How is the Virgin Mother considered in your chapter?
> The Abbot: I consider her, as far as I am concerned, the way any good Christian should.
> Y. Did she ever read?
> A. Yes, she did, but she never read those books.
> Y. What did she read then? It's never been heard of.
> A. Her Hours of Our Lady, piously.
> Y. That's easy. To which use?
> A. To that of Rome, I dare say[14].

In this excerpt, the comical effect is based on the fact that the Virgin is supposed to pray to herself in her recitation of the liturgy of the Hours, and on the fact that the abbot doesn't notice the anachronic absurdity of such a situation. Ysabeau's resistance, her confidence in her knowledge and values, allows her to face the abbot's condescension and informs the concept of mentorship in the Erasmian context: readers must grasp what they can from the exchange and be quick to follow the woman's wit.

AUTHORITY EMBEDDED IN FRIENDSHIP

In Erasmian thought, the master cannot be he who knows best, especially considering the importance of friendship for the Dutch humanist. At the beginning of the *Adagia*, which he also called the Treasury

---

croi bien que nôtre Dame lisoit: mais non pas ces sortes de livres-là. – M. Quelle étoit donc, à vôtre avis, l'étude de la Sainte Vierge? – A. Elle lisoit dans les heures Canoniales; ou bien Elle disoit son Rosaire, ou son Chapelet. – M. La réponse est tout à fait digne de vôtre docte et ingénieuse Révérence. Mais, s'il vous plait, à quel usage étoient ces Heures dont cette bienheureuse Fille et Femme se servoit? – Antrone. À l'usage du Grand Ordre de Saint Benoit. » (Gueudeville, p. 164-165)

14 « *Ysabeau (…) Que tient-on en vostre chapitre De la vierge mere? – L'abbé. J'en tien, Quant à moy, ce qu'un bon chrestien Doibt tenir. – Y. Elle ne lisoit Donc jamais de livres? – L'a. Si faisoit; Mais sans doubte, elle ne leut oncques En ces livres cy. – Y. En quoy doncques? Je ne l'ay encore apprins d'ame. – L'a. En ses heures de nostre Dame. Devotement. – Y. Voicy bon homme; Et à quel usage? – L'a. De Rome, Comme je croy.* » (v. 301-313)

of Minerva, Erasmus very purposely placed the words of Pythagoras "*Amicorum communia omnia*" [Between friends, all is common.] In a mentor/mentee relationship, failure too is part of this common property. There is, therefore, no shame in mentioning it.

For instance, in the *Le jeune dévot ou la piété puérile* [The devout youth or young piety, t. 5, p. 34-62], Erasmus exposes to Gaspar his ambition to imitate his virtues. Gaspar dismisses the possibility of any jealousy because of their friendship.

> Erasmus: If I become your contender in good behaviour, you won't be jealous, will you?
> Gaspar: Not in the least. Because of it, I'll appreciate you much more. As you know, conformity in manners and habits brings friends together as well as moods and nature. If the first one results in shared inclination, the other one leads to mutual attachment and complete intimacy.
> E. This is true, except for Competitors for the same civil office, though they have contracted the same disease.
> G. All the more for two Lovers who want to marry the same Lady, though they are sick and suffer from the same wound[15].

Therefore, the mentor differs from the rival in matters of love or the competitor in the race for office, because the content of his knowledge is of a different kind. Learning is inappropriate when dealing with being. This being said, Gaspar does not intend to make things easier for Erasmus: he refuses to be indulgent and will still strive to surpass himself. « *De ton côté, fais de ton mieux pour me dépasser* », [As to you, do your best to beat me] he concludes. Another example comes in Marot's version of « *La fille abhorrant mariage* » [The girl abhorrant of marriage] and « *La fille repentie* » [The repentant girl], in which Clement displays true concern for Catherine:

> Clement: What pleasant weather, don't you think? See, see, everywhere, everybody is smiling that the world is so youthful.

15 « *Erasmus: Si je me fais ton Rival en Conduite, tu n'en seras point jaloux, n'est-ce pas? – Gaspard: Tant s'en faut: tu m'en seras beaucoup plus cher par cet endroit-là. Car comme tu sais, la conformité des mœurs et des manieres ne contribue pas moins à unir deux Amis que celle des humeurs et du Naturel: si par la premiere on contracte une bienveillance reciproque, c'est par l'autre qu'on pousse l'attachement mutüel jusqu'à une entiere familiarité. – E: Cela est vrai: mais non pas entre les Concurrens d'une même charge dans la Magistrature, quoiqu'ils soient attaquez du même mal. – Gaspar. Encore moins entre deux Amans qui veulent épouser la même Maitresse, quoi qu'ils soient malades, et qu'ils aient le cœur blessé du même amour.* (Gueudeville, p. 62)

Catherine: It is true.
Cl.: Why then is your Spring not smiling too[16]?

Following Clement's diligent questioning, Catherine finally replies, « *Quel homme! Vous me pressez aussi fort comme s'il vous touchoit*[17] » [What a man! You insist so, it is as if it affected you]. This emphasizes Clement's attitude and their existing intimacy, so she finally confides in her friend her wish to become a nun. Refusing to oppose Catherine directly, it is in an aside to the reader, that Clement expresses his disagreement:

Clement: Ahem, she's mistaking bran for wheat.
Catherine: What are you saying?
Cl.: Nothing Catherine. I have a frog in my throat, go ahead[18].

Clement is very careful not to be directive after Catherine's failed monastic experience. This appears clearly in another Conversation between the two characters, which focuses mostly on the girl's critical appraisal of her failed attempt to become a nun. Clement continues to keep a low profile, while Catherine stresses that he was right in his mistrust "For sure, from all my friends, and I thought some of them very wise, I didn't receive more sensible advice, still you're the youngest"[19]. His questions help Catherine to tell her story, without any triumphant remark from his part in a way that is very reminiscent of Socratic maieutics.

In the conversation « *La femme qui se plaint de son époux, ou le mariage* » [The wife complaining about her husband, or marriage], Eulalie *la flatteuse* [Flattering Eulalie] offers her advice to a cantankerous and unhappily married woman, going by the name of Xantippe, « *nom de* cette fameuse Harpie, femme de Socrate[20] » [Name of *this famous Harpy, Socrates' wife*]. In this discussion too, friendship appears paramount as the matters broached are indeed delicate. Eulalie, however, does not patronize her friend and assures her that she too has experienced similar difficulties, conflicts and

16 *Clement.: Qu'il faict beau temps, quand je m'advise / Voyez, voyez tout à la ronde / Comment le monde rit au monde / Aussi est il en sa jeunesse. – Catherine: Vous dites vray. Cl.: Et pour quoy est-ce / Que votre printemps, ça et la / Ne rit aussi?* » (p. 267).

17 Gueudeville, p. 276.

18 « *Cl: Hem c'est prendre bran pour farine. – Cath: Que dites vous? – Cl: Rien, Catherine, je toussois dictes à loisir.* » (p. 277).

19 « *Cath. Je vous asseure qu'entre tant d'amys que congnoys, / Et que bien prudentz je tenoys, / Je n'ai point eu conseil plus saige / Que de vous, le plus jeune d'aage / De toute la troupe.* » (p. 300)

20 Gueudeville, p. 60.

matrimonial discontent but has managed to overcome such hiccups in married life. She is the living proof that improvement is possible.

> Eulalie: Do you mind, dear Xanthippe, if I talk to you open-heartedly to be of service to you as a good friend?
> X. A women definitely, but I wouldn't be foolish enough to refuse. Yes, Eulalie, my dear, do talk to me frankly.
> E. You'll have the same right over me. We are childhood friends as you know, and this durable friendship requires a mutual trust devoid of reservation or exceptions.
> [...]
> X. Is everything fine with your spouse? Do you live harmoniously?
> E. Thank God, everything goes smoothly now in our couple.
> X. Were you at war at the beginning? I feel relieved.
> E. Never a storm, but as it may happen among all Mortals, a few clouds from time to time.
> [...]
> X. Be obliging please, how did you manage to change your Spouse [i.e. to make him nicer][21]?

Eulalie is willing to explain what she did as long as Xantippe keeps this secret:

> E. I'll tell you then but only if you imitate me and my confiding in you can teach you something. [...] I won't hide from you my conjugal strategies. Leave it among us however, I beg you, I don't want to be turned into a hero of marital harmony and domestic peace[22].

Eulalie's reply reveals a risk present in the mentor/mentee relationship: if she accepts to be considered as a model she could be undeservedly praised

21 « *Eulalie: Voulez-vous bien, ma chère Xantippe, que je vous rende ici le service d'une bonne Amie, et que je vous parle à cœur ouvert? – Xantippe: Quoique Femme, je ne suis pas assez déraisonnable pour m'y opposer. Oui, ma chère Eulalie, vous pouvez me parler en toute liberté. – E. Vous aurez le même droit sur moi. Nous nous connaissons depuis l'enfance, comme vous le savez. Aussi cette longue amitié demande entre nous une confiance mutuelle qui soit sans réserve et sans exception. X. Tout va-t-il bien avec le vôtre? vivez vous angeliquement ensemble? – E. Dieu merci; la Paix règne à présent dans nôtre petit ménage. – X. Il y avoit donc guerre au commencement? Cela me soulage un peu. E. Il n'y a jamais eu de tempête chez nous. Cependant, comme cela arrive chez tous les Mortels, il s'élevoit, de tems en tems, entre mon Epoux et moi certaines petites nuées [...] – X. Mais obligez-moi de m'apprendre comment vous avez fait pour façonner vôtre Epoux [ie le rendre aimable].* » (Gueudeville, p. 67-71)

22 « *Eulalie: Je le veux bien: mais à condition que vous me prendrez pour modèle, et que ma confidence vous sera une bonne leçon. [...] Je ne vous célerai donc point ma manœuvre Conjugale. Cependant, que ce soit entre nous: je vous prie: car je ne pretens pas m'ériger en Heroine de bon Ménage et de Paix Domestique.* » (Gueudeville, p. 71-72)

and could become self-complacent. The passages commented here reveal two prevailing aspects of the mentor-mentee relationship: though the mentor can act as a model, he or she must be wary of the potential danger of narcissism, unless the relationship sits within the safeguard of friendship.

MENTORING STRATEGIES?

Gueudeville's *Colloques* display a very subtle view on the array of possibilities offered by the mentor for the mentee to improve his or her capabilities. « La femme qui se plaint de son époux ou le mariage » [The wife complaining about her husband, or marriage] addresses, from the start, the difficult social position of French women under the Old Regime:

> The position of an ill-married woman is deplorable: there is no other solution for her except a reasonable and patient obligingness. The debauched husband is a Devil for his wife. True hell is a home where, instead of Reason, passion rules both parties. Good advice on how to maintain a marital union. Never go to bed feeling angry. The sole option for an ill-married woman is to seek all opportunities to deserve the esteem of her tyrant. Often, the source of evil is to neglect to get acquainted. A good wife honours the female sex and is a priceless treasure for her husband[23].

Gueudeville clearly exposes the position of married women in his day and age in an introductory paragraph he added to Erasmus' conversation. For him, married women are not at liberty to confront their husbands, who are well aware of their power. They should be lauded for enduring the misconducts of their lord and master. It is for this reason that the text doesn't present divorce as an interesting solution, and tags it as a temptation:

> When this temptation arises, dismiss it. What is a women separated from her husband? How is she considered? Is she regarded with esteem?

23 « *La condition d'un (sic) Femme mal pourvuë est déplorable: point d'autre remède pour elle qu'une sage et patiente complaisance. L'Epoux debauché, c'est le Demon de l'Epouse. Vrai Enfer qu'un Menage où, au lieu de la Raison, la passion règne des deux côtez. Bons Conseils pour le maintien de l'Union Conjugale. On ne doit jamais s'y coucher sur sa colere. Le seul parti d'une mal Mariée, c'est de chercher toutes les occasions de gagner l'estime de son Tiran. Souvent la source du mal, c'est de ne s'appliquer point assez à s'entreconoîstre. La bonne Femme est l'honneur de son Sexe, et un Tresor inestimable pour le Mari.* » (p. 59-60).

> Were the husband a hundred times in the wrong, would the Spouse be less despised[24]?

For Gueudeville, following Erasmus' steps, divorce is not an option as the first drawback of this is marginalization. Eulalie's arguments, therefore, recognize Xantippe's marital difficulties with Nicolas for what they are, but favor Xantippe's interests in the matter. As a mentor, Eulalie prompts her friend to take action and the help she offers does bring Xantippe to react. Indeed, Xantippe's displeasure changes, and her anger towards her husband Nicolas leads to the brink of genuine destruction when she threatens to hit her husband with a stool. Having vented her resentment, however, she is finally ready to repair the situation, to renounce to violence and to express her wish to learn from Eulalie how she managed her own case. "Now, tell me shortly, what would you have had me do?", she asks[25].

Eulalie makes it very clear that she doesn't approve of Xantippe's violent reactions and explains that the angry Xantippe has to accept an unexpected solution and to put in more effort still. She shows this is possible by bringing herself to the same level as her friend and using herself as an example. For Erasmus, the mentor cannot initiate a process that has to be decided by the agent herself. The mentor, like Eulalie can only illustrate the solution proposed, thereby proving at a very personal level its efficiency. The mentor-mentee relationship thus appears to be one of equality, where the advisor has experienced what is suggested but lets the other decide for herself.

In many ways, Eulalie's advice is not an easy solution and one that requires the greatest effort from Xantippe. Xantippe notices this and is not fooled. So even though Paulinian submission is still very present in the text, Xantippe is spurred to act. This rejection of passivity and resignation is a way of avoiding submission as go to show the analogies used by Eulalie:

> Xantippe: What? You would have me fake love and answer the caress of such a husband? I am definitely more honest. My hypocrisy does not go so far.
>
> Eulalie: Where there is no restraint, there can be no profit. Please, tell me where lies your greatest interest? Isn't it that your husband stops behaving the

24 « *Quand cette tentation-là vous reviendra dans l'esprit, repoussez-la par ce raisonnement-ci: qu'est ce qu'une Femme séparée d'avec son Mari? Comment est elle regardée? Quel cas en fait on? Et le tort serait cent fois du côté de l'Epoux, l'Espouse en est elle moins méprisée?* » (p. 102).

25 « *Dites moi a present en abrégé, que faut-il que je fasse?* » (p. 105).

way you say, becomes easier and more accommodating, is it not? I ask you: if you were as able a sorceress as the famous Circe, if you had the knack for changing your husband into a pig or a bear, would you like to do so?
X. I don't know. It would depend on how I feel.
E. Don't you know? How can you hesitate? Would you prefer to be a sow, a female swine, rather than the wife of a man?
X. Let's be serious. Frankly, I'd rather sleep with a male of my own species than with a Pig.
E. Come now! If you had Circe's skills and a book of magic to drive your husband away from drunkenness into sobriety, from profligacy to economy, from laziness to care; if you could eventually make of your husband a man as perfect as he is bad, would you ponder so long[26]?

Eulalie's pedagogy suggests that every wife be a Circe. Circe's 'metamorphosing power' is 'the power of lust and especially, the spell of Love. It is your choice to use this spell and therefore your choice to have a good husband.'[27] By changing herself into a Circe, Xantippe turns herself into a powerful woman, even though her marriage remains full of constraints. Such a change is pushed even further when Eulalie reminds Xantippe of her success in taming a parrot:

> Eulalie: What! You spare neither your time nor your energy to find entertainment in a Bird. Yet you baulk, you dread the work, when it is question to gain a husband with whom you'll be happy to spend the rest of your life[28]?

---

26 « *Xantippe: Quoi! vous voudriez que je contrefisse assez l'amoureuse pour répondre aux caresses d'un tel Mari? Oh certes je suis de meilleure foi; et mon hypocrisie ne va point jusque-là. – Eulalie: Mais il faut se contraindre pour son profit. Or, dites moi, je vous prie, vôtre interet dominant, n'est ce pas que vôtre Mari cesse d'être tel que vous le dite, et qu'il devienne plus traitable et plus accommodant? Je vous demande: si, étant aussi habile Sorciere que la fameuse Circé, vous aviez le secret de metamorphoser vôtre Mari en Cochon ou en Ours, seriez vous d'humeur à faire une telle operation? – X: Je n'en sai rien, c'est selon que l'envie m'en prendroit. – E: Vous n'en savez rien? Y a-t-il donc ici tant soit peu à balancer? Est ce que vous aimeriez mieux être une truie, ou femelle d'un Pourceau, que d'être la Femme d'un homme? – X: Dans le serieux pourtant: franchement j'aimerais mieux coucher avec un Mâle de mon Espèce, qu'avec un Cochon. – E: Mais ça! si, par l'adresse et le grimoire de Circé, vous pouviez faire passer vôtre Mari de l'ivrognerie à la sobriété; de la prodigalité à l'économie, de la faineantise à la diligence; enfin, si vous pouviez faire de vôtre Epoux un homme aussi parfait qu'il est vicieux, Penseriez-vous longtemps à ce que vous auriez à faire?* » (Gueudeville, p. 95-96).

27 « *Eulalie: [...] la force de la Volupté, et principalement le charme de l'Amour. Il ne tient donc qu'à vous d'emploïer ce charme; et conséquemment il ne tient qu'à vous d'avoir un bon mari.* » (Gueudeville, p. 97).

28 « *[...] Quoi! Vous n'épargnez ni vôtre temps ni vôtre peine pour tirer quelque divertissement d'un Oiseau: et vous reculez, vous craignez la peine, lorsqu'il s'agit de mettre vôtre Mari sur le pié de pouvoir passer agréablement toute votre vie avec lui?* » (Gueudeville, p. 104).

Eulalie encourages Xantippe to tame her husband and to bring him to do good. This solution does not question feminine submission but offers the possibility of positive change within the context of society. Finally, Eulalie's strategy is not simply to reconcile husband and wife, it is to turn Xantippe into the mentor of her husband.

What does this say about the mentor/mentee relationship? The Eulalie/Xantippe conversation goes beyond the issue of friendship, as it puts the mentee into action, helps her to reconsider a blocked situation. A successful mentorship appears to be one that challenges the mentee, offers her the opportunity to reassess her position and to gain command over her own destiny. In short, Gueudeville's *Colloquie* is a lesson of empowerment allowing anyone facing a deadlock to overcome their difficulties, especially any internal ones.

To conclude, this brief overview of some French translations of Erasmus' *Colloquia* tells us a lot about mentorship. For French Erasmian authors, the complicity between mentor and mentee can only thrive thanks to friendship. More than just a value cherished by Erasmus himself, friendship is a prerequisite to the mentoring experience. The mentor's legitimacy rests on the fact that he or she has hurdled the same obstacles, and can share the journey, the end of which can only be full autonomy. The fulfillment of mentorship is the independence of the mentee: it is in this accomplishment that the mentor/mentee relationship dissolves. The presence of irony and implicit in the colloquies is a key element to warn the mentee: he or she has to decipher the subtleties of underlying meaning, to tame difficulties and charm adversity.

Anne-Laure METZGER-RAMBACH
Université Bordeaux-Montaigne
France

STAGING PAST AND PRESENT MENTORS ON THE GLOBAL THEATRE OF PRINTED KNOWLEDGE

Neoplatonic cosmography and ethos in Giovan Battista Ramusio's *Navigations and travels* (1550-1559)

INTRODUCTION

Renaissance authors and editors of travel narratives consistently employed paratextual apparatus, principally prefaces and commentaries, to shape their professional identities and illustrate their personal beliefs[1]. Ramusio's *Discorsi* present mentorship and friendship as the aspiration to universal harmony via a narrative praxis that drew profoundly, and creatively, on modern and ancient sources. Cicero's *De Amicitia* occupies a preeminent position amongst the classical Latin treatises on friendship, as it addresses the most commendable form of friendship, which is reciprocal love based on the performance of communal virtues in earthly life. While the historical filiation of Cicero's dialogue on friendship is customarily indicated in books VIII and IX of Aristotle's *Nicomachean Ethics*, the type of virtues Ramusio elected as ideals to be upheld by true mentors of humankind is indebted to the so-called second and third generation Neoplatonism and Hermeticism. These inter-disciplinary philosophical movements characterized a substantial part of Venetian cultural production in the

1 Augustus Pallotta, « The New World and Italian Readers of the Spanish Historie in the Sixteenth Century », *Italica*, 1992, vol. 69, n° 3 (Autumn), p. 347. While Pallotta discussed Iberian professionals translating Spanish narratives into Italian, early Italian writers of the Age of Discoveries, including Ramusio, regularly adopted the same praxis.

first half of the sixteenth century[2], finding their intellectual workshop in the *Studium patavinum*, the University of Padua, and intellectuals who operated there at the time.

Although Ramusio preferred to avoid publicity over the course of his long career as curator of modern publications and operated anonymously behind the scenes of the great Venetian editors and intellectuals of his time, he was no mere imitator. In the following pages, I will investigate the linguistic means and theoretical principles Ramusio employed to construe mentorship and friendship in semi-synonymous terms, thus contextualising the cosmological and ethical tenets of Florentine Neoplatonism at the onset of the Age of Discoveries.

ORIGINS OF VENETIAN NEOPLATONISM

The Paduan academic environment and Ramusio's own collaboration with friends and acquaintances represent the primary pathways to attempt to reconstruct the historical correlation between the secretary of the Venetian Republic and the early development of humanistic Neoplatonism. Deemed the most important Italian centre for Aristotelianism in the fifteenth and sixteenth centuries[3], the University of Padua was likewise an academic institution open to intellectual debate.

Ramusio's strongest and most enduring connection with the Venetian academic environment is plausibly to be found in his lifelong distinguished friend and mentor Pietro Bembo, whose commitments at the University of Padua prevented him from carrying out his duties as curator and chief librarian of the Nicena library. Ramusio agreed to act as custodian of this library from 1531 to 1543, although under the supervision of Bembo, replacing in that role their common friend Andrea Navagero[4]. The Nicena library stored and preserved a large number

2 John M. Headley, « The Sixteenth-Century Venetian Celebration of the Earth's Total Habitability: The Issue of the Fully Habitable World for Renaissance Europe », *Journal of World History*, 1997, vol. 8, n° 1 (Spring), p. 16.

3 Paul Oskar Kristeller, « Florentine Platonism and Its Relations with Humanism and Scholasticism », *Church History*, 1939, vol. 8, n° 3 (September), p. 201.

4 Veneri, « Giovanni Battista Ramusio » p. 169, p. 171.

of manuscripts, which cardinal Bessarion donated to the Republic of Venice. Ramusio's position at the Nicena library sheds light on both the context where he started devising the travel narratives he would later include in his collection, and the earlier critical debates that initiated the discourse regarding the suitability of Florentine Neoplatonism in informing the reading of the contemporary literary genre that developed parallel to the European exploration of the globe, the humanistic geographical treatise[5].

While acting as chief librarian and custodian of the library, Ramusio started collecting the materials concerning modern and ancient explorations of the Globe that he would publish in the *editio princeps* of his *Navigations and Travels* nearly two decades later. Consequently, he had the opportunity to critically compare the geographical information provided by early modern navigators and historians with the accounts presented by the great geographers of the past, delving into the philosophical and cosmogonic repercussions the new European discoveries had on classical and sacred geography.

Perhaps even more significant in tracing the convergence between Florentine Neoplatonism and Ramusio's geo-cosmogonic treatise is the donor of the collection. Cardinal Bessarion penned an apology of Plato

5 A former mentee of the renowned Platonist George Gemisthus Pletho, cardinal Bessarion donated a large number of Greek and Latin manuscripts to the Republic of Venice on 31st May 1468. Although the figures provided vary in terms of the exact number of volumes acquired, the manuscripts donated by Bessarion included rare geographical and philosophical treatises. Wiegand and Davis mention 482 Greek, and 264 Latin manuscripts, whereas Labowsky suggests more than 1,000 total volumes. Carlotta Labowsky, *Bessarion's library and the Biblioteca Marciana: six early inventories*, Rome: Edizioni di storia e letteratura, 1979, p. 44-45; Wayne A. Wiegand and Donald G. Davis, *Encyclopedia of Library History*, New York, Routledge, 2013, p. 548. It may be possible that these estimates are drawn from inventories compiled at different times. In his letters to Ramusio, Bembo urges his friend to demand that private citizens wishing to borrow items from the Nicena library leave a monetary deposit at least twice the value of the manuscripts, saying that the donor himself, cardinal Bessarion, set this rule upon donating his collection. This remark suggests that an unspecified number of books had been borrowed, but not returned, as Bembo lamented: "You need to keep in mind that, since those who were in charge of the books paid no attention to this rule, we found out that some of them were missing" ("*Vi dovete aricordare che, per non vi avere avuto tal cura quelli che li avevano il governo avanti noi, trovammo che ce n'erano di manco*"). Pietro Bembo, *Lettere*, Bologna, Commissione per i testi di lingua, 1987-1993, IV, p. 335. Regarding Bembo's lingering authority and influence on Ramusio as chief librarian of the Nicena library, see also Bembo, *Lettere*, III, 282-283; IV, p. 46-47, p. 342-343. Translations in this article are my own, unless indicated otherwise.

entitled *In Calumniatores Platonis*[6] in which he attempted to reconcile Christianised Platonic theories and Aristotelian philosophy, as Tomeo would endeavour to do after him, explaining that "the preference for one should not exclude the appreciation of the other."[7] He instead proposed there was substantial agreement between the two philosophers. Crucial to the future development of Neoplatonic readings of geographical discoveries was his depiction of Plato, whom Bessarion presented as a great mathematician and, more importantly, natural philosopher who demonstrated that the world, although not eternal in nature, reflects the eternal reality[8].

In the mid-1400s, the development of cosmographic representations concerned with accurately locating the exact position of terrestrial and celestial spheres initiated a prolonged, educated debate regarding the holistic interaction of forms, patterns, and meanings between earthly and heavenly places. This debate aimed to progressively reform medieval cosmogony according to the information derived from recent European explorations of the Western and Eastern Indies. The classical tradition of studying material spaces as new places[9] explains the cosmogonic nature of the *Theatrum Mundi* (Theatre of the World): a moralised theatre that connects the representation of the Globe, interpreted as physical space, with the *cosmos*: an ordered, harmonious creation where human and divine intellect meet to make sense of the universe, defined as cosmogonic place[10]. Modern and contemporary academic discourse has accommodated this pursuit into several definitions. Despite exhibiting different critical inclinations, several scholars pointed to the metaphysical nature

---

6 Bessarion, *Bessarionis cardinalis Sabini & patriarche Constantinopolitani capitula libri primi aduersus calumniatorem Platonis incipiunt feliciter*, Rome, Conradus suueynheym: Arnoldus pannartzque magistri Rome impresserunt talia multa simul. Petrus cum fratre Francisco Maximus ambo huic operi aptatam contribuere domum, 1469. The work was started in 1465 and was first published in Rome in 1469.

7 Nesca Adeline Robb, *Neoplatonism of the Italian Renaissance*, New York, Octagon Books, 1968, p. 51.

8 Robb, 1968, p. 47-54.

9 "The difference between a space and a place is not just a matter of semantics and even less a matter of utility but of affective capacity and that capacity cannot be easily regulated by authorities or planned in advance", E. Muir, « The 2001 Josephine Waters Bennett Lecture: The Idea of Community in Renaissance Italy », *Renaissance Quarterly*, 2002, vol. 55, n° 1 (Spring), p. 11.

10 Dennis Cosgrove, « Globalism and Tolerance in Early Modern Geography », *Annals of the Association of American Geographers*, 2003, vol. 93, n° 4 (December), p. 856.

of the project that informed the humanist geo-cosmogonic discussions. Through their undertaking, Neoplatonic humanists intended to retrieve the apparently lost harmony between the eternal place of God, and the geographical spaces inhabited by all living beings; what the Venetian philosopher and theologian Francesco Giorgi called *Harmonia Mundi*[11].

The philosophical debates that took place at the University of Padua[12] in the wake of Tomeo's lectures prepared a fertile background for a generation of scholars keen on investigating Platonic and Neoplatonic texts in relation to their expertise and research interests[13]. These intellectuals interpreted and applied Neoplatonic theoretical frameworks to diverse fields of knowledge: Francesco Giorgi, Niccolò Tartaglia, and Silvio Belli to mathematics; Pietro Bembo (*Della Historia Vinitiana*, book VI) and Gasparo Contarini (*De magistratibus et republica Venetorum*, 1453) to historiography; Sperone Speroni (*Dialogo d'amore*, 1542), Mario Equicola (*Libro de natura d'Amore*, 1525), Bembo (*Gli Asolani*, 1505) to philosophy and to the Love treatise, *trattato d'amore* – the 16th century literary genre evolving from Florentine Neoplatonism; Bembo (*De Aetna*, 1495), Gastaldi, Girolamo Ruscelli (*Le imprese illustri*, 1580 edition)[14]

---

11 Francesco Giorgio, *Francisci Georgii Veneti [...] De harmonia mundi totius cantica tria*, Venetiis: in ædibus Bernardini de Vitalibus chalcographi, 1525.

12 In 1497, the Venetian Neoplatonist Niccolò Leonico Tomeo (1456-1531) delivered a series of lectures specifically focused on Plato's philosophy, subsequently attempting to reconcile Platonic and Aristotelian positions on the theme of the soul in his *Alverotus sive De tribus animorum vehiculis*. See Niccolò Leonico Tomeo, *Nicolai Leonici Thomaei Dialogi nunc primum in lucem editi quorum nomina proxima pagina habentur*, Venetiis: in ædibus Gregorii de Gregoriis, Mense septembri 1524, p. XXX^r^-XLII^v^.

13 Anna Corrias, « Imagination and Memory in Marsilio Ficino's Theory of the Vehicles of the Soul », *The International Journal of the Platonic Tradition* 6, 2012, p. 85; Jonathan Davies, « Marsilio Ficino: Lecturer at the Studio fiorentino », *Renaissance Quarterly*, 1992, vol. 45, n° 4 (Winter), p. 788; the Niccolò Leonico Tolomeo entry in *Dizionario biografico degli italiani*, 2005, p. 64, http://www.treccani.it/enciclopedia/niccolo-leonico-tomeo_(Dizionario-Biografico).

14 In the given order: Giorgio, *Francisci Georgii Veneti*...; Niccolò Tartaglia, *La prima [-sesta] parte del general trattato di numeri, et misure [...]*, VI vols, in Vinegia: per Curtio Troiano de i Nauò, 1556-1560; Silvio Belli, *Libro del misurar con la uista [...]*, in Venetia: per Domenico de' Nicolini, 1565; Pietro Bembo, *Della historia vinitiana di m. Pietro Bembo card. volgarmente scritta. Libri 12*, in Vinegia: appresso Gualtero Scotto, 1552; Gasparo Contarini, *De magistratibus & republica Venetorum libri quinque, authore Gaspare Contareno patricio Veneto*, Parisiis: ex officina Michaëlis Vascosani, in uia quæ est ad diuum Iacobum, sub fontis insigni, 1593; Sperone Speroni, *I dialogi di Messer Speron Sperone*, in Vinegia: in casa de' figliuoli di Aldo, 1542; Mario Equicola, *Libro de natura de amore di Mario Equicola secretario del illustrissimo S. Federico 2. Gonzaga marchese di Mantua*, stampato in Venetia: per Lorenzo Lorio da Portes, 1525; Pietro Bembo, *Petri Bembi De Aetna ad*

and Ramusio (amongst others) to geography and cartography, thereby relating the theory of universal perfection to the political reformation of the Venetian Republic[15].

These names provide a reliable estimate of the popularity that philosophical treatises penned by members of the *Quattrocento* Florentine Platonic Academy enjoyed among scholars in charge of educating the Venetian patriciate and upper-middle class. Ficino's reading of the Platonic tradition in the *De Amore* (1484) was well-suited to repair the rupture between the *Theatrum Mundi* (cosmogonic space) of classical authorities, and what would later become the *Theatrum Orbis Terrarum* (geographical place) of late Renaissance geographers, thus initiating the early modern discourse concerning the modes of interaction between physical and metaphysical actors on the global stage.

In recent years, scholars have suggested that the collection of travel narratives devised and edited by Ramusio represents a turning point in the evolution of the geographic literary genre. Horodowich observed that the *Navigations and Travels* provided an innovative stylistic and conceptual framework subsequently adopted by renowned Renaissance editors and compilers of travel narrative collections, such as Richard Hakluyt's *Divers Voyages*, Samuel del Purchas' *Pilgrims*, and Theodore di Bry's *Grand Voyages*[16]. Ramusio's *Navigations and Travels* introduced the first systematic, inclusive description of the modern world[17], thus offering an innovative interpretation of European explorations based on space (continents), rather than the Iberian political spheres of influence. Furthermore, the collection openly staged the disciplinary and political repercussions the *Cinquecento* discoveries brought forth on the diplomacy of printed culture[18].

Two crucial components of Ramusio's early humanistic and political career in the period preceding the composition of the *Navigations and Travels* offer a useful insight into his cosmological ideas, moral beliefs, and his links to humanistic Neoplatonic philosophy. In addition to the

Angelum Chabrielem liber, impressum Venetiis: in aedibus Aldi Romani, mense februario, 1495; Girolamo Ruscelli, *Le imprese illustri con espositioni, et discorsi del s.or Ieronimo Ruscelli. [...] Con la giunta di altre imprese tutto riordinato et corretto*, in Venetia: presso a Francesco de' Franceschi, senese, 1580.

15 Cosgrove, 1992, p. 76, 80, 82.

16 L. Horodowich, « Armchair Travelers and the Venetian Discovery of the New World », *The Sixteenth Century Journal*, 2005, vol. 36, n° 4 (Winter) p. 1043.

17 Veneri, 2012, p. 162, 164, 190.

18 *Ibid.*, p. 166.

scholarly and courtly environments where Ramusio lived and operated, or had been exposed to through his acquaintances, a number of his friends and mentors participated in the debates that emerged from the Ficinian revival of Plato.

RAMUSIO AND HIS INTELLECTUAL CIRCLE
The reciprocity of mentorship and friendship in *Navigations and Travels*

In the heterogeneous society that constituted Ramusio's scholarly and political network, the most important figure that comes to mind is his lifelong friend and mentor Pietro Bembo. Bembo was among the first intellectuals to initiate the second stage of Florentine Neoplatonism in Italy, turning it from a philosophical (and philological) debate on the nature of Love into the literary Love Treatise[19]. Composed in Ferrara between 1497 and 1502, Bembo's Neoplatonic dialogue *Gli Asolani* (1505) accepts the principles of Ficinian philosophy without altering or reforming its theoretical premises. Instead, the dialogue develops the theme of love that occurs between human beings in a style that is primarily aesthetic and poetic in nature[20]. The modes of interaction between lovers and friends develop into a refined, elegant etiquette that appealed to the literary taste of the courtly Italian society, thus becoming "the great prototype of the courtly Neoplatonic treatise."[21]

A conspicuous number of extant letters[22] attest to the reciprocal mentorship and friendship that existed between the cardinal and the

19 Robb, 1968, p. 176-211. Family ties have contributed to arouse Pietro's interest in Florentine Neoplatonism. Bernardo Bembo, Pietro's father, resided on two different occasions in Florence as ambassador of the Venetian Republic (1475-1476; 1478-1480). The young Pietro accompanied his father to Florence, and attended at least one meeting of the Platonic Academy. A generous patron of Florentine humanists, Bernardo became a close associate of Ficino, who profusely praised the Venetian ambassador on multiple occasions, addressing numerous letters to him in the 1470s and 1480s. Hankins, 1991, p. 447; Robb, 1968, p. 184.

20 Robb, 1968, p. 192, 194.

21 *Ibid.*, p. 184.

22 Bembo's letters to Ramusio may be consulted at the Marciana Library (Ms. Marciano It.X.143), while Ramusio's letters to the cardinal are held at the Ambrosiana Library

secretary of the Republic, a disciplinary and moral bond that led to an unremitting collaboration on different editorial projects. Ramusio revised the 1525 edition of *Prose della volgar lingua*[23], as well as most of Bembo's posthumous historiographical treatises. Ramusio also advised both Bembo and their common friend Girolamo Fracastoro on matters of classical philology.

As a result, Ramusio became well acquainted with his friend's literary style and philosophical ideas, adopting some of Bembo's stylistic traits and theoretical precepts in the paratexts he inserted in his *Navigations and Travels*. Romanini notices that in his *Discorsi*, Ramusio adopted the style and lexicon of *Gli Asolani*[24], thus situating his commentaries within Bembo's Neoplatonic cultural and linguistic framework. Romanini's observations are further supported by a letter Bembo addressed to Ramusio, where the cardinal misinterpreted Ramusio's silence on the copy of *Gli Asolani* he had sent to him as a sign of disappointment[25].

Bembo's letters to Ramusio constitute a valuable source to identify the modes of interaction among Ramusio's network of friends and mentors, showing how their reciprocal mentoring and learning embraced treatises focused on Plato, the modern Neoplatonic love treatise, cosmogony and cosmology. The cardinal praised his friend for printing the complete collection of Plato's works: "Send my regards to my distinguished friend [lit., *compare*] Aldo Manuzio. What a great accomplishment is your printing of Plato['s work]."[26] Other letters reveal their shared passion for

(Ms. Ambrosiano D. 335). Massimo Donattini, « Giovanni Battista Ramusio e le sue 'Navigationi'. Appunti per una biografia », *Critica Storica*, 1980, vol. 17, n° 1, p. 63, 87, 91. Bembo's letters are available in the modern edition mentioned above.

23 Pietro Bembo, *Prose di. m. Pietro Bembo nelle quali si ragiona della volgar lingua scritte al cardinale de Medici che poi e stato creato a Sommo Pontefice et detto papa Clemente Settimo diuise in tre libri*, Impresse in Vinegia: per Giouan Tacuino, nel mese di Settembre, 1525.

24 Fabio Romanini, *Se fussero più ordinate, e meglio scritte...: Giovanni Battista Ramusio correttore ed editore delle Navigationi et viaggi*, Rome: Viella, 2007, p. 283-284.

25 "[The fact that] you did not want to say anything about *Gli Asolani* tells me much about what you think of it, that is you did not like it. Never mind", ("*Del non mi aver voi voluto dir cosa alcuna degli* Asolani *è stato un dir assai, cioè che e' [sic.] non ve sono piaciuti. Pazienza.*"), Bembo, *Lettere*, II, p. 206.

26 "*Al mio onorato compare M. Aldo Manuzio mi fate raccomandato. Oh quanto fate bene a imprimere Platone*", Bembo, *Lettere*, II, p. 56-60. Considering that the letter is dated 30th July, 1512 (in the text, "St Peter's day"), in this instance Bembo is plausibly referring to the first Greek edition of Plato's complete works Aldo Manuzio and Andrea Torresano published the following year. This edition was curated by the Greek scholar Marco Musuro: Plato, *Hapanta ta tou Platonos. Omnia Platonis opera*, Venetiis: in aedib. Aldi, et Andreae soceri,

classical and modern cosmographers (ranging from Ptolemy to Francesco Maurolico's *Cosmographia*)[27], and contemporary geographical treatises, particularly Oviedo's *Historia general delas Indias.*

If one were to expect to find detailed discussions about the tenets of modern philosophical trends in Bembo's letters to Ramusio, one would probably find very little material of use, apart from a few very concise glimmers. What does transpire from their correspondence, though, are traces of two aspects of Ficino's philosophy that have been obscured in the literary tradition of the Love Treatise: Neoplatonic cosmology and ethics.

The reciprocity that characterises the process of mentoring and learning in Ramusio's network of mentors and friends extends to the cultural formation of their friends' offspring. This is instanced in Bembo's request to Ramusio to mentor Carlo da Fano's son (Carlo Gualteruzzi): "I would like you [Ramusio] to be the fourth among such *prudence* and *wisdom* (lit., *quarto tra cotanto senno*, Italics in the original) in teaching those pupils about ancient and modern cosmography, which will be a noble and useful deed [...]."[28]

First registered in Dante's *Divine Comedy* ("lasciali digrignar pur a lor senno", *Inf.* XXI, v. 134), the word *senno* used by Bembo indicates the faculty and actual capability to understand, evaluate, and act upon

---

mense Septembri 1513. Although Ramusio is not explicitly mentioned in the dedicatory letter, Bembo's words suggest he may have contributed to the preparation of this edition.

27 Bembo's letters requesting a copy of Ptolemy's 'book' held at the Nicena library (probably the *Geographia*) date back to 1531; Veneri suggests Ramusio started collecting the narratives that would later form the *Navigations and Travels* precisely in this period. Bembo, *Lettere*, III vol. 278, p. 282, 285, 295; Veneri, 2012, p. 164. In 1541, Bembo sent a, probably hand-written, copy of Maurolico's *De Astrologia* to Ramusio, enquiring about the present state of negotiations with 'new printers' to have it published. Maurolico is called 'il messinese', as he was born in Messina into a Greek family that migrated to Sicily around the time of the Sicilian Vespers (1282), according to Rosario Moscheo, the curator of the entry in the *Dizionario Biografico degli Italiani.* The reference probably alludes to the *editio princeps* of the treatise, printed in Venice two years later by Lucantonio Giunta: Francesco Maurolico, *Cosmographia Francisci Maurolyci Messanensis Siculi, in tres dialogos distincta: in quibus de forma, situ, numeroque tam coelorum quam elementorum, alijsque rebus ad astronomica rudimenta spectantibus satis disseritur*, Venetiis: apud haeredes Lucae'antonij Iuntae Florentini, mense Ianuario 1543. Bembo, *Lettere*, IV vol., p. 372, 392; Treccani, *Dizionario Biografico degli Italiani*, 2008, vol. 72 http://www.treccani.it/enciclopedia/francesco-maurolico_(Dizionario-Biografico)/.

28 "*Piacemi che voi siate il quarto fra cotanto senno in instruir quei fanciulli nello [sic.] cosmografia e antica e moderna, che non sara poco utile e nobile opera [...]*", Bembo, *Lettere*, IV, p. 559. Unless stated otherwise, italics in the extracts indicates my own emphasis.

reality with wisdom and prudence[29]. Wisdom and Prudence are precisely the two virtues Ficino associated with, respectively, the understanding of the *cosmos* (a term that interprets the physical universe as a direct manifestation of the metaphysical Divine Will), and human history, as I discuss in the second section of this chapter.

The epistolary exchange between Ramusio, Bembo, and Fracastoro is invaluable for appreciating how their reciprocal mentoring operated. The familiar, affectionate tone that transpires from the letters reveals their disposition to discuss in an informal fashion the minutiae of natural phenomena and the rationale of cosmogonic theories, where the universal virtues of their interlocutor constitute the guiding principle in evaluating the dialectical nature of human knowledge.

For instance, the extract from Fracastoro's letter XXX on the fluctuation of the river Nile illustrates how diverse hypotheses represent an opportunity to learn from Ramusio:

> I could not have received a more welcome gift than your amendments, which made me informed, *prudent*, and, possibly, more learned. [...] Regarding the fluctuation of the river Nile, I, with the greatest anticipation [lit., desire], look forward to apprehending its true cause, and what the ancients thought about it [...] Hence, I encourage and exhort you [to shed light on it], since *the matters concerning rivers, mountains, and land, although not eternal, are nonetheless close to the eternal ones*[30].

From a philosophical perspective, Bembo, Ramusio and Fracastoro shared the same belief in the *harmonia mundi*. A reflection of the undocumented discussions that occurred among the circle of friends concerns the Platonic theory of the *plenum*, according to which God's infinite wisdom did not leave any part of the Earth uninhabited. In the sixth book of his *Historia Vinitiana* (begun after 1530, and first published in 1551), Bembo critiqued the classical notion which asserts that only two out of five climate zones were habitable, countering it with the Platonic

29 "*Facoltà, e capacità abituale, d'intendere, giudicare e operare con prudenza e saviezza*", *Treccani*, 2005, http://www.treccani.it/vocabolario/senno/.

30 "*Non poteva ricever cosa più grata, che le vostre correzioni, che m'han fatto avvertito, e prudente, e, se sarà possibile, più colto [...] Quanto al crescimento del Nilo, io con grandissimo desiderio aspetto d'intender la vera cagione, e quello che gli antichi pensarono. Tanto più mi sarà grata, quanto per il mezzo vostro venirà in luce. Al che vi esorto, ed inanimo, perché ancor che queste cose non sieno eterne, cioè le cose de' fiumi, de' monti, e della terra, sono però vicine all'eterne*", Fracastoro, *Operum* 92 (second part).

theory of 'rational plenitude' (*plenum*), which would evolve over the course of the sixteenth century into the idea of the Earth's total habitability. While discussing the arguments Christopher Columbus employed to convince Isabella I of Castile and Ferdinando II of Aragon to lend their financial support to his first voyage, Bembo writes:

> And Columbus showed the Catholic Monarchs that what almost all antiquity believed was a vain fable of the ancients, a subdivision not supported, nor confirmed by true reasons: that is the sky is divided into five parts. [According to the ancients,] of these parts of the sky, the middle one is afflicted by heat, and the ones at the furthest ends by cold, and the three parts of Earth that are beneath them are inhabitable by men, and only the two parts located between those three are habitable. If this were true, it would be almost necessary to believe God to have been imprudent, since he shaped the world this way, leaving the greater part of Earth without men due to the harsh elements, thus making it useless. [...] This way, the whole globe partakes of the vital aura[31].

Ramusio presents the exact same principles of plenitude and sufficient reason in the *Discourse of messer Giovan Battista Ramusio about the fluctuation* [lit., growth] *of the river Nile*, [addressed to] *the most excellent messer Ieronimo Fracastoro*:

> [...] Contrary to the ancients and their erroneous imagination concerning this globe of earth, which is now clearly known to be all inhabited, nor is there any part either hot or cold, discounting deserts and oceans, that is not full of men and animals, that everyone exists there as in a temperate region. I say temperate according to the constitution given to them by nature[32].

Ramusio restates the same theory in the *Discourse on the third volume of the Navigations and Travels on the part of the new world*, dedicated to his friend and mentor Girolamo Fracastoro[33].

The acknowledgment of Plato's fame and the cosmological importance of his *Timaeus* in Western discourse, as evidenced in the sixteenth century

---

31 Pietro Bembo, *Della historia vinitiana di m. Pietro Bembo card. volgarmente scritta. Libri 12*, in Vinegia: appresso Gualtero Scotto, 1552, p. 72^{v}-73^{r}.

32 *Discorso di messer Gio. Battista Ramusio sopra il crescer del fiume Nilo, allo eccellentissimo messer Ieronimo Fracastoro.* The citation and translation are taken from John M. Headley, « The Sixteenth-Century Venetian Celebration of the Earth's Total Habitability: The Issue of the Fully Habitable World for Renaissance Europe », *Journal of World History*, 1997, vol. 8, n° 1 (Spring), p. 14-16. For the original Italian text, see Giovanni Battista Ramusio, *Navigazioni e viaggi*, ed. Milanesi, Marica, II vol., Turin: Einaudi, 1978-1988, p. 404-405.

33 Headley, 1997, p. 14-16; Ramusio, *Navigazioni e Viaggi*, V, p. 5-17.

by the publication of numerous commentaries on Plato's treatise, reveals the reciprocity of friendship and mentorship in Ramusio's dedications. The idea that "all that exists should exist in some spot and occupying some place" (*Timeaus*, 52b), which scholars defined retrospectively as the theory of rational plenitude, represents the founding principle of a treatise on cosmogony and astronomy Fracastoro composed after the death of their mutual friend Giambattista della Torre (1534). In this fictional Neoplatonic dialogue, Fracastoro has Della Torre's brother Marcantonio explain to his sibling that the entire universe is filled with a spatially limitless *materia prima* that excludes the possibility of cosmic vacuum, confers unity to the universe, and harmonic proportionality to all its parts[34]. Peruzzi noted that the influence of Plato's *Timaeus* on Fracastoro's cosmogonic studies goes beyond the implicit reference[35]. It takes the form of the explicit citation in his *Homocentrica*[36], a work Fracastoro mentioned in a letter to Ramusio[37].

RAMUSIO'S UNDERSTANDING OF MENTORING
The Sharing of communal virtues for the continuity of human sapientia

In recent years, scholarly investigation has ascertained in what measure Ramusio staged in the narratives, and partially in his *Discorsi*, the competition for colonial and cultural supremacy in terms of comparative nationalism. In order to acquire reliable and up-to-date written and visual materials illustrating ancient and contemporary European voyages, he

34 Enrico Peruzzi, *La nave di Ermete: la cosmologia di Girolamo Fracastoro*, Florence: Olschki, 1995, p. 1-2; p. 61-62.

35 *Ibid.*, p. 19-20.

36 Girolamo Fracastoro, *Hieronymi Fracastorii Homocentrica Eiusdem De causis criticorum dierum per ea quae in nobis sunt*, Venetiis, Bartolomeo Zanetti, 1538.

37 Girolamo Fracastoro, *Operum Hieronymi Fracastorii Veronensis quaedam fragmenta ex codice autographo nunc primum vulgate*, Patavii, Excudebat Jospephus Cominus, 1738, p. 69. This edition contains several previously unpublished writings by Fracastoro, and it is divided into two separate sections, each one having its independent pagination. The reference relates to the second part of the volume, entitled *Operum Hieronymi Fracastorii Veronensis quaedam fragmenta ex Codice Autographo nunc primum vulgata*.

relied upon his extensive international network of friends and mentors[38]. This varied community included humanists, academics, publishers, bibliophiles, merchants, navigators, pilots, and Venetian resident ambassadors such as Andrea Navagero, who assisted him in obtaining copies of travel accounts and information about the navigators involved in the explorations.

In his *Commentaries*, Ramusio explores the controversial nature of historical events and natural phenomena of his time, striving in the paratext to appear a humble archivist concerned with the re-evaluation of classical, medieval, and contemporary geo-ethnographic learning. The literary projection of Ramusio's scholarly self often combines with commentaries that reveal the *Navigations*' cultural diplomacy. This is particularly true in those passages in which he enthusiastically affirms the primacy of Venetian and Italian explorers in the discovery of territories and peoples beyond Europe. While the geopolitical evolution of European colonial history openly displays the contest of human greed and hunger for power, the universal, cosmogonic harmony that reconciles culture and nature resides in the personal qualities that inform the reading of contemporary events and explorations[39].

In addition to the celebratory and faintly nostalgic commemoration of past Italian travellers and explorers, Ramusio adopted a complementary form of writing that transcended the mutually exclusive nature of political entities and colonial competition. Inverting the traditional representation of the elitist and restrictive relationship between mentor and mentee, Ramusio's commentaries established a parallel historiographical praxis where the inner qualities of individuals, and not their literary *personae*, acquire the status of the authentic, transcendent mentors of the mature scholar. In doing so, he subscribes to the metaphysical origin of both mentorship and friendship: mutual love in its highest and most noble interpretation; Ciceronian and Ficinian love based on the performance of communal virtues[40]. The performed unity of those virtues ensures the

38 Veneri, 2012, p. 176, 179, 185-187.

39 Regarding the critical re-examination of the dualism nature – culture in subaltern and gender studies, see Cosgrove, 2003, p. 852.

40 "[XXVII] It is goodness, human goodness, I say, [lit., *Virtus, virtus inquam*] Gaius Fannius, and you, Quintus Mucius, which both brings friendships together and preserves them. In it is found all harmony, stability and trust. Whenever it rises up and shows forth its light, and sees and recognises the same thing in another, it moves out towards it and in

continuity of human *sapientia* (knowledge and wisdom) in the *Theatrum Mundi*, thus echoing Pico Della Mirandola's assertion of knowledge as a prerequisite of Love[41].

The re-establishment of a line of continuity between the *Theatrum Mundi* of classical and religious authorities (cosmogonic place), and the *Theatrum Orbis Terrarum* (geographical space) of modern navigators and historians, such as Ramusio, was facilitated by Marsilio Ficino's erudite and syncretic[42] reinterpretation of the Platonic tradition thus perpetuating the early modern discourse concerning the modes of interaction between physical and metaphysical forces, Man and the Divine, on the global stage. Being the most celebrated exponent of Florentine Neoplatonism, Ficino's popularity in Italy and Europe during the late fifteenth and the larger part of the sixteenth century has been meticulously demonstrated[43].

---

turn receives what the other has to give. Thence love, or friendship (for both have their origin in loving) blazes forth; and loving is nothing other than showing affection for the object of love for his own sake, not because of any lack in oneself, or the prospect of any advantage; though advantage does indeed flower from friendship even if one was not particularly aiming at it." For the original Latin text and the English translation see Marcus Tullius Cicero, and J. G. F. Powell, *Cicero: Laelius, on Friendship (Laelius De Amicitia), & The Dream of Scipio (Somnium Scipionis)*, Warminster, Aris & Phillips, 1990, p. 72-73.

41 "But in what way can anyone either judge or love things which are unknown?" G. P. della Mirandola, *On the dignity of man*, Indianapolis, Bobbs-Merrill, 1965, p. 8.

42 On the convergence and creative combination of classical and medieval sources in the *Commentary*, see M. Ficino and S. Jayne, *Commentary on Plato's Symposium on love*, Dallas Tex, Spring Publications, 1985, p. 4-7.

43 The bibliography discussing Ficino's fame, and the impact of his ideas on contemporary and later intellectuals operating in diverse fields of knowledge are extensive and diversified in scope. In the wake of Kristeller's classic analysis of Ficino's thought and the Florentine Neoplatonic Academy, in the last fifty years scholars have investigated the profound impact of early Neoplatonism and its development in sixteenth-century humanist culture. The following are the studies I consulted to better understand the breath of Neoplatonic influence on the Renaissance geographical and historical discourse; as such, they represent only a starting point to retrace the history of Neoplatonism in Italy from its rise to its decline towards the middle of the sixteenth century: Alison Brown, « Platonism in Fifteenth-Century Florence and Its Contribution to Early Modern Political Thought », *The Journal of Modern History*, 1986, vol. 58, n° 2 (June), p. 383-413; Brian P. Copenhaver, « Scholastic Philosophy and Renaissance Magic in the *De vita* of Marsilio Ficino », *Renaissance Quarterly*, 1984, vol. 37, n° 4 (Winter), p. 523-554; Corrias, 2012; Jonathan Davies, « Marsilio Ficino: Lecturer at the Studio fiorentino », *Renaissance Quarterly*, 1992, vol. 45, n° 4 (Winter), p. 785-790; Konrad Eisenbichler and Olga Zorzi Pugliese, eds, *Ficino and Renaissance Neoplatonism*, Ottawa Canada, Dovehouse Editions Canada, 1986; James Hankins, « The Myth of the Platonic Academy of Florence », *Renaissance Quarterly*, 1991, vol. 44, n° 3 (Autumn), p. 429-475; Paul Oskar Kristeller,

As I mentioned earlier, love in its Ciceronian and Ficinian understanding, was a key ingredient of Ramusio's own conceptualisation of mentoring. In Ficino's reading, Love represents the antonym of the original Chaos. It is a unifying force that confers shape to material and immaterial beings, 'forms and ideas', and harmonises single parts of the creation with the totality. As a result, Love is primarily the underlying *logos* that 'paints' the cosmological substance of the *fabrica del mondo*, the World Machine:

> The Platonists define *chaos* as an unformed world [lit., "world without shapes"], and *world* as a formed chaos [lit., the world is chaos painted by forms]. [...] The forming of the Ideas, [we call] the perfecting of Love. The combination of all the forms and ideas we call in Latin a *mundus*, in Greek a *cosmos*, that is, an ornament[44].

Despite being a mere manifestation of the authentic Love it embodies, the *mundus* represents the dialectical response of the human intellect to undifferentiated chaos, or *essentia* (essence).

In the introductory *Discourse on the third volume of the Navigations and Travels on the part of the new world*[45], addressed to his mentor and friend Girolamo Fracastoro, Ramusio reveals the Neoplatonic roots of his cosmography. The *Discourse* opens with a commendation of Plato's *Timaeus* as the treatise that commenced the European discourse on the nature of cosmology. Plato's 'nature of the universe' implicitly refers to the theory of the *plenum* as the foundational principle that informs the relation between the part and the totality in the World Machine. Platonic and Bembian rational plenitude converges to redeem the world from the vacuum of primordial chaos, explaining the inner harmony that unites the variety of natural phenomena:

> [...] Investigating the variety (of natural phenomena) with the *eye of the intellect*, [...] one would see that it is accomplished with so such *harmony* and *consonance*, and by such a perpetual and immutable law, that if one point were missing,

The Philosophy of Marsilio Ficino, trans. Virginia Conant, Gloucester MA, Peter Smith, 1964; Kristeller, 1939, p. 201-211; Cecilia Maier-Kapoor, « Marsilio Ficino's Medico-philosophical Language of Love: its Genesis and its Reception amongst Sixteenth-century Italian Love Treatises », Diss., Johns Hopkins University, 2010; Robb, 1968.

44 Ficino and Jayne, 1985, p. 38-39.

45 *Discorso di messer Gio. Battista Ramusio sopra il terzo volume delle Navigazioni e Viaggi nella parte del mondo nuovo*, Giovanni Battista Ramusio, *Navigazioni e viaggi*, V, p. 5-17.

> all other elements would become merged together [lit., *si confondessero insieme*], and would return to primordial *chaos*[46].

In Ramusio, the authentic discovery of the material world equals to the discovery of the world of ideas. Similarly, in Ficino (Speech V, chapter 4), the contemplation of the "face of God shining in the machine of the world, and manifest to the eyes" leads the human soul to contemplate the universal beauty, ubiquitous and incorporeal in nature, through the manifestation of universal Love[47].

In both Ficino and Ramusio, the diversity of natural phenomena represents the external cause that enables the writing subjectivity to initiate a process of self-understanding made possible by the harmony that bonds together the actors and their stage, i.e. human beings and the world they inhabit. The genuine significance of the empirical, visual dimension of contemporary European explorations needs to rise above the physical to return to its metaphysical origin in the 'eye of the intellect'. If such is the true substance of human explorations, it remains to determine what magical means the perfecting of Love, that is the forming of ideas, employs to manifest itself in the individual, and how it informs the relationships human beings establish with their mentors in the development and progression of human knowledge.

In the *Preface on the beginning of the book of the magnificent sir Marco Polo*[48], addressed once more to his mentor and friend Girolamo Fracastoro, Ramusio identifies Ficinian *logos* as the authentic human magic, the shaping force of the cosmos, and the founding principle of geography:

> The degree of esteem enjoyed by geography among the ancients, excellent sir Ieronimo, may be easily appreciated. In order to come to understand it, one needs to have great *knowledge* [lit., gran dottrina] and *contemplation*; [this

46 Ramusio, *Navigazioni e viaggi*, V, p. 9.

47 "When the body is mature, and the reason has been awakened, it considers by contemplation the face of God shining in the machine of the world, and manifest to the eyes. Through this contemplation it is led to behold the face of God which shines within itself. But since the face of a parent is pleasing to the children, it is necessary for the face of God the Father to be most pleasing to souls. The splendor and grace of this face – to repeat the same thing very often – whether in the Angel or in the Soul, or in the Matter of the World, is to be called universal beauty. And the impulse toward that is to be called universal love. That this beauty is everywhere incorporeal we do not doubt", Ficino and Jayne, *Commentary* p. 90.

48 *Di messer Giovambattista Ramusio prefazione sopra il principio del libro del magnifico messer Marco Polo. All'eccellente messer Ieronimo Fracastoro.* Ramusio, *Navigazioni e viaggi*, III, p. 21-35.

> is the reason why] some of the most illustrious writers of the past decided to write about it. Among them was Homer, who could not find a better *form* than *words* to describe a man both *perfect* and full of *sapientia* (wisdom) than saying that he [i.e., Homer] had visited different parts of the world and has seen many cities and customs of peoples: he believed that the cognition of this *scientia* (science; knowledge) seemed fit to make a man *wise* and *prudent*[49].

The extract outlines the key virtues that constitute the authentic, universal mentors of Man, virtues in this case ascribed to Homer, the father of European epic poetry and, according to Ramusio, geographical literary canon.

Ramusio's ladder of virtues echoes the intimately humanistic categorisation formulated by Ficino who, in his *De Amore* (Speech VI, chapter 18), describes the operational forces that bind human beings to one another. Ramusio diverges from Ficino's thought solely in the hierarchical relevance of qualities, attributing equal prominence to moral and intellectual virtues[50]. The genuine understanding of the inner cosmological essence of the world machine stems from acumen of interpretation, intended as the diachronic evolution of empirical knowledge that occurs among human beings. In turn, the knowledge that resides in the 'eye of the intellect' leads to spiritual contemplation via Ficinian *logos*, the human magic that mentors the intellect[51] in fulfilling its true purpose, thus reaching the metalinguistic wisdom God infused in the soul of humankind.

This ideal epitomises the theoretical opposite of the simple observation and recording of events and natural phenomena, thus differentiating

---

49 Ramusio, *Navigazioni e viaggi*, III, p. 21.

50 "Among these, two kinds of virtues are included; I mean the moral virtues and the intellectual, which are superior to them. The intellectual virtues are Wisdom, Knowledge, and Prudence; the moral virtues are Justice, Courage, and Temperance. [...] The intellectual virtues are more mysterious, because of their hidden truth. However, anyone who is brought up on the moral virtues, since he is purer than other people, can easily ascend to the intellectual virtues [...] But realize you can immediately rise above the moral virtues to the clearer truth of Wisdom, Knowledge, and Prudence, if you will consider that these virtues are granted to the soul brought up on the best moral virtues, and that in them is contained the highest form of moral life", Ficino and Jayne, 1985, p. 143. This extract outlines one of the key differences between Plato and Ficino, that is, the agency accorded to Man in learning how to re-join the One's love through the intellectual gifts bestowed upon humanity.

51 Regarding the long-standing contemplative tradition of interpreting the globe as a moral space in order to transcend cosmic knowledge (*scientia*) and achieve self-knowledge (*sapientia*), see Cosgrove, 2003, p. 862.

collectors of stories and natural occurrences (chroniclers) from authentic historians and cosmographers. In Ficino's *De Amore*, acuity of contemplation and subtlety of interpretation represent two of the seven preeminent gifts God bestowed upon men through his heavenly ministers[52]. Ramusio explicitly mentions all three intellectual virtues that in Ficino's *De Amore* manifest the divine Truth in the world, *sapientia*, *scientia*, and prudence:

> Truth [...] through its various effects acquires the name of various virtues. Insofar as it deals with divine things, it is called Wisdom (lit., *sapientia*) [...]; insofar as it deals with natural things, it is called Knowledge (lit., *scientia*); with human things, Prudence[53].

The harmonic continuity between classical and early modern cosmographers translates into a meta-temporal friendship that engraves past and present mentors within the confines of the printed page to celebrate the universal communality of human discovery, a cosmological revelation that correlates the intellectual exploration of the *Theatrum Mundi* to the moral understanding of the historical events performed by human actors.

Since Neoplatonic truth is transcendental and immanent, it encompasses and rises above the analytical and provisional nature of human knowledge, thus crossing the boundaries of time to accommodate past and present mentors insofar as the virtues they share manifest themselves through their logos.

Ramusio reaffirms the intimate connection between the unity and continuity of geographical matter and its poetical expression in other interludes, as in the *Discourse on the navigation of the most ancient merchant Iambolo*[54], when he mentions classical and modern sources that probed the reliability of Diodorus Siculus' account of Iambulus' story:

> [...] Homer's poetry (that most wise [lit., *sapientissimi*] men deemed to be the first *form* of philosophy due to its antiquity, and those men took from it all their principles) [...] In addition, although the duty [*officio*] of poets is to

52 "Of these gifts seven are preeminent: acuity of contemplation, [...], subtlety in interpreting [...]", Ficino and Jayne, 1985, p. 111.

53 *Ibid.*, p. 142-143.

54 *Discorso sopra la navigazione di Iambolo, mercante antichissimo*, Ramusio, *Navigazioni e viaggi*, I, p. 903-908.

> make the things they describe great and marvellous, nonetheless we know that most of the time they express the truth in this *form* of *words* [...][55].

Being the origin and final destination of the cosmos[56], Ficinian Love is the omnipresent "creator and the preserver of all works that are according to nature [lit., the creator and preserver of all natural things] ... [and it is] the master and lord of all the arts"[57], Love presides over the formation, unity and continuity of the natural world and its phenomena, positioning itself as the first mentor of all arts. As such, Love permeates the historical languages that attempt to understand the geo-historical progression of humanity, giving it shape and order in their respective languages. In order to fulfil its cosmogonic purpose, Love correspondingly imbues the relationship between mentors and mentees in the creation, configuration, and advancement of the highest virtue of the human mind, *sapientia* (Wisdom), linking the desire to discover the unknown to the Ciceronian pleasure learning generates in the mentee:

> It remains [...] that we explain in what way he [Love] is the master and governor of all the arts. That he is certainly the master of all the arts we shall understand if only we shall consider that no one can discover or learn any art unless the pleasure of learning and the desire of discovering move him, and unless he who teaches loves his students, and the students thirst very eagerly for that learning. [...] For, whoever greatly loves both works of art themselves and the people for whom they are made executes works of art diligently and completes them exactly[58].

The recognition of love between the mentor and the mentee as a prerequisite in the cultural formation of students defines Neoplatonic love as the intangible force that generates authentic learning. The ensuing eagerness it provokes in the students leads to the desire to discover what lies beyond the masters' factual knowledge. Learning

55 *Ibid.*, I, p. 904.

56 "And thus the power of Love and the power of Necessity alternately succeed each other. This succession certainly takes place in divine things according to the hierarchy of being; in other things according to intervals of time. In such a way, however, that Love is the first and last of all." Ficino and Jayne, 1985, p. 100.

57 *Ibid.*, p. 63. The role of Love as the master of human arts is restated in almost identical terms in Speech V, chapter 8 (p. 97-98), where the universal mentorship is presented as the result of the fourth virtue of Love, Wisdom.

58 *Discorso sopra alcune lettere e navigazioni fatte per li capitani dell'armate delli serenissimi re di Portogallo verso le Indie orientali*: Ramusio, *Navigazioni e viaggi*, I, p. 599-600.

and discovering are tied to the innate desire of human beings to seek the Truth which, originating from the pleasure of self-understanding, leads to excellence when the love of the individual encompasses both the discipline he masters, and those to whom his works are addressed; in our case Ramusio's mentors, and his readership. Ramusio explicitly mentions pleasure as the primary purpose of learning and discovering in the *Discourse on some letters and navigations towards the Eastern Indies done by the captains of the armies of the most serene kings of Portugual*: "[...] We would presently have a marvellous history which, for the unique and unheard things that would be told in it, would provide infinite pleasure to those who would read it."[59]

The Ficinian and Ramusian pedagogical approach, which is partially indebted to Quintilian's *Institutio Oratoria* (Institutes of Oratory), represents a significant point of departure from a perception of disciplinary progression based solely on the scholarly, disciplinary knowledge of the master. Since the exploration of truth aspires to understand the ultimate cosmogonic relations that connect the Soul and Body of the World to the Angelic Mind, mentorship has to be inclusive in nature, going beyond the traditionally exclusive bond between mentor and mentee. Accordingly, the only lesson a true mentor can deliver to posterity through his disciples is the experiential application of the eternal virtues of the intellect and of the soul, thus differentiating true *sapientia* from mere mnemonic erudition. The mentor's ultimate objective is to reach the soul of his disciples through the transmission of knowledge.

Ficino's discussion of the mentor-mentee relationship in the light of its cosmogonic nature is not confined to portraying general principles and cultural aspirations via a peculiar terminology that Ramusio adopted both in letter and in spirit. It also expounds the exact roles that the Mind and the Soul, respectively, perform in the continuity of the human discourse.

> [...] The Mind confers organized shape [lit., *specie artificiosa*; that is intellect-born typology] and order. The Soul confers life and motion [...] the Mind seems to be higher than the Soul, because life, the gift of the Soul, is not given to all bodies. The Mind, however, does give them all shape and order[60].

59 *Ibid.*
60 Ficino and Jayne, 1985, p. 138.

Organised shape, meaning the partition of the totality into disciplinary spheres of enquiry, and order, that is the inherent harmony that informs human languages in mirroring the perfect Harmony of the Cosmos, became the most prominent Neoplatonic intellectual virtues Ramusio consistently attributed to his chosen mentors, and to the travel narratives included in his collection.

The metaphysical category of 'order' acquires in Ramusio two distinctive connotations, both reminiscent of medieval rhetorical standards. It represents both the preordained disposition (*dispositio*) of the subject matter, and the accurate narration of its individual parts (*narratio*). For instance, the editor of the *Navigations and Travels* laments the absence of order in the letters and travel accounts concerning the Portuguese explorations of the Eastern Indies (*Portuguese navigations to the Eastern Indies*)[61], and in Francisco Álvares' account of his voyage in Ethiopia (*Discourse on the voyage in Ethiopia*)[62]. Ramusio also uses it to criticise the anonymous painter that altered the 'perfect' order Fra Mauro conferred on his famous World Map, which in turn mirrors the absolute excellence of a map of Asia that Marco Polo supposedly drew over the course of his sojourn in the Celestial Empire and brought back to Venice upon his return. The metaphysical nature of this order as the mentor of the Mind provides the theoretical foundations to transcend the oppositional character of human political affairs and cultural dialectics, representing the conciliatory global approach the disciple proposes in order to harmonise past and present contributions to the field of cosmography and geography.

While discussing the accuracy and reliability of Marco Polo's *Milion*, Ramusio not only highly commends Abu l'-Fida's geographical compendium, *Taqwim al-buldan* (*Sketch of the Countries*)[63], but he also extends his admiration to the whole tradition of Arab cosmographers, geographers, and men of letters, praising "the truly magnificent (lit., *bellissimo*) and consistent (lit., *risoluto*) order that is proper to, and characteristic of Arab writers."[64] In a historical period marked by a generalised

61 *Navigazioni portoghesi verso le Indie orientali*, Ramusio, *Navigazioni e viaggi*, I, p. 599.

62 *Ibid.*, I, p. 79-80.

63 Veneri, 2012, p. 170. The compendium was written in 1321 and consisted of a selection of Ptolemy's and Arabic geographers' writings that described a total of 28 countries. See Ramusio, *Navigazioni e viaggi*, III, p. 24.

64 Ramusio, *Navigazioni e viaggi*, III, p. 24.

apprehension towards the rise of Middle Eastern powers that scholars have aptly defined as "Turkish obsession,"[65] Ramusio decided to praise the Arab written cultural tradition in its entirety. In doing so, he implicitly suggested an exemplary mentor to whom modern writers may wish to relate in translating the ideal principle of order into a well-defined, accessible writing praxis. The ideal nature of the universal mentor allows Ramusio to commend a commercial partner and military adversary (that did not always coincide with an enemy) of the Republic he faithfully served for his whole life, thus offering his mentors and readership a liberal and cosmopolitan notion of the Republic of Letters.

The same inclusive principle based on the performance of Neoplatonic virtues extends to certain members of the indigenous populations and Spanish travellers described in the travel accounts. In the *Discourse on the discovery and conquest of Peru*, Ramusio ascribes the virtue of prudence to a select few Spanish and indigenous observers who condemned the civil wars that took place in Peru prior to, and after the arrival of the *conquistadores*. He attributes these conflicts to human greed and malice:

> The Indians of that country, old and *wise* men, along with many Spaniards say that these deaths and wars originate from the shape [lit., *constellazione*, constellation] and wealth of that land; but the most *prudent* attribute them to the malice and greed of human beings, since they say that, as far back as they can remember (and they are 100 years old), there has always been war in Peru[66].

By freely combining and translating two different accounts (both first published in Seville in 1534)[67] recounting the conquest of Peru, Ramusio makes selective use of his literary creativity characteristic of his philological praxis. The identification of malice and greed as the authentic causes of conflicts is based on the selective use of the prudential virtue. In this regard, the extract above translates, almost to the word, Bembo's statement concerning the essential virtue that differentiates 'good' from 'bad' accounts of human events in a letter he addressed to Ramusio in 1529: "[...] Prudence, which is the foundation of good histories [...]."[68]

65 See Giovanni Ricci, *Ossessione turca: in una retrovia cristiana dell'Europa moderna*, Bologna: Il mulino, 2002, as cited in Veneri, 2012, p. 167, 201.

66 Ramusio, *Navigazioni e viaggi*, VI, p. 670.

67 Veneri, 2012, p. 182.

68 Bembo, *Lettere*, III, p. 57. The context is the History of Venice, which the Council of Ten invited Bembo to write.

Furthermore, the conversation of the prudent interlocutors reflects the contemporary Venetian political debate about the political renewal of the *Serenissima*, associating it with the traditional Republican myth of civic harmony. The universal mentor of all human beings, Ficinian Prudence (intended as the divine manifestation of Truth in human affairs) represented the political ideal the conservative patrician factions used to defend the relevance of traditions in conducting external and internal politics. In the terminology employed at the time, the debate focused on "how the absolutes of *prudentia*, which implied justice, good government, *origine* and universal time, could be reconciled with *novitas*."[69]

In other parts of the narrations he edited, Ramusio explicitly denounced the custom of Spanish *conquistadores* of working American native populations to death, and the ensuing destruction of their native cultures[70]. Thus Ramusio's commentaries reveal that many early Renaissance historians and cosmographers in Italy and elsewhere in Europe were focused on discovering and learning about the *Theatrum Mundi*, its protagonists, and the philosophical narrative that unite the theatre and actors to the totality, which in the *Navigations and Travels* equals the same cosmological Love that binds mentors and mentees. Hence, if the aforementioned literary consonance may be easily interpreted as a clichéd projection of the European voice imposed on the conquered, i.e. the trope of 'noble savage', it nonetheless condemns greed and malice on a meta-ethnographic basis. In addition, Ramusio identifies generosity and benevolence as two virtues that could represent a common moral ground on which to establish peaceful coexistence and mutual cultural enrichment, thus allowing entire populations to serve each other as reciprocal mentors in the literary evaluation of human affairs through the universal virtue of prudence.

On the earthly dimension of human discovery, immanent Love translates into a set of extrinsic virtues of the Mind and of the Soul that may be performed equally by different individuals in their own disciplines, be they narrators (theatre directors), the numerous named and anonymous characters staged in the narratives they edited (*dramatis personae*), or cartographers (scenographers) who provided visual

69 Cosgrove, 1992, p. 77.

70 To be precise, in the *Discourse on the third volume of the Navigations and Travels on the part of the new world*, Ramusio, *Navigazioni e viaggi*, V, p. 10, when discussing the nature of syphilis, as indicated in Horodowich, 2005, p. 1057.

substance to the different stages on which the actors perform. The visual dimension of knowledge establishes a correspondence between the ordered disposition of texts and the cartographic representations and illustrations of their content.

In Ramusio's historiographical methodology, social status and the level of education, or lack thereof, do not prevent the coming into being of the mentor-mentee relationship, on the condition that individuals demonstrate their willingness and actual capability to confer proper shape to the *scientia* (disciplinary content knowledge) they present in an orderly manner. By suspending social and ethnographic differences, Ramusio's historical remarks offer an egalitarian implementation of human virtues. Only through this peculiarly phenomenological manifestation of the Neoplatonic order can the virtues of the individual reveal their authentic inclusive nature, thus replacing the elitist inclination to consider the theoretical, written dimension of *sapientia* superior to its oral[71] tradition.

The above considerations may extend to include a comprehensive study of the Neoplatonic virtues of the Mind and of the Soul to all characters present in the *Navigations and Travels*, potentially offering an innovative insight into Ramusio's distinctive philological praxis, constantly fluctuating between Neoplatonic idealism and Venetian nationalism. Applying the fine art of philological manipulation employed by earlier Italian humanists in editing historiographical texts, e.g. Leonardo Bruni[72], Ramusio removed

71 In assessing the reliability and trustworthiness of cosmographic and geographical sources, Ramusio confers equal importance and dignity to oral and written evidence. The deciding factor in choosing between divergent or contradictory information is generally not their material provenance, but the Neoplatonic qualities of the individuals who first provided them, as well as the "order" through which these virtues are manifested. Furthermore, Veneri observes that "[...] the experience that gives value to the oral text is used by Ramusio to validate, verify, or update the classical text." Veneri, 2012, p. 189. It should be noted, however, that Ramusio's patriotic agenda prevents him from evaluating the entirety of his sources impartially, resulting in nationalistic philology that assigns priority to past and present Venetian intellectuals and travellers.

72 "By refusing to recognize the Villani chronicle as either authoritative or normative, Bruni reduced it to the level of a storehouse of information that he could use freely to fashion his own radically new interpretation of the city's past. Cabrini shows how he does this by calling into play a range of manipulative techniques, including selection, modification, and omission." G. Ianziti, « Bruni on Writing History », *Renaissance Quarterly*, 1998, vol. 51, n° 2 (Summer), p. 369; Anna Maria Cabrini, « Le *Historiae* del Bruni: Risultati e ipotesi di una ricerca sulle fonti », *Leonardo Bruni, Cancelliere della Repubblica di Firenze*, ed. Paolo Viti, Florence: Olschki, 1990, p. 248. The parallels between Ramusio's and

the authors' commentaries, moral examples, and historical details he deemed to be relevant solely to the original audience. It is worth noting that he systematically and methodically removed all celebratory propaganda about the conquest in order to free the identity and stability of geographical space from the socio-political domination of the *conquistadores*, while complementing the travel accounts with his own commentaries, notes, and geo-historical details[73]. Whereas this *modus operandi* demonstrates little love towards the original *lectio* of the text, it aligns with Ramusio's aspiration to offer his viewership a consistent representation of the cosmos and the virtues and vices of the actors that perform on it.

CONCLUSION
On the role mentorship performs in the ultimate quest for human knowledge

The refined, erudite application of the Ficinian reading of the Platonic tradition constitutes the moral and theoretical substance of Ramusio's historical cosmology. Florentine Neoplatonism influences both the paratextual interludes devised to assist and direct his readers in retrieving the *Harmonia Mundi* which the same narratives presented in his *Navigations and Travels* seemed to challenge, and the inclusive textual relationships he established with his mentors. The manifestation of the divine Truth via the contingent application of the virtues of the Intellect finds an archetypical representative in a friend and mentor that endows the transcendental origin of human *sapientia* with the immanent, earthly dimension of Ciceronian love based on the performance of the same Neoplatonic *scientia*. In Ramusio's affectionate depiction, the polymath Girolamo Fracastoro embodied the aspiration to cosmic harmony, inscribing it in his poetry and prose dedicated to scientific, geographical, astronomical, philosophical, and medical studies. The warm, beautifully penned, and unequivocally

Bruni's editorial-translation techniques and theory are a topic worthy of further studies, particularly in regards to the nationalistic celebration of the state inscribed into the philological praxis they applied to their editions of classical (Bruni) and contemporary (Ramusio) historiographical narratives.

73 Veneri, 2012, p. 182, 185.

celebratory portrayal of Ramusio's friend summarises the qualities of the universal mentor I have thus far outlined: wisdom (*sapientia*), knowledge (*scientia*), and prudence. The celebration of mentorship and friendship illustrates the role of human memory, intended as the Ficinian aspiration of the mature learned man to overcome the oblivion of time through the generational transmission of knowledge in writing and disciplinary mentorship[74]. The salvific value of entrusting the "treasures of the soul" to the printed page aspires to "provide some benefit to men."[75] The ultimate purpose of the human progression of knowledge and mentorship is elaborated upon in the final paragraph of Ramusio's *Discourse on the book of sir Hayton the Armenian* (Hayton or Hethum of Corycus, who authored *La Flor des Estoires*, History of the Tartars):

> Since it seems to me I have said enough about what I intended to, I shall conclude, reassuring scholars operating in the same field (lit., *di simil lezione*)[76] that I, with the intention of bringing them joy and delight, endeavoured to collect from different books the things narrated above, and with the same intention, I continuously applied to these volumes of the Navigations and Travels all the care I was capable of, knowing that it is the proper duty of Man to benefit others in everything he is capable of[77].

The highest achievements of Neoplatonic truth, that is human wisdom or *sapientia*, reveal the ultimate purpose of the Platonic love that unites mentor and mentee, including in it all humanity, whose mind and logos shape the inner substance of our cosmos.

Gianluca CAPUTO
RMIT University
Australia

---

74 "Once the soul is mature, the love of procreation inspires it with a burning desire to teach and to write, so that by propagating its knowledge, either in writings or in the minds of students, the knowledge and truth of a teacher may remain among men eternally", Ficino and Jayne, 1985, p. 131.

75 Ramusio, *Navigazioni e viaggi*, I, p. 3.

76 Ramusio is here using the word *lezione* in its etymological declination, meaning the manner of reading a text choosing between different testimonies, thus applying his personal interpretation of Ficinian moral philosophy to the teachings of humanistic textual philology.

77 Ramusio, *Navigazioni e viaggi*, III, p. 309.

MOLIÈRE AS A MENTOR

Literati and learned ladies in contemporary Australia

INTRODUCTION
Adaptation and mentoring

In 2022, the world will celebrate the 400th anniversary of Molière's birth. Molière's works continue to be staged and adapted all over the world, most recently by the esteemed Australian playwright, Justin Fleming, who has established himself as the foremost translator and adaptor of Molière's works for stage production in Australia today. To date, he has adapted five of Molière's major works: *Tartuffe* (*Tartuffe: The Hypocrite*), *L'École des femmes* (*The School for Wives*), *Les Femmes savantes* (*The Literati*), *Le Misanthrope* (*The Misanthrope*) and *L'Avare* (*The Miser*). According to Fleming, Australians embrace Molière because his works speak to a shared suspicion of authority, hypocrisy and extremes[1]. As one of his characters, Uranie, affirms, Molière's satirical works serve as potent 'public mirrors'[2], exposing common human failings. According to one reading then, adaptations perform a didactic function – they appear to transcend cultural and linguistic boundaries to tell us something about the human condition. In this way, adapting Molière constructs the French playwright as a timeless and global social commentator and mentor.

Adaptations can perform a didactic function because they promote an explicit exchange between the past and present. While the distinction between adaptation and translation can sometimes be blurry, adaptations allow for a degree of freedom and flexibility in terms of

1 Justin Fleming, « My adventures with Molière », *The Sydney Morning Herald*, August 3, 2018.

2 Molière, *La Critique de l'École des Femmes*, IV.

exactly what is transposed[3]. In doing so, adaptations acknowledge that "art is derived from other art, stories are born of other stories."[4] Far from servile copying, they are today regarded as works in their own right, the product of a creative, interpretative and intertextual enterprise[5]. More specifically, while there is considerable disagreement within the field concerning the theoretical position and analysis of adaptations[6], Hutcheon and Corrigan[7] provide a useful starting point. They argue that understanding adaptations involves three interrelated perspectives: process, product and reception. As process, adaptations necessarily involve interpretation, appropriation and salvaging; adaptors must decide what to keep and why based on a certain reading and contextual considerations. The result of this process is a transposition or transcoding: adaptation as product. Hutcheon notes that as a product, adaptations are commonly analogised to translation and paraphrase, they emphasise a freedom to amplify a core meaning, while also engaging in a cultural and linguistic transaction. Finally, as receptive act, adaptations acknowledge the idea that no text is ever completely original, but a mixture and tapestry of other texts. Readers and audiences recognise an adaptation because of an explicit or implicit recollection of, and relationship to a source text.

This chapter proposes a case study of the adaptation of particular social critiques within satirical works for contemporary audiences. In particular, it will examine how Fleming's adaptation of Molière's, *Les Femmes savantes* (*The Literati*) deals specifically with Molière's critique of the education of women and their social status more broadly. In many respects, *Les Femmes savantes* can be regarded as an attack on an exaggerated version of 17th century salon literary culture and the women at its centre, whose activities played into debates around women's education and self-determination. In order, it would seem, to shift the focus away from a critique of women's education, Fleming changes the learned Vadius into the female scholar, Dr Athénaïs Vadius. This

3 See 'Adaptation' and 'Translation' in Patrice Pavis, *Dictionary of the Theatre: Terms, Concepts and Analysis*, Toronto, University of Toronto Press, 1998.

4 Linda Hutcheon, *A Theory of Adaptation*, New York, Routledge, 2006, p. 2.

5 Hutcheon, 2006.

6 Kamilla Elliot, « Adaptation Theory and Adaptation Scholarship », *The Oxford Handbook of Adaptation Studies*, ed. Thomas Leitch, New York, OUP, 2017, pp. 679-697.

7 Hutcheon, 2006 and T. Corrigan, « Defining Adaptation », *The Oxford Handbook of Adaptation Studies*, ed. Thomas Leitch, New York, OUP, 2017, pp. 23-35.

adjustment goes some way to refocusing the satire squarely on literary pedantry. However, this change and the apparent removal of women from the title does not necessarily negate the problematic portrayal of aspiring women and their education. Instead, the choice of book clubs as a substitute for salons and the maintenance of conservative voices appear to turn the critical spotlight back on women in the play. What emerges from Fleming's irreverent Molièresque reworking of *Les Femmes savantes* is a timely reflection on how far women have come in terms of education and a critique of the modern-day cultural contradictions that still hold them back.

BACKGROUND TO *LES FEMMES SAVANTES* AND *THE LITERATI*

A five-act comedy in alexandrines, *Les Femmes savantes* was first performed in March 1672 at the Palais Royal. The play was written during a turbulent time in Molière's career: he began to lose favour with the king and his health deteriorated to the point that just under a year later he lost his life after a performance of *Le Malade imaginaire.* The play was not terribly well received by the king at first and attracted the criticism of antifeminism, notably a century later by Voltaire[8]. Like many other of Molière's comedies, the action centres on a dysfunctional family; instead of a delirious bourgeois father as in *Le Bourgeois gentilhomme*, this time it is the mother who is the destabilising force. Philaminte, her sister-in-law, Bélise, and her daughter Armande attempt to establish a high-minded, Platonic-like academy to facilitate and flaunt their apparent scientific learning and linguistic refinement. Implacable, the women deride the rest of the household's lack of learning and obsession with the physical and sensual. As part of her project of domestic reform, Philaminte arranges for the outrageously pretentious writer, Trissotin, to marry her other daughter, Henriette, who wants to

8 In the *dédicace* to *Alzire* (1736), Voltaire accuses Molière of legitimising unnecessary prejudice. He writes: « *Le ridicule même que Molière & Despreaux ont jetté sur les Femmes Scavantes, a semblé, dans un siécle poli, justifier les préjugés de la barbarie* ». (Voltaire, « Epistre à Madame la Marquise du Chastelet », in *Œuvres choisies*, t. 3, Genève, 1756, p. 4.)

marry Clitandre instead. For his part, Philaminte's husband, Chrysale, sides with Henriette but struggles to assert his patriarchal authority. In the end, a fake legal emergency invokes the spectre of imminent financial ruin and Trissotin's money-tainted intentions are revealed as he refuses Henriette; Clitandre and Henriette marry, while Philaminte is dignified in the face of humiliation.

Encapsulated in the title, arguably the main, but not only critique[9] running through *Les Femmes savantes* is the education of women and their status more broadly. With the backdrop of the Counter Reformation, there were intense debates in the period regarding the equal provision of education to women and their freedom to choose a spouse[10]. Molière picks up these two themes in denouncing a "specific female type: pretentious but untalented middle-class ladies."[11] More specifically, *Les Femmes savantes* continues and expands the critique of *préciosité* in *Les Précieuses ridicules*[12].

Although much of what is known about the movement of *préciosité* comes from contemporary satirists[13], it is possible to identify some defining features. Broadly speaking, the term *précieuse* refers collectively to the well-spoken women who frequented salons[14]. In historic terms, the emergence of salons was part of the recognition of the growing social and cultural influence of the city over the court[15], while they also performed a political function of controlling a transition from an established nobility to a more open elite[16]. That said, they were not all alike; indeed there appear to be two distinct waves in salon-culture in Seventeenth Century France[17]. The

9 Thomas Finn, « Bookish Women: Female Readers and Women's Education in Molière », *Women in French Studies*, Special Issue, 2012. Finn makes the point that while learned ladies receive a fair share of criticism in the play, their sometimes noble and high-brow intellectual pursuits along with the contemptable treatment of Trissotin and Vadius, make it problematic to establish a single target of satire.

10 David Shaw, « *Les Femmes savantes* and Feminism », *Journal of European Studies*, 1984, vol. 14 n° 1.

11 Shaw, 1984, p. 28.

12 Faith Beasely, *Salons, History and the Creation of 17th Century France*, Aldershot, Ashgate Publishing, 2007.

13 James Gaines, *The Molière Encyclopedia*, Westport, Greenwood, 2002.

14 Gaines, 2002.

15 William Beik, *A Social and Cultural History of Early Modern France*, New York, Cambridge University Press, 2009.

16 Steven Kale, *French Salons: High Society and Political Sociability from the Old Regime to the Revolution of 1848*, Maryland, Johns Hopkins University Press, 2005.

17 Wendy Ayres-Bennett, *Sociolinguistic Variation in Seventeenth Century France*, Cambridge, Cambridge University Press, 2004.

first period, from 1610-1650, is most strongly associated with Mme de Rambouillet, who established the perhaps most prestigious *chambre bleue* in approximately1608[18]. Contrastingly, the second period, from 1650-1665, is most commonly epitomized in the salon of Madeleine de Scudéry. In light of the increasing influence of an ascendant bourgeoisie, salon culture transformed during this period in way that privileged games of manners and fashionable social intercourse over serious scientific and philosophical conversation[19]. It is this second wave that Molière derides most forcefully in *Les Précieuses ridicules*, while in *Les Femmes savantes*, he exaggerates the caricature, so that the provincial female upstart becomes a more "generalized female pedant imbued with the philosophy of Descartes and fascinated by astronomy and physics."[20]

Three centuries later, *The Literati* was first performed in 2016 by Bell Shakespeare, in collaboration with Griffin Theatre Company[21], directed by Lee Lewis. It built on the success of Fleming's other adaptations of Molière's works, including *Tartuffe (Tartuffe: The Hypocrite)* in 2014 and *The School for Wives* (*L'École des femmes*) in 2012. Reviewers treated the play as both a translation and adaptation, describing it as a "merciless sendup of literary pretension and social snobbery"[22] capturing "much of Molière's critique [...] while including a witty commentary on modern life."[23] Other reviews noted the challenge of updating the work to make the characters and ideas more palatable, with opinion divided as to how well Fleming accomplished this. Several reviews identified the reconfiguration of Vadius as a new world feminist as a way of creating a distinctly feminine authoritative voice and thereby mitigate Molière's

18 Established around this date, the salon was perhaps most influential between 1624 and 1648. See Beasely, 2007.

19 Jean-Luc Vincent, « Vie littéraire: Théâtre et société à l'époque classique », Molière, *Les Précieuses Ridicules*, Paris, Gallimard, 1998, pp. 67-76.

20 James Gaines, ed., *The Molière Encyclopedia*. Westport, Greenwood, 2002, p. 182.

21 In 2018, both theatre companies will again jointly produce Molière's *The Misanthrope*. Established in 1990, Bell Shakespeare is a national theatre company, committed primarily to promoting the works of Shakespeare and other classics. Based in Sydney, Griffin Theatre Company celebrates Australian theatre – staging new works that are written about Australia and performed by Australians.

22 June Albert, « Playwright Justin Fleming on Helpmann, Molière and the joy of theatre », *The Australian*, May 28, 2016.

23 Lisa Thatcher, « The Literati – Molière Brought to New by Justin Fleming », *Theatre Review*, last modified June 2, 2016, https://lisathatcher.com/2016/06/02/the-literati-moliere-brought-to-new-life-by-justin-fleming-theatre-review/.

undermining of women's education[24]. While this was regarded as a welcome change, for one reviewer it did not remove the spotlight on the poor choices of women[25]. Furthermore, Fleming's cheeky humour and comic linguistic interplay between the poetic and Australian colloquialisms was both applauded[26] and regarded as burdensome[27].

In terms of what is adapted and how, Fleming attempts to strike a mix of both 'then and now'[28]. For one, the play is curiously set in modern-day Paris, in a fashionable living room that, at least from images of the original production, could double just as a well as the interior of an affluent apartment in Sydney. Indeed, the play is clearly meant for an Australian audience, demonstrated most vividly in the ample servings of Australian slang and colloquialisms. While much of the text is translated into English, like Molière, Fleming attempts to embed a consistent rhyme scheme. In particular, Fleming adjusts Molière's rhyming couplets to suit his purpose – AABB for passages of pure pedantry, ABAB for love and when expressing wisdom, ABBA. On the other hand, in terms of characters, Fleming reduces the number or characters while also anglicising and contemporising their names. Thus, Chrysale and Philaminte become Christopher and Philomena, Martine and Armande to Martina and Amanda and the two lovers, Clitandre and Henriette morph into Clinton (Clint) and Juliet, while Trissotin (meaning three times 'sot' or stupid) is aptly renamed, Tristan Tosser. Most importantly, Fleming feminises both the attorney and Vadius, the male 'savant', becoming instead a female scholar, doctor Athénaïs Vadius.

24 Jason Blake, « *The Literati* review: Justin Fleming's Linguistic flair brings comedy up to date », *The Syndey Morning Herald*, June 2, 2016 and Ben Neutze, « *The Literati* Review », *Daily Review*, last modified June 6, 2016, https://dailyreview.com.au/literati-review-griffin-theatre-sydney/43638/.

25 Cassie Tongue, « *The Literati* – Bell Shakespeare Co/Griffin Company », *Aussie Theatre*, last modified June 6, 2016, https://aussietheatre.com.au/reviews/literati-bell-shakespeare-cogriffin-theatre-co-.

26 Blake, 2016.

27 Tongue, 2016.

28 Fleming, 2018.

A NEW VADIUS FOR A NEW ERA

One of the most notable changes relating to the satire of women's education in *The Literati*, relates to the reconfiguration of Vadius. In Molière's work, Vadius is a 'savant' and according to Couton[29], the character is most probably based on Gilles Ménage, whose latinised given name was Aegidius. Known for literary squabbles with l'Abbé Cotin, the likely source for Trissotin, Ménage was a linguistic authority on the French language as well a scholar of antiquity. Like the great satirist, Fleming draws inspiration for his female Vadius from the 17th century context, this time from Françoise Athénaïs, marquise de Montespan (1641-1707), a witty and intelligent mistress of Louis XIV and friend of Molière.

As reviewers noted, the change from a male to female scholar has significant implications for the play and the critique of women's education. In addition to this transformation, Fleming's Vadius also takes on the role of Ariste, Chrysale's wise brother who encourages him to support Clitandre (Clint) and Henriette's (Juliet) alliance. Clint's introduction to Vadius in *The Literati* establishes Vadius' authority in a way that *Les Femmes savantes* does not. In *Les Femmes savantes*, Ariste is introduced in terms of his role in the plot, whereas the modern adaption stresses the character's credentials. Clint thus remarks:

> Who better than a true scholar to push our worthy cause?
> Doctor Athénaïs Vadius, in black, with calm voice and manner;
> An old friend of Juliet's father, there's nobody better than her:
> She's a respected learned woman, in letters and scientific laws. (II, 1)[30]

The passage stresses Vadius' intelligence; she is a 'true scholar', 'a respected learned woman', there being 'nobody better'. Not only is she learned in the humanities, but her knowledge of science as well deepens her authority in a technologically-savvy, twenty-first century context. However, she also embodies a restrained femininity – she wears black and has a 'calm' demeanour. In many ways, Fleming contrasts Vadius

29 *Œuvres complètes de Molière*, texte établi par Ch. Louandre, Paris, Charpentier, 1910.
30 Justin Fleming, *The Literati*, Currency Press Pty Ltd, Strawberry Hills, NSW, 2016.

with Philomena and Amanda, who parade a "bookish pomposity" (II, 8) rather than a real claim to scholarly knowledge.

Yet Fleming's Vadius is not just an intellectual but as Ariste, a wise guide and support. She tutors Christopher, who, as Chrysale for him, is baffled by how to assert himself in his relationship with Philomena. Her mentoring role comes to the fore after Christopher's confrontation with Philomena over his endorsement of Clint as Henriette's future spouse. As in many other occasions, the text allows for a direct comparison of both the old and the new.

CHRISTOPHER

If I'd pushed her about Clinton, she would have completely lost it.
She's a dragon full of fire, and when she takes that tone with me,
I call her Dear Heart and Sweetie-Pie.

VADIUS

Then the fault lies with you, too:
You can't blame Philomena for being strong, and making a firm decision:
It's your weakness that gives her strength, your timidity augments her position.
It's not your wife, but your own cowardice, that reigns supreme over you.
Marriage is an institution, which has rules, like any polity.
If you stoop, you lend her height; if you cringe, you increase her authority;
Hand her the halter, you'll be led by the nose, as you place her in seniority.
Marriage can't function in harmony if you abandon the concept of
equality.

[...]

CHRISTOPHER

Starting today I have to change, and make Philomena understand
If we're to be equal partners, then I play an equal part, and
That Juliet's my daughter too, and it follows that I'm her father. (II, 9).

CHRYSALE

Elle me fait trembler dès qu'elle prend son ton;
Je ne sais où me mettre, et c'est un vrai dragon;
Et cependant avec toute sa diablerie,
Il faut que je l'appelle, et « mon cœur », et « ma mie ».

ARISTE

Allez, c'est se moquer. Votre femme, entre nous,
Est par vos lâchetés souveraine sur vous.
Son pouvoir n'est fondé que sur votre foiblesse.
C'est de vous qu'elle prend le titre de maîtresse.

Vous-même à ses hauteurs vous vous abandonnez,
Et vous faites mener en bête par le nez.
Quoi! Vous ne pouvez pas, voyant comme on vous nomme,
Vous résoudre une fois à vouloir être un homme,
À faire condescendre une femme à vos vœux,
Et prendre assez de cœur pour dire un Je le veux?

[...]

CHRYSALE
Et je lui veux faire aujourd'hui connoître
Que ma fille est ma fille, et que j'en suis le maître
Pour lui prendre un mari qui soit selon mes vœux. (II, 6, v. 673-686; 703-705).

The references to husbandry in both texts are telling. For Ariste and Chrysale, steeped in the deeply patriarchal society of 17th century France, being led about like a beast represents a perversion of natural order, it should be the husband who metes out orders. On the other hand, for Vadius, the master to be served is not one spouse or the other, but the full and equal institution of marriage; he is not less than a man because he fails to be master of his own abode, but rather because he is not fully realising his role as an equal partner. In this way, the texts diverge in the ideological implications of the erring husband's behaviour and this reflects a clear shift in context. Crucially, it is Vadius, a woman, who is the voice of pragmatic reason here – combining feminist intellect with the sound voice of a trendy family psychologist or life coach.

In her display of superior wisdom and judgment, Vadius thus plays a vital role in the adaptation. As Blake notes[31], Philaminte is an important new feminine authoritative voice and this goes some way in helping to displace the central critique of women's learnedness. While it might be conceded as Shaw has argued, that Molière's Henriette displays qualities of independence, tact and good judgement[32], in her opinions on education she can be regarded not as a shining feminist antidote but simply as an alternative to her sister Armande[33]. Furthermore and perhaps most importantly, unlike Henriette and Armande, Fleming's Vadius embodies sound instinct, discernment as well as intellectual excellence. If the play is to satirise anything then, it appears that it cannot be

31 Blake, 2016.
32 Shaw, 1984.
33 Finn, 2012.

learned women in an academic sense, a proposition that would rightly seem out of place in the 21st century. This desire to modernise the play marries well with Fleming's change of title to *The Literati* to reflect the self-purported[34] target of his satire, literary pretention.

SALONS TO BOOK CLUBS

Whereas Molière's source of satire was arguably the women of Parisian salons, Fleming takes issue with the wordy frequenters of book clubs. The choice of contemporary book clubs seems natural, and is arguably intended to refocus the audience on literary pretentiousness instead of women's education. However, from a sociological standpoint, book clubs actually seem to retain much of the gendered and status-enhancing character of the salons of old, and this then problematises the apparent shift away from the critique of women.

The choice of book clubs preserves much of the utility but not all of the social and political significance of the salon. Beasley, in her extensive analysis of women and the literary culture of salons in 17th century France, argues that literary taste was considered an innately feminine quality, so much so that the judgement of women attending salons was sought and valued by authors. Most famously is perhaps Corneille, who is said to have read drafts of his compositions to his sister, Madame de Fontenelle, for her critical feedback[35]. This appeal to feminine instinct is significant inasmuch as it positioned salons and thereby women as rivals to the newly established, powerful state institution of the male-dominated *Académie*. In effect, salons became "private academies"[36], each with a distinct character, membership and subject matter, all arranged by the female host. Such status positioned women at the centre of learning and learned society.

34 Jonathan Llewellyn, « An interview with Australian Playwright, Justin Fleming about *The Literati* », *Riverside*, December 2015, https://riversideparramatta.com.au/2015/12/an-interview-with-australian-playwright-justin-fleming-about-the-literati/.

35 M. de Vigneul-Marville (Argonne), *Mélanges d'histoire de la littérature*, 3 vols, Rotterdam, 1702, I, p. 156.

36 Joan DeJean, « The Salons and Preciosity », *A New History of French Literature*, ed. Dennis Hollier, Harvard University Press, Cambridge Massachusetts, 1994, p. 299.

In a similar way to salons, from a sociological standpoint, book clubs today are important social, cultural and political spaces for women. In her extensive and ground-breaking study of reading groups in the United States, Elizabeth Long[37] argues that book clubs, which tend to be predominantly populated by women, perform a range of important functions. On the one hand, without minimalising the central pleasure of reading itself, one of the cultural roles of women's reading groups is to encourage collective reflection. Long makes the case that unlike their male counterparts, middle-class women today struggle with uncertain and often conflicting identities. She muses that while the primary life trajectory for men continues to be career with family on the side, middle-class women are stranded between traditional notions of womanhood and domesticity on the one hand and the increasing range of life choices available to them thanks to the liberalisation of the labour market and increasing social and political equality. In this way, discussions around texts connect creatively with the wider narratives that structure the lives of women. Given their ability to bring women together, to inspire and carry out 'identity work', Long argues that book clubs are far more than just sites of cultural reception. Yet as she further notes, the central practice of reading also suggests that book clubs can be a tool for social distinction and life-long learning, as a continuation rather than as a supplement for those in possession of higher education.

There are striking similarities between the book club in *The Literati* and what amounts to a simulated salon *Les Femmes savantes.* In particular, both portray women in them as uncouth and unwitting reproducers of culture, desperately in need of social advancement. This point is established in the way Philomena and Amanda greet Tristan Tosser as their Author of the Week.

PHILOMENA

Welcome to the Tuesday Book Club! And hail to our Author of the Week!
It's Tristan Tosser! and his stunning new work on which he's going to speak!

AMANDA

I burn to read it! [...] Do hasten!

PHILOMENA

Yes, quick! Thrust some gems in my general direction!

---

37 Elizabeth Long, *Book Clubs: Women and the Uses of Reading in Everyday Life*, University of Chicago Press, Chicago, 2003.

AMANDA
Soothe our impatient hunger with an epigrammatic orgasm!

PHILOMENA
Let your sumptuous syntax plunge deep through my ectoplasm! (III, 1).

In a similar but somewhat more explicit tone than Molière, the text positions Amanda and Philomena from the outset as passive participants in a spectacle orchestrated by Tristan. True it is that criticism is not only reserved for Amanda and Philomena, but for Tristian too. However, the fact that Tristan is devoid of originality seems irrelevant here, as both mother and daughter perceive him as an authority. Ironically, the women fail to see or admit that like themselves, Tristan's claim to cultural capital depends on what Riggs aptly describes as "performance mistaken for property, pretence buttressed by association."[38] More damningly, Philomena and Amanda's series of imperatives ("thurst", "soothe", "plunge") give graphic weight to the debasing idea that women "must be fertilised by male intellect"[39] in order to obtain culture and influence. As in *Les Femmes savantes*, the status-enhancing functions of literary arenas are perverted, and instead they become excessively transactional spaces in which women lose out. Crucially then, Philomena and Amanda's naivety blurs the shift in critique from women's education to literary pedantry and leaves the audience wondering who exactly is being ridiculed.

Yet the book club is but the beginning of a wider educational endeavour for Philomena and Amanda. As their predecessors, Philaminte and Henriette, they have the goal of establishing a Platonic academy with the aim of "the removal from our language of every unpleasant syllable" (« *C'est le retranchement de ces syllabes sales* »)[40], uttered "where the illiterate congregate" (« *Ces fades lieux communs de nos méchants plaisants* »)[41]. What is of interest here is not the translation, but Fleming's transposition of the idea of an academy bent on linguist prescriptivism.

Molière's text is steeped in a context of linguistic purism. 17th century France was the era of the linguistic prescriptivists or *remarquers*, the most well-known being Vaugelas, who published his '*Remarques sur la Langue*

38 Larry Riggs, « The Formation and Exploitation of Cultural Capital in Molière, », *Seventeenth-Century French Studies*, 2005, vol. 27, p. 89.
39 Larry Riggs, 2005, p. 89.
40 II, 2; II, 7, v. 913.
41 II, 2, II, 7, v. 915.

Françoise' in 1647, in which he promoted a courtly style of language based broadly on the ideals of purity and clarity and the eschewal of the language of the masses[42]. Moreover, the lofty linguistic ambition of the *remarquers* was shared by the newly created *Académie Française*, established by Cardinal Richelieu in 1635, with the express charter to

> *travailler, avec tout le soin et toute la diligence possibles, à donner des règles certaines à notre langue et à la rendre pure, éloquente et capable de traiter les arts et les sciences*[43].

In the light of prescriptive linguistic developments in 17th century France, Philaminte's desire to remove 'filthy syllables' has contextual relevance. She embodies her era – the absolutism of Louis XIV manifested in a misguided project of linguistic purification. As a symbol of a women's social mobility, her aggression is revolutionary. However, Philomena's similar project seems out of place in a contemporary context. Fleming makes some attempt to contemporise her approach to language in her dealings with Martina, the household maid, whom she fires for her apparent stylistic vulgarity.

PHILOMENA
She has, with unequalled insolence, done something even sicker;
Despite some thirty lessons in how to speak correctly,
She has grossly insulted my ears by addressing me directly
With so brutal an abuse of words as to butcher our beautiful language;
Her ignorance of the Macquarie Dictionary causes terrible anguish.
[…]
'Um, yeah, like, whatever.' Exactly which language is that in?
And 'vunerable' has an L, it's from 'vulnus', a wound, in Latin
God knows what is meant by 'sitch', and you should have spoken better.
And 'StrenGth' and 'LenGth' have a G, the seventh alphabetical letter! (II, 7).

The references to contemporary conversational fillers such as 'um', 'yeah,' 'like' and 'whatever' are welcome updates. However, what is odd about Philomena's as opposed to Philaminte's overly condescending attitude regarding linguistic variation (reflected appropriately in the choice of rhyming couplets), is that she is out of kilter with what is known and accepted about linguistic variation today. As David Crystal writes about prescriptivism, "as a means of surviving high society, 'always' and 'never'

42 Mireille Huchon, *Histoire de la langue française*, Paris, Livre de Poche, 2002.
43 *Statuts et Règlements de L'Académie Française*, XXIV, 1635.

may have their place. As a means of surviving society as a whole, and especially in a modern multidimensional society, which makes a multiplicity of ethnic, specialist, and technological demands upon all of us, they are a disaster."[44] Moreover, while certainly dictionaries play a role in codification, her insistence on the authority of the Macquarie Dictionary shows her own ignorance of the dictionary's descriptive approach to the inclusion of new lexical items, one based on use rather than correctness[45]. These factors combined render Philomena and Amanda more outlandish and indeed pretentious than their historical counterparts.

CONSERVATIVE VOICES

Compounding the difficulties for women, their status and education in Fleming's adaptation is the maintenance of the critiques of Chrysale and to a lesser extent, Clitandre regarding the educational pursuits of Philaminte and Armande. Whereas in *Les Femmes savantes*, Chrysale's critique is based on an apparent disruption to patriarchal norms in the *The Literati*, Christopher's attack takes the form of a contradictory assault on learning itself. Importantly, in reading the adaptation as a self-conscious, reflexive reworking, the perpetuation of these opinions draws attention to lingering and subtle forms of cultural sexism in contemporary societies – in this case, Australia.

Christopher presents conflicting views on education. Curiously he suggests that knowledge is worth pursuing for its 'own sake' and yet he denigrates Amanda and Philomena's engagement with writers and scientific learning. Likewise, he suggests that intellectualism is the province of universities, but equally that knowledge is not "a key to some ivory tower."[46] Another reading of his criticism would be to treat it, like Chrysale's, as an attempt to assert authority and maintain domestic order. The marriage aside, a key point of dispute is Martine's (Martina) sacking, which both characters decry.

44 David Crystal, *The Fight for English*, New York, Oxford University Press, 2006, p. 104.

45 « Dictionary Editor FAQs », August 11, 2015, https://www.macquariedictionary.com.au/blog/article/279/.

46 II, 8.

CHRISTOPHER
So she doesn't know the dictionary; she's not a bloody linguist;
Does it matter? It's the kitchen where her talents are distinguished.
I have to say I'd much prefer that she choose the right herbs,
Even if, while doing so, she mightn't use the right verbs;
I'd rather she repeat a hundred times some inappropriate phrase
Than burn the roast, congeal the soup or screw the bouillabaisse.
When I'm having a bowl of soup, accompanied by a little tipple
I'm not there thinking how I'd kill for a perfect participle.
I mean, Molière and Shakespeare, sure, they put language on the map,
But stick them in a kitchen, and they might be absolute crap. (II, 8).

CHRYSALE
Qu'importe qu'elle manque aux lois de Vaugelas,
Pourvu qu'à la cuisine elle ne manque pas?
J'aime bien mieux, pour moi, qu'en épluchant ses herbes,
Elle accommode mal les noms avec les verbes,
Et redise cent fois un bas ou méchant mot,
Que de brûler ma viande, ou saler trop mon pot.
Je vis de bonne soupe, et non de beau langage.
Vaugelas n'apprend point à bien faire un potage;
Et Malherbe et Balzac, si savants en beaux mots,
En cuisine peut-être auroient été des sots. (II, 7, v. 525-534).

What unites both of these passages is the perpetuation of a gendered worldview. That is to say that the choice to maintain Martina[47] as maid and select male authors as cultural reference points positions men as creatures of learning and power and women as generally better suited to the domestic realm, Vadius being the anomaly and not the rule. This outlook underpins Chrysale's lamentation of the inappropriateness of girls seeking learning, « *Il n'est pas bien honnête, et pour beaucoup de causes, / Qu'une femme étudie, et sache tant de choses*[48] », Honesty becomes necessity in *The Literati* and Christopher interrogates the reasons for and depth of Philomena and Amanda's educational aspirations. He questions whether the women "really need" the volumes on science they have acquired and complains about the telescope "frighten[ing] the hell out of the neighbours."[49] Indeed, as he notes, his "patch of the earth is in tatters", and his "personal life [...] completely upside

47 The example of Vadius is proof that maintaining the identity of characters is a given.
48 v. 571-572.
49 II, 8.

down."[50] Christopher seems to imply that ambitious women are a disorderly force, he is suspicious of their educational intentions and this amounts to a mere dilution of Chrysale's patriarchal ideology. While Christopher apparently has no problems with 'truly' learned women (as his friendship with Vadius attests) nor domestic female servants, he cannot cope with socially mobile women, especially when their endeavours lead to domestic upheaval. Strikingly, this is precisely what Perrault, a contemporary of the great French playwright, remarked of Molière[51].

In addition to Christopher's undermining of their intellectual pursuits, Clint adds fuel to fire by casting pretentiousness as an undesirable feminine trait. He makes this clear when attempting to explain to Juliet his objection to flattering Philomena in order to win her over.

CLINTON
Yeah, but I really find flattery hard, because I was born sincere.
And I like to keep it real, you know, and not put on some veneer,
I find with clever ladies that it's sort of insulting to flirt;
If women want to be scholars, fine; whatever lifts your skirt
But: the ones who treat you like fools are unbelievable shockers,
Like they have to tell the entire world their brain is totally chockers.
I love a truly erudite woman, without any pomp or pretence
Who doesn't have to parade the fact that her knowledge is immense,
She spreads her knowledge warmly, like light through a prism.
She doesn't use gigantic words like antidisestablishmentarianism;
Take the case of your mother: now you know that I respect her,
But every time she opens her gob, you get a bloody lecture. (I, 3).

CLITANDRE
Mon cœur n'a jamais pu, tant il est né sincère,
Même dans votre sœur flatter leur caractère;
Et les femmes docteurs ne sont point de mon goût.
Je consens qu'une femme ait des clartés de tout:
Mais je ne lui veux point la passion choquante
De se rendre savante afin d'être savante;
Et j'aime que souvent aux questions qu'on fait,

50 II, 8.

51 In *Les Hommes Illustres*, Perrault remarks that Molière considered aspirational intellectual women a blight on society. According to Perrault, Molière believed that « *les femmes avoient une violente inclination à devenir, ou du moins à paroistre, Sçavantes, ce qui n'accorde pas avec l'esprit du mesnage, si necessaire pour conserver les biens dans les familles* ». Charles Perrault, *Les Hommes Illustres*, Paris, Antoine Dezallier, 1696, p. 80.

Elle sache ignorer les choses qu'elle sait:
De son étude enfin je veux qu'elle se cache,
Et qu'elle ait du savoir sans vouloir qu'on le sache,
Sans citer les auteurs, sans dire de grands mots,
Et clouer de l'esprit à ses moindres propos.
Je respecte beaucoup madame votre mère;
Mais je ne puis du tout approuver sa chimère (I, 3, v. 215-228).

While Clinton certainly does not spare his criticism for women only and the audience may have sympathy for his attitude, nevertheless his ideal female counterpart leaves much to be desired. His description of a woman who "spreads her knowledge warmly" and does not use "gigantic words" suggests modesty, self-censure and restraint. Yet, as with Clitandre, the audience is left troubled by Clinton's double standards as he feels at liberty throughout the play to voice his own opinions. Furthermore, Christopher and Clinton's success in obtaining their preferred marriage arrangement can be regarded as a validation of their bourgeois common-sense and values[52], while the episode further compounds the characterisation of Philomena and Amanda as hopelessly delusional. Such a characterisation goes some way to maintaining what Mosconi[53] describes as Molière's apparent antifeminist strategy of transforming female knowledge into pedantry and devaluing women's ideas by making them appear tyrannical and authoritarian. To a contemporary audience then, these passages serve to highlight the ways in patriarchal interests persist in discourse – the ideal woman being constructed in 'common-sense' ways which ultimately suit the male characters. Such forms of cultural sexism would seem at least to be markedly out of place in a nominally developed society like Australia, and therein lies a compelling albeit subtle critique.

52 Ralph Albanese, « Molière and the teaching of Frenchness: *Les Femmes savantes* as a case study », *The Cambridge Companion to Molière*, David Bradby and Andrew Calder eds, New York, Cambridge University Press, 2006, p. 151-163.

53 Nicole Mosconi, « *Les Femmes Savantes*: Figure de l'idéologie sexiste dans l'histoire de l'éducation », *Revue française de Pédagogie*, 1990, n° 93, p. 27-40.

CONCLUSION

Amongst other things, adaptations are a mix of appropriation, salvaging, paraphrase, transposition and cultural and linguistic transaction. This contribution has attempted to demonstrate the complexity of this process. On the one hand, adaptors can transform characters to ensure that a work is more sensitive to contemporary contexts. This is certainly the case with Vadius, who is refashioned as a learned female scholar, whose combination of credentials and pragmatism ensures that she is an endearing authoritative voice. The change in this role appears to dislodge the focus of satire of learned women, encapsulated in the title of Molière's work. However, for historical and sociological reasons, the decision to make light of book clubs runs the danger of countering this shift. Instead, aspiring women appear to be placed back into the centre of ridicule as naïve consumers of what they suppose is status enhancing cultural capital. Moreover, Fleming maintains the voices of prominent conservative voices in the play, namely Chrysale (Christopher) and Clitandre (Clint), who under the guise of necessity and attractiveness, mount a sustained, albeit at times subtle attack on Philomena and Amanda and their pursuit of knowledge and social mobility. Importantly though, it is argued that in crafting a mix of old and new, the work draws attention to continuities in cultural sexism in contemporary societies. As such, this reading suggests that Fleming's work actually offers a substantive critique of the very undermining of outwardly mobile women in Australia today embodied by characters such as Christopher and Clinton.

What emerges from his reworking is the picture of a world in which women's pursuit of culture is not so much officially contested anymore, as much as it is, at least in some contexts, culturally problematic or undesirable. Unlike their predecessors, Philomena and Amanda are able to attend university and become as learned as Vadius, but cultural opportunities outside the common sense of domestic life or the lofty realms of higher education are treated as presumptuous and pompous. Indeed, tall poppy syndrome is said to be characteristic of Australian culture. Ultimately, as a work of social critique, Fleming's *The Literati* invites us to consider what sort of social and cultural mobility we are happy to settle for in a 'progressive' society.

Kirk WEEDEN
Monash University
Australia

SECOND PART

MENTORING IN THE 19TH AND 20TH CENTURY

"I NEVER WAS, AND NEVER WILL BE [...] ANYONE'S MASTER"

Pietro Giordani and the fabulous young man

INTRODUCTION

In the line-up of iconic, larger-than-life figures who shaped the romantic imagination, Italian poet Giacomo Leopardi (1798-1837) represents a conspicuous oddity. He lacked the *physique du rôle* of a Byron, a Pushkin or a Goethe. His entire life was afflicted by ill-health and the torments caused by bone tuberculosis which severely affected his spine and posture and would leave him bed-ridden for weeks. In an 1837 document, the Roman Apostolic Minister requested the Neapolitan authorities to exempt Leopardi from joining the security guards, claiming that he was "so small in stature and so badly crippled that even in the most critical circumstances he should not be serving in the army."[1]

Giacomo was constantly mindful of his condition; however, in a letter to Luigi De Sinner in May 1832, he lamented that he would rather destroy all his works if readers were even remotely tempted to see them as the product of his torments[2]. In fact, pages after pages of poetry and prose testify to the writer's struggle to rise above his personal afflictions, and poetically contemplate human frailties and sublimities from the outside. Critic Luigi Malagoli saw this perceptiveness as the result of a process of self-growth emerging from a time-transcending confrontation with the inner self. A disillusionment with the world that has led to "that pristine, most high

1 Quoted in Vincenzo Guarracino, *Guida alla lettura di Leopardi*, Milan, Mondadori, 1992, p. 13. All translations from the Italian texts are my own unless otherwise specified.

2 Giacomo Leopardi, Letter to Prof. Luigi De Sinner, Florence, 24 May 1832, Giacomo Leopardi, *Epistolario di Giacomo Leopardi, Nuova edizione ampliata con lettere dei corrispondenti e con note illustrative*, ed. by Francesco Moroncini, vol. VI (1830-1837), Florence, Felice Le Monnier, 1940, p. 178.

objectivation of the self, which is the peak of Leopardi's poetry."[3] Such attitude enables the poet to embrace his past delusions as expressions of the universe's vulnerability, and face both with a Socratic smile, as in the epilogue of "Aspasia" (1831): "*[...] su l'erba / qui neghittoso immobile giacendo / Il mar la terra e il cielo miro e sorrido*" ("[...] to laze / here listless, still, upon the grass and gaze / across the sea, the earth, the sky – and smile")[4].

Few coeval intellectuals really understood his greatness; amongst them, Pietro Giordani, a classicist and translator who, in a letter dated 12 March 1817 – Leopardi was not yet nineteen at the time – expressed his sincere admiration for the young poet's talent which he hoped would restore the long-lost dignity of Italian letters in the centuries to come. This marked the beginning of Giordani's apprenticeship to Giacomino, nourished on the veneration of the mentor towards the young Leopardi's "boundless, frightening greatness."[5] In hindsight, such proclaimed admiration does not look like an ideal case scenario for a mentor/mentee relationship. What is more, Giordani never took on the role of intellectual guide to anyone, as he confirmed in a letter to Leopardi of 16 May 1817: "I never was, and never will be either Benedetto Mosca's, nor anyone else's *master*; a word that makes me nauseous and angry."[6] Leopardi retorted, on a slightly vexed tone, that he would stop calling him 'master' if that displeased him: "I meant to say advisor and guide in my studies, and I hope that you will not refuse this task on my behalf, if you refuse that name."[7] In truth, Giordani, who had won the reputation of being the 'dictator' of Italian

3 Luigi Malagoli, *Il grande Leopardi*, Florence, "La Nuova Italia" Editrice, 1937, p. 335: "*Quella originaria altissima oggettivazione di sé, che è il vertice della poesia leopardiana.*"

4 Leopardi, « Aspasia », *Opere*, ed. by Mario Fubini, Turin: UTET, 1977, p. 344, lines 111-112. Specific reference will be made to a further edition of the « Canti », edited by Niccolò Gallo and Cesare Gàrboli, Turin, Einaudi, 1962. English edition: Leopardi, *Canti*, selected and introduced by Franco Fortini and translated by Paul Lawton, Dublin, UCD Foundation for Italian Studies, 1996, p. 141, lines 111-112. Unless otherwise specified, all English translations of the *Canti* refer to this edition. A further English version, *The Canti*, with a selection of his prose, translated by J.C. Nichols (Manchester, Carcanet, 1994), is occasionally referred to as *The Canti*.

5 Letter by Giordani to Pietro Brighenti, 25 June 1819, Pietro Giordani, *Epistolario. Edito per Antonio Gussalli*, vol. V, Milan: Borroni e Scotti, 1854, p. 24: "*Grandezza smisurata, spaventevole.*"

6 Giacomo Leopardi, *Epistolario*, vol. III, p. 40: "*Nè di Benedetto Mosca, nè di niun altro sono mai stato, nè mai vorrò essere maestro: parola che mi fa nausea e ira.*"

7 Giacomo Leopardi, *Epistolario*, vol. I, p. 73. "*Io volea dire consigliere e guida negli studi, e spero ch'ella non rifiuterà quest'ufficio in favor mio, se rifiuta quel nome.*"

literature, also had a propensity for mentoring, as he candidly stated in another letter to Brighenti: "If a well-intentioned talent trusted me, I believe I would raise him to no ordinary heights in this art that so few understand and many spoil."[8]

GIACOMO, THE OUTSIDER

Most Italian *literati* were ready to dismiss Leopardi's poetic voice as incompatible with the emerging Romantic movement ever since the song *All'Italia* (1818), one of his brief forays into patriotic poetry. The song is conceived as an ideal dialogue between Leopardi and a neglected Greek poet, Simonides of Ceos, author of an encomium for the defeated Spartans in the battle of the Thermopylae, celebrating Leonidas' "perennial fame"[9], of which only a fragment, retrieved by the Greek historian Diodorus Siculus, has remained. This same fragment had been translated by Pietro Giordani, whose influence definitely sets the polemical, heroic tone of the whole poem. Leopardi, who lends his voice to Simonides, inveighs against the Italic people, the intelligentsia's shameless disregard for Italy's past glories and their lack of commitment in a strong emphatic reprimand: *"L'armi, qua l'armi: io solo / combatterò, procomberò sol io"* ("To arms, to arms: I'll fight / Alone, and fall face forward, I alone")[10]. This diptych is tinged with sarcasm; firstly, the poet chooses the expression "*procomberò*", which has an archaic ring even in the 1800s. Significantly, anachronisms abound in his writings: through them the author takes a moral distance from his own age. Secondly, the verb makes quite explicit that the poet is bound to perish under the foreign invaders along with his fellow countrymen. He will certainly suffer the same fate as them, but with a difference:

8 Giordani, Letter to Brighenti, 28 September 1819, *Epistolario*, vol. V, 41: "*Se un ingegno ben disposto volesse fidarsi a me, credo che lo potrei indirizzare a un'altezza non volgare in quest'arte che pochissimi intendono e molti guastano.*"

9 "*Fama perenne*"; from Pietro Giordani's translation of Diodorus, XI, 11, 6, mentioned in *Opere* 83, note 79.

10 Leopardi, « All'Italia », *Opere* 81, lines 37-38. English version: *The Canti* 3-4, lines 37-38. The "*intelligenti*" society in Bologna (at the time under the State of the Church) insinuate that this fight against an unknown enemy reminds of Don Quixote's battle against the windmills.

only he will die facing the enemies, not turning his back on them like a fugitive. The poem caused a turmoil. The *Dizionario della lingua italiana*, compiled by Niccolò Tommaseo[11], possibly the main execrator of Leopardi, gives a definition of *procombere*, launching an underhand jab at his enemy. Tommaseo refers to a certain poet who, despite his clear incapacity to "manfully bear his own sufferings" displays nothing but "rhetorical pedantry"[12]. Apart from this criticism, the evasive tenor of this stanza also suggests the impending danger of confusing enemies and supposed friends, a point that early critics of the song did not quite grasp. In truth, Giordani was among the first readers who perceived the poem's concluding lines as a poetic symbiosis between Simonides and Leopardi: "There and until the last line it is always Simonides speaking; Greek and coeval to that famous battle."[13]

Many readers have built Leopardi's posthumous fame upon the easy myth of his physical frailty and, by consequence, his pessimistic, almost cynical outlook on humanity. Contemporaries like Niccolò Tommaseo, instigated by personal contrasts with Leopardi, dismissed his works as the expression of something "mortified while being alive" and "squalid within the most exquisite elegance"[14]. As Giordani demonstrated in his *Di una grave ingiuria fatta a Giacomo Leopardi morto* (1839) (About a severe offence done to the last Giacomo Leopardi), Tommaseo, then among the Italian intellectuals who migrated to Paris – the *"Italia parigina"*, as Giordani wrily calls them – plotted to suppress the publication of Leopardi's work by Baudry in France.

An amiable and dignified personality in Leopardi's eyes, Alessandro Manzoni could not be more remote from the poet's sceptical materialism. The novelist limited his praise to the style of the *Operette morali*, a controversial work that was even condemned to the *Index Librorum Prohibitorum* for scepticism, stoicism and the denial of original sin in 1850. A similar case of censorship awaited Giordani's prologue to

11 The 'official' reason for the conflict is Tommaseo's rejection by the publisher Stella for the role of translator of Cicero in favour of Leopardi, but there would have been no point of contact between such opposing personalities anyway. See Raffaele Ciampini, *Vita di Niccolò Tommaseo*, Florence, Sansoni Editore, 1945, p. 129-131.

12 Nicolò (sic) Tommaseo, Bernardo Bellini, *Dizionario della lingua italiana*, vol. XV PRIMI-REVE, Milan, Rizzoli, 1865, p. 46: *"Sostenere virilmente i dolori"* and *"rettorica pedanteria"*.

13 Letter by Giordani to Brighenti, 6 July 1819, *Epistolario* 275-277, note 1: *"Ivi sino all'ultimo verso è sempre Simonide che parla; greco, e contemporaneo a quella famosa pugna."*

14 Guarracino, 1992, p. 349: *"Mortificato nel vivente"* and *"squallido nella più squisita eleganza"*.

the Operette, which was rejected by Viesseux's liberal, but obliging Florentine journal *Antologia* in 1826. Historian Pietro Colletta, a close acquaintance and material supporter of Leopardi, sanctioned Giacomo's irredeemable desolation and monotony, an opinion that will also resonate in De Sanctis' restraint in even calling Leopardi a poet[15]. Animated by a late-romantic, idealistic historicism, De Sanctis could not help but see Leopardi as a "deeply religious" soul, who "feels God in himself and denies it to the world."[16] He was generally critical of all of Leopardi's works except the *Consalvo*, a poem which blatantly imitates the lachrymose sensationalism of minor romantic poetry.

De Sanctis' separation between Leopardi's 'intellect' and his 'heart', between the supreme poet of affection and the pure philosopher of the *Operette*, has permeated critical thinking for decades, until the original contribution of C. Luporini, whose essay *Leopardi progressivo* (1947) attempted to overcome this dualism – a prejudice that Giordani himself had strived to dismantle. Giosue Carducci, who edited the first edition of Leopardi's *Zibaldone*[17], delineated two stages in the sensibility of "that great and unhappy mind"[18], which were further developed into the somehow reductive categories of 'historical' and 'cosmic' pessimism. Idealist critic Benedetto Croce undermined the relevance of Leopardi's work as the result of an unaccomplished personal growth, "a stifled life"[19], which only finds its short-lived consolation in the lines of the *Idilli*.

In his own lifetime, Leopardi's position in the literary arena, especially in the progressive circles of Florence and Milan, was highly disputable: he was a love-or-hate character. Acclaimed as the new talent, he was a

15 Guarracino, *ibid.*, p. 350-351.

16 Luigi Tonelli, *Leopardi*, Milan, Dall'Oglio Editore, 1987, p. 17: "*Profondamente religiosa*", "*[s]ente Dio in sé e lo nega nel mondo*".

17 The current title, taken from a quote by Leopardi, will be first used in the Mondadori edition, edited by Francesco Flora, in 1937. The text, compared by Joshua Cohen of Harper's Magazines "one of the greatest blogs of the nineteenth century" (https://harpers.org/blog/2013/11/giacomo-leopardis-zibaldone/) has been translated into English by the University of Birmingham: *Zibaldone*, ed. by Michael Caesar and Franco D'Intino, translated from the Italian by Kathleen Baldwin, Richard Dixon, David Gibbons, Ann Goldstein, Gerard Slowey, Martin Thom, Pamela Williams, New York, Farrar, Straus and Giroux, 2013.

18 Giosue Carducci, *Ceneri e faville. Serie terza e ultima, 1877-1901*, Bologna, Nicola Zanichelli Editore, 1923, p. 34.

19 Benedetto Croce, *Poesia e non poesia*, Bari, G. Laterza & Figli, 1955, p. 105: "*Una vita strozzata*".

reluctant guest at social gatherings – he abhorred the sight of people wearing masks. His works were soon dismissed as sad and outmoded. In his *Storia della letteratura italiana* (1865), for example, Cesare Cantù recognises the formal influence of Giordani on the young Leopardi, but finds faults in the former's "polished and marble-cold style" and "a natural turn of phrase but with little content."[20] A catholic liberal animated by post-Risorgimento ideals, Cantù rebuffs Giordani for failing to instil in his pupil "national and religious thoughts" and the "need for originality"[21].

Overall, for 19th century optimism Leopardi was a nuisance, a voice in the desert. In many ways, he was a sceptical romantic, whose patriotic fervour faded away quite soon, replaced by a more philosophical, time-transcending view of human destiny. He was an atheist, in the best of Enlightenment tradition, with a tormented thirst for spirituality. He was somehow a rationalist, but with a tinge of absurd and dream-like grotesque. His works often stand on the border between an eclectic imaginative power and the voice of reason, both of them engaging in an epic battle against an inexorably rational, un-ethical nature.

PIETRO AND GIACOMO

Along with ill-health, which prevented him from leaving his native village of Recanati until the age of twenty-four, for a brief stay in Rome, Leopardi's family upbringing was equally forbidding. He was raised in a small-country aristocratic, utterly conformist family in one of Italy's most backwards states, the State of the Church, extending from Lazio to Marche and Romagna. A state where, in Alfredo Panzini's words, "sloth and nettle grow luxuriant"[22] and the "barbarous birthplace" ("*natio borgo selvaggio*")[23] was inhabited by an uncivilised, coarse-mannered, spiteful populace – as

20 Cesare Cantù, *Storia della letteratura italiana*, Florence, Sansoni, 1865, p. 611: "*Stile lindo e freddo come il marmo*" and "*una frase naturale ma scarsa di concetti*".

21 Cantù, 1865, p. 613: "*Pensieri nazionali e religiosi*" and "*bisogno dell'originalità*".

22 Alfredo Panzini, *Il libro dei morti*, in *Romanzi d'ambo i sessi*, Milan, Mondadori, 1941, p. 10: "*L'accidia e l'ortica crescono rigogliose*".

23 « Le ricordanze », *Opere* 279, line 30. English version: *The Canti* 89, line 30.

Leopardi describes them. Recanati was at the same time a safe haven, a golden cage, a confined space that gave the young poet high expectations about what could hide beyond its confines. His father Monaldo was a strange combination of post-Restoration intransigence and classical erudition and humanism, which he tried to instil in his first-born son Giacomo and his younger siblings, Pietro and Paolina. Giacomo proved the most studious of the three: at the age of fourteen his private tutor admitted he had no more to teach to his formidable pupil, who had already embarked on the self-study of Greek, Hebrew, French, Spanish and English. Around the age of ten, he had written one of his earliest poems, *Against Soup*, already denoting his self-ironic approach to life:

> *Si dice, che risusciti, quando sei buona i morti;*
> *Ma oh detto degno d'uomini invero poco accorti!*
> *Or dunque esser bisogna morti per goder poi*
> *Di questi beneficj, che sol si dicon tuoi?*
>
> "They say that, when you are good, you resuscitate the dead;
> But only insensible men could say this!
> Must we then be dead to enjoy
> those benefits that you claim to be yours[24]?"

The only connection with the outside world was through correspondence, and this is how the friendship between Giordani, "a sensitive man already disenchanted by the world"[25] and the blooming talent begins.

Despite his natural inclination for an Oblomov-like idleness, Pietro Giordani had an outright adventurous life. He was born in conservative Piacenza from a *parvenu* aristocratic family in 1774. His mother was a concentrate of bigotry particularly unpleasant to her son, but he also had a strained relationship with his authoritarian father. His education was fragmentary and, as he reports, "most sufficiently bad"[26], which oriented him to self-teach classical and modern languages. After a nervous

24 Giacomo Leopardi, « Contro la minestra. Versi martelliani », Giacomo Leopardi, *Tutti gli scritti inediti, rari e editi 1809-1810*, ed. by Maria Corti, Milan, Bompiani, 1972, p. 68.

25 Leopardi, 20 January 1820, in *Zibaldone di pensieri*, annotated edition by Giuseppe Pacella, Turin, Einaudi, 1991, vol. 1 [104]: "*Un uomo di sentimento già disingannato del mondo*". The numbers in square brackets identify the original pagination of the *Zibaldone*, a common page reference for most editions.

26 Pietro Giordani, *Pagine scelte*, ed. by Giovanni Forlini, Piacenza, Cassa di Risparmio di Piacenza, 1984, p. 15: "*Sufficientissimamente cattiva*".

breakdown caused by a stormy love story with aristocrat Rosa Milesi and a suicide attempt, Giordani decided to willingly enter a Benedectine convent to look for solitude and devote himself to his studies. He soon after proved rebellious to the impositions of the monastic rule and the abuses of authority, a defiance that would characterise all his life. In 1800, he escaped from the convent during the French invasion of Parma and migrated to Milan in the hope of a better life in Napoleon's Cisalpine republic, but soon decided to move to Ferrara seeking a career as a paedagogue in the state administration.

Giordani obtained a replacement position at the university of Bologna in 1803 but, accused of underperforming, was dismissed, and this episode occasioned a satirical pamphlet against the academic authorities, one of the early examples of Giordani's clashes with the powers that be. He distinguished himself as an exceptional orator and extemporary writer of short encomia which more and more often collided with the censors. The first instance was an « *Orazione per le belle arti* » (Speech for the fine arts) of 1806 in Bologna, in which he hoped that Napoleon's reformist thrust would restore Italian reputation, assuming that the current administration was far from efficient in that sense. Giordani did not admire Napoleon's heroism and military victories but appreciated his presumed efforts to promote equality and uproot the medieval practices of Italian society. His famous « *Panegirico di Napoleone* » (Eulogy of Napoleon), read in 1807 at the Academy of Cesena, where he had obtained a job as educator, was heavily amended, especially those passages against the church and the obsolete public education system. His only rewards for a then celebrated piece of writing were a small amount of money and a snuffbox.

Giordani's political views were obviously ostracised by the post-1815-restoration intelligentsia; this is why Monaldo, Leopardi's father, looked at his son's friendship with Giordani with suspicion and hostility[27]. With the acquisition of Bologna to the State of the Church, every immigrant citizen was banished from public offices, and Giordani was forced to leave the city. In 1816, after settling in Milan, Giordani started a

27 In a note, Monaldo expresses concern with his son's new friend: "In the year 1818 Giordani stayed at my home for four days, here in Recanati. With his pleasant manners, he managed to corrupt my children's minds, and it took much of God's intervention to prevent the poisonous seed of his words from germinating", ("*Nell'anno 1818 il Giordani alloggiò in casa mia quattro giorni qui in Recanati. Procurò con bel modo di guastare la mente ai miei figli, e non ci volle poco aiuto di Dio perché il seme velenoso delle sue parole non germogliasse*"). Quoted in Alfredo Panzini, *Casa Leopardi*, Florence, Le Monnier, 1948, p. 170.

yearly collaboration with the moderately liberal journal *Biblioteca Italiana*, directed by the sycophantic Giuseppe Acerbi[28], where he provided a translation of one of the most important manifestos of romanticism in Europe, the letter by Madame de Stäel on the usefulness of translations. This article was a polemical encouragement to Italian letters to move forward, to give up the classicist pedantry of the last century and embrace the innovative themes and aesthetics of the northern European bards.

Both Leopardi and Giordani reacted to this 'rebuff' by Stäel with disapproval, and this is a point that helps modern readers understand to what extent Leopardi thwarted the literary categories of neo-classical and romantic poetry. While accepting poetry as the creative simulation of ancient imagination, Leopardi denied the "association of poetry and eloquence, namely of poetry and truth" of the classicists[29]. He aspired to a sort of anti-modern, though innovative, poetical language that would treasure the lessons of the past.

MENTOR AND MENTEE ON ROMANTICISM

Mentor and mentee share quarters in the fight against the new romantic vogue from abroad. In *Discorso di un italiano intorno alla poesia romantica*, Leopardi contests de Stäel's drive to innovation in the letters, and substantiates his objections towards the optimism of the romantics by tracing a parallel between the ancient classical age and our childhood. The romantics have forgotten the impact of childhood memories on everyday life, as much as they have underrated the impact of the classical age, the childhood of our civilisation, in their own poetics; the young poet invokes a return to a pristine state of poetical imagination inspired by the classics[30].

---

28 Giordani qualifies himself sarcastically as "laundryman and pastry cook" ("*lavandaio e pasticcere*") for the compromises he had to suffer in order to have his articles accepted. From a letter by Giordani to Cornelia Martinetti, 7 February 1815, quoted in Giordani, 1984, p. 27.

29 Guido Guglielmi, *L'infinito terreno. Saggio su Leopardi*, Lecce, Piero Manni, 2010, p. 12: "*Associazione di poesia ed eloquenza, cioè di poesia e verità*".

30 Leopardi, « Discorso di un italiano sulla poesia romantica », *Poesie e prose, volume secondo: Prose*, Milan, Mondadori, 2003, p. 357: He urges Italians to "return with our imagination

Leopardi will strive to reach that 'poetry of sensations' as opposed to the purely romantic 'poetry of sentiment' – akin to Wordsworth's 'emotions recollected in tranquility'. In *Zibaldone*, he opposes the current inclination to sentimental poetry, and his opinion is in line with Giordani's condemnation of the "shitty century"[31], "age of midgets" where intellectuals feed on "beliefs" and "emotions"[32] (expressions that echo in Leopardi's "*superbe fole*", supreme fibs)[33].

However, as it usually happens with brilliant mentees, who end up outdoing their mentors' own teachings, Leopardi will elect poetic imagination as its inspiring motive. He conceives it as a child-like state of immediacy of a perception which arises from an unforced plainness of representation, a sublime perception that has gained a great author like Homer the appellative of "simple poet". In *Zibaldone*, he says: "Everything has improved from Homer onwards, except poetry."[34] Mature poets arrive at imaginative poetry only after a process of disillusion about the world, where sentiment has been silenced by the encounter with science and experience. Only after that necessary process are they ready to return to a state of clear-eyed innocence, typical of children, and reinstate a new solidarity with all the elements, the "beings" ("*esseri*"), in Leopardi's own words[35].

In stark opposition to Giordani's faith in scientific progress, Leopardi adopts a counter-historical point of view that will pervade his poems from the very beginning, with the purely subjective 'I' reshaped into a spokesperson for humankind. This depersonalisation and co-inclusion in human and more-than-human destinies will find their most striking expression in his last *canzone*, « *La ginestra o il fiore del deserto* » ("The Broom or The Flower of the Desert"), composed in 1836. As Cesare Gallo and Niccolò Gàrboli comment about this poem, "when you read something by him it seems to be living for the first time, or even to

as well as we can to the pristine state of our greatest" ("*rimetterci coll'immaginazione come meglio possiamo nello stato primitivo de' nostri maggiori*"), with the poet identified as "master of fantasising" ("*padrone delle fantasie*").

31 Pietro Giordani, letter-dissertation on Leopardi's *Operette morali*, submitted to the magazine *Antologia*, but never published; quoted in Giordani, 1984, p. 280.

32 Giordani, 1984, p. 290.

33 Leopardi, « La ginestra », *Opere* 393, line 154. English version: *Canti* 161; translated as "boastful dogma".

34 Leopardi, *Zibaldone*, vol. 1 [58]: "*Tutto si è perfezionato da Omero in poi, ma non la poesia*".

35 Leopardi, 23 agosto 1821, *Zibaldone*, vol. 2 [corollary to 1448,1].

be discovering how to live."[36] This is a very appropriate definition of Leopardi's all-pervading lyricism, presumably developed from his classical studies, but also from conversations with Giordani, among others.

Elsewhere, Leopardi questions an opportunistic, 'engaged' poetry, crowded with the horrid, the pathetic and the sublime, all of them products of a rationalising process. He also takes a significant distance from the concept of art as useful commodity – for example, in *Zibaldone*. There, he departs from Giordani's traditional view of art as pure imitation of nature, in favour of art as self-imitation of a poet's sensibility[37]. On the other hand, this belief elevates genuine lyrical poetry to the *locus* in which nature speaks within ourselves, but it also instigates a return to nature as a reaction to rationality, exhorting all living beings to an epic passive resistance against an "unpitying Nature" ("*empia natura*")[38], a "hard-hearted nurse" ("*dura nutrice*")[39], "our mother by our birth, but stepmother by enmity" ("*madre di parto e di voler matrigna*")[40].

Giordani, twenty-four years older than his mentee, saw Leopardi as the inheritor of his own literary and ethical leanings, based on the rediscovery of true classical art, the exaltation of Italy's common history and a yearning for liberation from foreign oppressive power forms. Some of these aspects were taken over by the young mentee, who addressed him using Dante's own words for Brunetto Latini, "dear and good father figure" ("*cara e buona immagine paterna*"), but his disappointment about the petty hostilities of the so-called civilised man led him to a more philosophical, time-transcending outlook. Giordani saw in Leopardi a poet "giving an Italian voice to Greek thoughts."[41] In fact, the mentor's idea of the perfect style was a combination of ancient Greek sobriety and the purity of thirteenth century vernacular language. Giordani invites the young talent to start writing prose and opt for poetry at a later stage in life, as a more mature genre[42],

36 Leopardi, introduction to « La ginestra », *Canti*, p. 273: "*Quando si legge qualcosa di lui sembra di vivere per la prima volta, o addirittura di scoprire di vivere*".

37 Leopardi, *Zibaldone*, vol. 3 [4356] and [4372].

38 « La ginestra », *Opere*, p. 393, line 148; English version: *Canti*, p. 161, line 149.

39 « La ginestra », *Opere*, p. 386, line 44; English version: *Canti*, p. 155, line 43.

40 « La ginestra », *Opere*, p. 391, line 125; English version: *Canti*, p. 159, lines 125-126.

41 Pietro Giordani, *Opere*, vol. II, Florence, Felice Le Monnier, 1846, p. 382: "*Dare voce italiana a pensieri greci*".

42 Letter by Giordani to Leopardi, Milan, 15 April 1817, Giacomo Leopardi, *Epistolario di Giacomo Leopardi, nuova edizione ampliata con lettere dei corrispondenti e con note illustrative*, ed. by Francesco Moroncini, vol. I (1810-1890), Florence, Felice Le Monnier, 1934, p. 73.

but the mentee polemically answers that only poetry can magnify his soul-searching inspiration and literally drag him out of himself: "It would seem to me to commit a deadly sin if I ignored it, and let this eagerness of youth disappear, and become a good prose writer."[43]

Nevertheless, between 1825 and 1828 Leopardi will face a more intense philosophical phase, in which the experience of prose writing encouraged by Giordani will reflect in the immediacy of syntax structures and the argumentative tone of his later poems and idylls. The influence of Giordani manifests itself then in two passionate corollaries to his poems: some notes (*Annotazioni*) to the *Canti* (1818-1824) and a « Presentazione » (1825) to the ten *Canzoni* which had already been published a year earlier. They both point the way towards a reaction to the purists of classical and Petrarchan form and the fanatics of Gallicisms and foreign coinages. The *Annotazioni* appear as the manifesto of a radically innovative poetic language rooted in the past, and grounded on long-neglected, or non-canonical authors that the Crusca Academy, the leading institution for the preservation of the 'purity' of Italian language, had dismissed as 'barbaric', such as Ludovico Ariosto, Torquato Tasso and Annibal Caro[44]. This re-evaluation is definitely the result of Giordani's exhortation to his mentee to read Tasso's prose works (letter of 1 November 1817). Leopardi initially responded with reluctance to this invitation (21 November 1817), but Giordani continued to urge him in this endeavour (30 November 1817)[45]. In this sense, the *Annotazioni* reflect Leopardi's interest in a reformed literary language, as the numerous references to Tasso's peculiar lexicon and turn of phrase adopted by the poet testify. Leopardi would later discard Tasso the epic poet on behalf of Tasso the persecuted intellectual, a figure that will become the protagonist of one of his *Operette Morali*[46].

The second paratext, the « Presentazione », on the other hand, declares the songs' peculiar character: none of them talks about love; not all of them are reminiscent of Petrarch; they do not follow any of the most

43 Letter to Giordani, Recanati, 30 April 1817, *Epistolario*, vol. I 61: "*Mi parrebbe peccato mortale a non curarmene, e a lasciar passare questo ardore di gioventù e a voler divenire buon prosatore.*"

44 For the linguistic influence of the last two authors on Leopardi's poetic works, see Paola Italia, *Il metodo di Leopardi*, Rome: Carocci editore, 2016, chapters 4 and 6.

45 Giacomo Leopardi, *Epistolario. Volume 1*, p. 135, 141, 143, respectively.

46 « Dialogo di Torquato Tasso e del suo Genio familiare », translated as "Dialogue Between Torquato Tasso and his Familiar Spirit" (1823).

popular authors in the genre, including Parini and Monti; the songs' titles are always misleading about the content; the themes in the poems are peculiar and not easy to understand at first sight[47]. On many occasions, his lines abound with classical references and borrowings, but with an eye to innovative concise turns of phrase – for example, the reluctance to similitude and extended secondary clauses, or rhymes and metric norms imposed by the traditional *canzone*. As Paola Italia points out in her book about the paratext of the *Canzoni*, Leopardi's terminology adopts original etymologies and unusual registers – for example terms like "*Evviva Evviva*" (long live: modified to "*oh viva, oh viva*" from 1831), "*smozzicare*" (to crumble, but also to slur), "*credere*" (to entrust), "*sollazzo*" (relief), "*incombere*" (to loom), "*ferrata*" (both irony and iron-coated) – which were considered outside the 'canon' established by the Crusca Academy. Italia persuasively argues that Leopardi formulates a systematic program about poetic language, the "theory of the *pellegrino*"[48], with the specific meaning of "unusual, peculiar, outside common use." In a page from *Zibaldone* (14 July 1821), he contends:

> If you observe the style of Virgil or Horace, models of elegance in all centuries, you will notice that their elegance consists primarily and generally on their strange, wandering modes and voices, or their implementation in that particular use, place, meaning, in their strange, wandering metaphors[49].

Horace and Virgil are established classics nowadays but, in their day and age, initiated an experimental style which challenged the norms of previous ancient models by introducing the unusual, the uncommon in terms of language and meaning, a choice that closely resembles that of Leopardi's "bitter truth"[50] as a source of aesthetic pleasure. Still, the careful use of the term *pellegrino* does not prevent Leopardi's poetic language from what Mario Fubini defines as "simplicity of vocabulary", expressed through a "vague and indeterminate word" in order to introduce the readers to the poet's intimate discovery which, in turn, brings

47 Italia, 2016, p. 10-11.

48 Italia, *ibid.*, p. 14-15 and 64.

49 Leopardi, *Zibaldone*, vol. 1 [1323-24]: "*[S]e osserverete lo stile di Virgilio o di Orazio, modelli di eleganza a tutti secoli, vedrete che l'eleganza loro principalissimamente e generalmente consiste nel pellegrino dei modi e delle voci, o delle loro applicazioni a quel tal uso, luogo, significazione, nel pellegrino delle metafore.*"

50 Leopardi, « Al conte Carlo Pepoli », *Opere*, p. 255, line 140: "*Acerbo vero*".

new meaning to their own lives[51]. More significantly, the *pellegrino* (with the meaning of pilgrim) also impinges on the idea of the fragment, a significant stylistic solution which finds quite certainly its inspiration from Giordani's peculiar, almost archaeological interest for details. In Leopardi, this fascination emerges in the poetic contrast of objective and subjective elements, description and introspection, both of which find their exceptional synthesis in the later *Grandi Idilli* (Great Idylls). A fragment is not meant by Leopardi simply as the basic unit of his vague, allusive style, but also as a poetic declaration of intent. Discussing the ability of poets to engage the readers' or spectators' imagination and heart, Leopardi observes about Dante:

> Dante [who] in two words gives life to an image, and leaves much to do to fantasy; but I say to do, not to overdo, because it spontaneously conceives that image and adds what is missing to the poet's traits, which are able to recall almost by necessity the idea of the whole. And the same was among the ancients in any kind of imitation of nature[52].

Through fragments, seen as "objects untouched by civilization", the poet finds timeless remains of that "inclination for the primitive" that roused the first poets in the contemplation of an intact nature[53].

The fragment technique features in the *Idilli* through the use of parallel images that usually draw from an objective observation of nature and human beings, but these images are not evocative of a further introspective dimension. The confines between the outside world and the poet's personal ordeal are still clear-cut and hardly communicate with each another. For example, in « Il sabato del villaggio » (1829), parallel 'snapshots' of village life contribute to create a landscape that is only contemplated, rather than re-lived through the poet's own sensibility. According to Mario Fubini, Leopardi sees a lyrical poem not as an "architectural organism, self-enclosed and accomplished"[54], but as

51 Leopardi, « Introduzione ai Canti », *Opere*, p. 61: "*Semplicità del suo vocabolario*" and "*parola [...] vaga e indeterminata*".

52 Leopardi, *Zibaldone*, vol. 1, [57]: "*Dante, [che] con due parole desta un'immagine, lascia molto a fare alla fantasia; ma dico fare, non già faticare, giacché ella spontaneamente concepisce quell'immagine e aggiunge quello che manca ai tratti del poeta, che son tali da richiamar quasi necessariamente l'idea del tutto. E così presso gli antichi in ogni genere di imitazione della natura.*"

53 Leopardi, *Prose e poesie*, ed. by Rolando Damiani and Mario Andrea Rigoni, with an essay by Cesare Galimberti, vol. II, « Prose », Milan, Mondadori, 2003, p. 358.

54 Leopardi, « Introduzione ai Canti », *Opere*, p. 62: "*Organismo architettonico, in sé chiuso e compiuto*".

the game of a gradual clustering of affections, in which even pauses in the discourse and changes of scenario engage the reader in this process of accumulation of sentimental accents.

Thus, with a sensibility to detail that reminds of his mentor's inclination to sensualism, and the reverence for the works of Antonio Canova, Leopardi's odes are closely reminiscent of those surviving fragments of ancient sculptures that barely suggest their earlier shape, and engage the spectators to hypothesise the original appearance of the object: in their incompleteness those fragments become even more evocative than the complete sculpture could ever do.

BEAUTY AND TRUTH
The Mentee Finds his Way

In a quite memorable biopic of Leopardi, *Il giovane favoloso* (The Fabulous Young Man, 2014)[55], directed by Mario Martone, Giordani accompanies Leopardi to Macerata and exhorts him to appreciate classical art simply by touching it. He introduces an element of sensuality in the perception of classical beauty that was unknown to Leopardi's exquisitely philological experience of the ancients. The scene translates visually Leopardi's concept of poetry as a "commerce with the senses"[56], using "*sensi*" in both material and spiritual terms. Against the spiritualist Catholicism of many intellectuals and patriots of his time, imbued with Jansenism, Hegelian idealism and Leibniz's *Theodicy*, a work which Giordani particularly despised, the intellectual opposes a neoclassical form of materialism, in which moral behaviour does not depend on religious experience and it is not inborn, but acquired.

Giordani had pronounced a famous « Panegirico ad Antonio Canova » (1810) in which he elected the neoclassical Italian sculptor as an example of the eternising virtue of art, which preserves the memory of great men and women from the ravages of nature. Its only object should be truth,

55 *Il giovane favoloso*, directed by Mario Martone, Rai Cinema, 2014.

56 Giacomo Leopardi, « Discorso di un italiano intorno alla poesia romantica » ("Discourse of an Italian on Romantic Poetry"), *Tutte le opere*, vol. I, p. 915: "*Commercio coi sensi*".

the imitation of nature, "but not the obvious or the imperfect, but the refined, the accomplished and the rare."[57] It is an aristocratic view of art as imitation, with no dark corners and little room for imagination. Still, according to Giordani's own pragmatic sensism, art has the power to propagate the pleasure of the senses even to the illiterate. Therefore, the artist must be an example of virtuous gravity and moral rectitude, a lesson Giordani has taught to Leopardi.

Certainly, this confrontation with truth and beauty drew from Giordani and his devotion to the classical world, as clearly evidenced in the songs « Bruto Minore » (1821) and « Ultimo Canto di Saffo » (1822). However, the mentee once again outpaced the mentor. Leopardi had compared himself to Brutus in a letter to Giordani of 1819 because he sympathised with his extreme gesture of taking one's own life in defence of moral rectitude against the degeneration of the new emperors and the "unworthy fate", or "vile fate"[58] – "*fato indegno*"[59].

In a comment published a year after the song, Leopardi interrogates the reasons for Brutus' presumed last sentence before his death: "Oh miserable virtue, you were a naked word, and I used to follow you as if you were a thing: but you were subject to fortune."[60] Unpopular as this sentence could be in his own time, the poet argues that it encapsulates the revolutionary spirit of Brutus, who alone dared oppose the idea of a superior virtue or glory that surpasses individual actions, and revealed the role of fortune – itself a manifestation of the 'bitter truth'. Leopardi searches for a new discovery of that titanic spirit of rebellion to the supernatural forces that subjugate humanity inexorably, but still cannot suppress a gesture of defiance. Even now, when the laws of rationality have revealed the cruelty of nature, committing suicide is an act of civil and human vindication, an act against nature, although, even in the age of Leopardi, nature itself has already been brutally disfigured by progress and scientific inquiry. Brutus witnesses the end of that age of the imagination that belonged to the classical world; on the other hand, science and introspection start disclosing

57 Giordani, « Panegirico ad Antonio Canova », *Scritti*, Milan, Istituto Editoriale Italiano, 1930, p. 128: "*Ma non dell'ovvio e manchevole, ma scelto e compiuto e raro*".

58 Leopardi, *Canti*, p. 33, line 38.

59 Leopardi, *Opere*, p. 138, line 38.

60 Leopardi, « Comparazione », *Canti*, p. 381: "*O virtù miserabile, eri una parola nuda, e io ti seguiva come tu fossi una cosa: ma tu sottostavi alla fortuna.*"

the inconsistency of the creative mind. The advent of Christianity and other religions is explained by Leopardi as the disillusionment with earthly life and the need to look for virtue and fulfilment in the phantom of religion.

In the aforementioned letter to De Sinner of 1832, the poet confirmed that his attitude to destiny has not departed from the example of Brutus of ten years earlier. Leopardi's considerations on the role of nature as supreme manipulator of human destiny are much subtler than they appear. The poet does not engage in an epic struggle with nature, but he deprecates how our supposedly civilised society had stripped nature of its role of provider of happiness. The only glimpse of that pristine happiness is in the natural cultures that live in faraway lands and in children; yet, both of them are doomed to see happiness bestowed by nature vanish with time. As the poet states in the *Zibaldone*[61], our civilisation is living a second nature, in which rationality has destroyed all illusions, leaving behind only one 'idea', religion, which has inculcated doubt and prejudice, while passing them for certainties[62]. Religion is the "sombre pondering"[63] – "*tenebroso ingegno*"[64], searching to penetrate the mystery of afterlife. Brutus' suicide is the affirmation of this impasse: while our first nature would condemn self-destruction as a violation of its purpose of universal happiness, our second nature ultimately justifies it rationally as a challenge to an already inherent unhappiness.

Elsewhere, Leopardi explains how the great suicides of ancient times – Cleopatra, Mithridates, Otho the short-lived Roman emperor – were never driven to their extreme gestures by sentimental reasons, or melancholy, but contemplated self-destruction as an escape from present or impending disasters that threatened to overthrow the glory that their imagination had confused with the peak of human happiness[65].

In Sappho, the tragedy of unrequited love is combined with the beauty of a human soul entrapped in "an ugly and young body" – "*un*

61 Leopardi, *Zibaldone*, vol. 2, [2202-4].
62 Leopardi, *Canti*, p. 56-58.
63 Leopardi, *ibid.*, p. 35, line 68.
64 Leopardi, *Opere*, p. 141, line 70.
65 Leopardi, *Zibaldone*, vol. 1, [57-58] and « Dialogo di Plotino e di Porfirio » ("Dialogue Between Plotinus and Porphyry"), *Operette morali. Essays and Dialogues*, translated with an introduction and notes by Giovanni Cecchetti, Berkeley, Los Angeles, London, University of California Press, p. 468 and 469 (parallel text).

corpo brutto e giovane"[66] – the insoluble conflict between truth, virtue and beauty. With the tragic assumption that "merit lodged within a graceless body [...] sheds no light"[67] – "*virtù non luce in disadorno ammanto*"[68], suicide represents the only option to quench desire and passion. In fact, according to the legend, which had been perpetuated by Ovid, only those who were healed from the torments of passion would not lose their lives – a fate that did not occur, and neither seems welcome, to Sappho[69].

In both poems, the classical characters struggle with urgent, timeless moral dilemmas: Brutus as a historical character living the uncertainties of the present, Sappho as a symbolic figure invested with a metaphysical role. Sappho begins her story with the subject pronoun "*noi*" (we), used in its classical singular sense, by celebrating the ravishing spectacle of the natural elements as they strike human beings with their fury – certainly a universal experience. The *noi* is then interrupted by a tragic first-person account, a solipsism against the seductions of nature – similar to a reluctant lover – that finds no sympathy in either human or non-human beings. At the end of the Canto, the universal sense of *noi* re-emerges, in striking dissonance with the *tu* (you) of Phaon, the only survivor who may perhaps enjoy a doomed happiness:

> *Morremo. Il velo indegno a terra sparto,*
> *rifuggirà l'ignudo animo a Dite,*
> *e il crudo fallo emenderà del cieco*
> *dispensator de' casi. E tu cui lungo*
> *amore indarno, e lunga fede, e vano*
> *d'implacato desio furor mi strinse,*
> *vivi felice, se felice in terra*
> *visse nato mortal.* [...][70]

> And we shall die. The worthless veil will fall,
> the naked soul will flee to Tartarus,
> and so the harsh offence of sightless power
> that orders all will be redressed. And you,

66 Leopardi, « Preambolo », quoted in *Opere*, p. 167.
67 Leopardi, *Canti*, p. 47, lines 52 and 54.
68 Leopardi, Opere, p. 174, line 54.
69 For a rare example of Sappho's iconography, see C. Densmore Curtis, « Sappho and the 'Leucadian Leap' », *American Journal of Archaeology*, 1920, vol. 24, n° 2 (Apr.-Jun.) p. 146-150.
70 Leopardi, *Opere*, p. 174-175, lines 55-62.

> to whom long hopeless love and endless faith
> have bound me with unquenched and mad desire,
> live on in happiness, if here on earth
> mortals were ever happy. [...][71].

Stylistically, Leopardi engages once again in a polemical battle against the Crusca dictionary by invoking uses of the language that escaped the norm of codified language, although he justifies his choices by quoting ancient and modern authors: for example, he discusses the direct-object use of *giovare* with the meaning of "to please", as in the line "*natar giova tra' nembi*"[72] – "we love to float amid this turbulence"[73], or he introduces innovative linguistic juxtapositions, such as "*spettacol molle*"[74] – "tender scenes"[75]. He does so by mentioning the daring expressions of Horace as a justification[76], in a perfect balance between classicism and innovation, between Sappho the celebrated poet and Sappho the archetype of the tragic lover, where the "great space between Sappho and ourselves [...] leads to that vagueness and uncertainty which utterly favours poetry."[77]

Both « Bruto Minore » and « Ultimo Canto di Saffo » testify to a growing distance from Giordani's pragmatic sensism. First of all, the poet sees pleasure, including artistic enjoyment, as inevitably derived from sorrow, owing its existence to sorrow. In a page from *Zibaldone* dated 1822[78], Leopardi still held the belief in happiness as the final goal of natural order, but he already voiced the idea that evil and sorrow are the only means to savour ephemeral pleasures and goodness to the full. A superbly concise line from the poem « La quiete dopo la tempesta » ("Calm after the Storm") of 1829, incapsulated this idea that "pleasure is affliction's child"[79] – "*piacer figlio d'affanno*"[80]. Leopardi also objects to humankind's tendency to invest their actions of eternal significance:

71 Leopardi, *Canti*, p. 47 and 49, lines 55-62.
72 Leopardi, *Opere*, p. 171, line 15.
73 Leopardi, *Canti*, p. 45, line 14.
74 Leopardi, *Opere*, p. 170, line 7.
75 Leopardi, *Canti*, p. 45, line 6.
76 Leopardi, *Opere*, p. 170, note 7.
77 Leopardi, « Annuncio delle Canzoni » (1825), « Canzone ottava », *Canti*, p. 359-360: "*Grande spazio frapposto fra Saffo e noi [...] dà luogo a quel vago ed incerto che favorisce sommamente la poesia.*"
78 Leopardi, *Zibaldone*, vol. 2 [2601-2].
79 Leopardi, *Canti*, p. 109, line 32.
80 Leopardi, *Opere*, p. 305, line 32.

in « La ginestra » he proclaims that "man presumes and boasts he is eternal"[81] – "*l'uom d'eternità s'arroga il vanto*"[82]. Elsewhere, he points out how unhappiness increases in direct relation to the amount of self-love, sophistication and sensibility in an individual or society – a price to pay for civilisation, and a new form of slavery[83]. Secondly, in light of the meditation on *goût* as an artistic ideal by Montesquieu, whom Leopardi avidly read in 1820, the aesthetics of beauty consists of elements of 'naturalness' and 'surprise'. Montesquieu's view is surpassed by Leopardi in his theory of the *grazia*, the 'je ne sais quoi' that identifies grace with a gradual appreciation of its constituent parts. Beauty as grace, far from being absolute and universal, is a harmonised sequence of fragments[84]. In his definition of *grazia*, the poet condenses both beauty and pleasure:

> [G]race consists of a certain outrage about things that belong to the beautiful and pleasure [...] grace should be called an appetizer, rather than the satisfaction of appetite[85].

Departing from his mentor's symbiotic bond between truth and beauty, Leopardi claims that the beautiful has to be sacrificed for the sake of the true, a point which Leopardi argued since the beginning, in a letter to Giordani of 30 May 1817[86], and later conflated in the expression "the bitter truth". In an earlier comment to Brutus and Theophrastus on the myths of ancient glory and virtue, he even defines "the truth / the true" – "*il vero*" – as the beautiful's "greatest contrary" – "*maggior contrario*"[87]. The 'truth/true' animates the poet's intention to investigate the mortal and eternal things, encompassing individual and universal human destinies from an intimately objective standpoint, which interlocks the admiration of the world's wonders and mysteries and the unflinching wisdom which comes from the experience of human failures.

81 Leopardi, *Canti*, p. 169, line 296.

82 Leopardi, *Opere*, p. 400, line 296.

83 Leopardi, *Zibaldone*, vol. 2 [2414].

84 Italia, 2016, p. 59-63.

85 Leopardi, *Zibaldone*, vol. 1 [203]: "*La grazia consiste in un certo irritamento nelle cose che appartengono al bello e al piacere [...] potendo la grazia chiamarsi piuttosto uno stuzzica-appetito, che una soddisfazione di esso.*" Quoted in Italia, 2016, p. 63.

86 Letter to Giordani, 30 May 1817, *Epistole, Volume Primo*, p. 75-77.

87 Leopardi, « Comparazione delle sentenze di Bruto Minore e di Teofrasto vicini a morte », ("Comparison of the sentences of Brutus the Younger and Theophrastus approaching death"), *Canti*, p. 385.

As Karl Vossler points out, Leopardi sets himself on that vantage point between illusion and reality, temporal and eternal, not in the sense of a dualism, but in an extraordinary fusion of the two perspectives[88]. Likewise, Leopardi confronts the mystery of the otherworld, not in a transcendental or spiritualistic way, but through the parallel observation of these mysteries in fragments of earthly life.

CONCLUSION

Giordani undoubtedly influenced Leopardi's sensitive approach to antiquity and offered a springboard for the talented poet to reach a modern form of poetry, incompatible with both neo-classicists and romantics. He was not a constant presence in Leopardi's life ever since, but the vocation as a mentor continued in his later years with an increased pedagogic concern that manifested itself in his criticism of Latin language teaching and the encouragement to study exact sciences and practical subjects.

But Giordani also brought his liberal ideas to more socially relevant reformist endeavours: in 1819, two years after discontinuing his full-time employment in the literary journal *Biblioteca*, he embarked in the defence of lower-class students from the punishments inflicted to them by religious or secular educators in Piacenza (the so-called *Causa dei ragazzi*). The safeguard of the lowest in society, young people and women, a commitment which also characterised his subsequent years in Parma (1831), won the approval of public opinion, but also cost Giordani the suspicion of the institutions, who feared his excessive reformist zeal. In fact, in 1824 he was expelled from Piacenza after the publication of an offensive poem against the newly appointed bishop and found a new home in Florence, where he would reside until 1830. This year Giordani faced what he called "the glory of the second exile"[89], being sent away for suspect sedition in the eyes of the Austrian authorities; he then set off to Parma.

88 Karl Voss, *Leopardi*, Munich, Musarion Verlag, 1923, p. 143.

89 Giordani, 1984, p. 36: "*La gloria del secondo esiglio*".

Although he was sceptical of the revolutionary movements of 1831, and strenuously defended his non-commitment, Giordani was arrested for political sabotage in 1834, after incessant scrutiny and censorship on the side of pro-Austrian prosecutors. Giordani's political activism continued until the insurrections of 1848, when Piacenza decided to separate from Parma and be annexed to Piedmont, a decision that he decried, fearing that extremism may work against the project of a unified Italian nation. He will not be able to see the further developments towards the Italian Risorgimento, since he died between 1 and 2 September 1848 in Parma, under the Austrian occupation.

It is around 1832 that the relationship between Giordani and Leopardi started to deteriorate. From 1820 the two friends had left aside discussions on poetry and mostly devoted their attention to health issues. Some letters were never delivered, and Giordani himself admitted that he rarely used to keep copies of any. One of the last communications we have from Giordani to Leopardi was sent to the latter's sister Paolina in Recanati, on 20 February 1830. In 1832, they only exchanged some courtesies, with a clear evidence that Giordani could not do much to alleviate his friend's misfortunes, despite Leopardi's still fervid admiration for his former mentor. The very last letter, sent by Giordani on 5 June 1837 with a request to Leopardi to provide a piece of writing to be published in Milan, will never reach the addressee, who presumably died of lung dropsy on 14 June in Torre del Greco.

One is led to investigate the reasons of this separation. Distance, perhaps, health deteriorating for both, Leopardi's intellectual progress, his new friendship with Antonio Ranieri, whom Giordani disliked. Giordani himself explained the possible reasons behind the end of their close friendship:

> He envied me and stopped loving me; and it was certainly not my fault. I have never envied him; and I have always taken pain to let him have over me and over everyone his place in fame. [...] He was very unhappy; and the maker of his unhappiness; partly due to his talents which transcended common understanding; partly due to his flaws, inconvenient to such a great mind. I am nothing but a mediocre man; but more coherent and sincere than others and himself[90].

---

90 Letter by Giordani to Pietro Brighenti, 12 October 1841, quoted in Giordani, 1984, p. 284: "*Egli mi ha invidiato e disamato e certo non per mia colpa. Io non l'ho mai invidiato*

Giordani's celebrity and/or notoriousness may have caused frictions or misunderstandings with Leopardi, at the time languishing in neglect and unpopularity. Besides, Giordani's political commitment may have sounded odd to dispassionate Leopardi. However, as a last posthumous tribute to 'Giacomino', Giordani compiled a substantial prologue to the first edition of Leopardi's philological works under the auspices of the publisher Le Monnier in 1845.

Sharing a similar fate with his fabulous young mentee, Giordani's own legacy can be summarised in these few enigmatic lines from one of the last letters he wrote to Pietro Brighenti: "If they want to put a stone to cover these poor bones, I will entreat them to write these simple words: Pietro Giordani was not known."[91]

Luigi GUSSAGO
La Trobe University
Australia

e sempre mi sono affaticato perché egli avesse sopra me e sopra tutti il suo posto nella fama. [...] Egli è stato infelicissimo; e fabbro di sua infelicità; parte co' suoi meriti trascendenti la comune comprensiva; parte co' suoi difetti, sconvenevoli a sì altissimo ingegno. Io non sono più che uom mediocre; ma più conseguente e più sincero degli altri e di lui."

91 Letter by Giordani to Pietro Brighenti, 1 February 1835, quoted in Giordani, 1984, p. 13: "*Se vorranno mettere una pietra che coprirà queste povere ossa, raccomanderò che vi scrivano queste sole parole: Non fu conosciuto Pietro Giordani.*" A very last, formal farewell to his friend was given by Giordani in the epitaph to Leopardi's tomb in the cemetery of the Virgilian Park, behind the church of Piedigrotta: "*Al conte Giacomo Leopardi recanatese / filologo ammirato fuori d'Italia / scrittore di filosofia e di poesie altissimo / da paragonare solamente coi greci*" – "To count Giacomo Leopardi from Recanati / admired philologist outside of Italy / writer of philosophy and of excellent poems / comparable only to the Greeks."

PRIVATE PASSIONS AND COMPANY PRIORITY

The love and work story of Sergei Diaghilev and Vaslav Nijinsky

> I have always maintained, Vassili, that no one in the Ballets Russes is indispensable. So, it is only logical to suppose that no one in life is indispensable either. We'll see.
> Sergei DIAGHILEV in *Nijinsky* (Herbert Ross, 1980).

In Herbert Ross' film *Nijinsky* (1980) Sergei Diaghilev (Alan Bates) demonstrates that if the famous impresario's assertion about workplace culture is usually true, his point about personal relationships rarely is. Having just fired Vaslav Nijinsky (George De La Pena) from his company, Sergei's words read like the type of cold articulation of experience and authority that we might consider – albeit begrudgingly – the mentor's priority. His performance, however, resounds with a strong note of the mentor's doubts. It also implies the strength of the mentee's claims to a dynamic of equal or near equal authority. In this case it appears that the mentor may dispense with the mentee. Once dispensed with, however, the younger man's demise may well cause the decline and fall of the elder. If no one is indispensable in the Ballets Russes, Sergei's claim can therefore refer as easily to himself as *patron* as to Vaslav, his *protégé*. If that relationship can ever be confined within professional boundaries, the mentee can just as easily dispense with the mentor.

In light of these complications, the logic of Sergei's rhetorical assertion is shown to be impossible. At the point where the mentee has become part of the mentor's 'life', as is so often the case in such relationships, the prospects of strict professionalism and a viable indispensability for either party appear to be few. As in *Petrushka* (1911), one of Diaghilev and Nijinsky's most celebrated ballets together, the all-powerful and domineering character of the Showman may assert for a moment at the end of the ballet that Petrushka is merely a lifeless prop, redundant to his ultimate needs. Within seconds, however, he will be confronted by a lively, mocking apparition of his creation that will never be left behind and will continue to haunt him forever.

Sergei Diaghilev (1872-1929) and Vaslav Nijinsky (1889-1950) were employer/employee, creative colleagues, business and financial partners and, indeed, lovers – the very model of mentor-mentee unprofessionalism. Exploring the notorious and multi-dimensional relationship between this impresario and his premier dancer and later choreographer, I want to reflect on the Diaghilev/Nijinsky relationship as a case of mentoring partnership. In doing so, I assess this unprofessional mentorship dynamic and what it tells us about the inevitable conflicts of desire and emotion that lie at the centre of even the most passionless, professionally distant mentor-mentee encounter. Analysing memoirs, autobiographies and reflections written by members of the Ballets Russes during the influential 1909-1913 period of the company and undertaking close-readings of sections of *Nijinsky* and Emile Ardolino's screen version of *Petrushka*[1], I construct a creative practice account of the Diaghilev/Nijinsky relationship from which I make certain observations about the role of emotional and personal factors involved in mentor-mentee relations generally[2]. Principally I argue that this performing arts case

1 Emile Ardolino, *Nureyev and the Joffrey Ballet / In Tribute to Nijinsky*, Great Performances in American Dance, 1981.

2 As I have employed it elsewhere, the creative practice account stands as a useful method in understanding the somewhat obscure notion of social history within the creative arts. See: Mark Nicholls, « Scythian Rhapsody: *The Red Shoes*, *Le Sacre du Printemps*, Creative Youth and Regenerative Rage », *Quarterly Review of Film and Video*, vol. 34, n° 5, 2017, p. 425-444; Mark Nicholls, « The French Lieutenant's Woman: Charles Smithson beyond the Pale and Mike beyond the Run », *Lost Objects of Desire: The Performances of Jeremy Irons*, Oxford, Berghahn Books, 2012, p. 82-101; and Mark Nicholls, « Crazy Days at Culver City: Reflections Hollywood Histories and the Popular Documentary », *Ormond Papers*, vol. 14, 1997, p. 175-182. It engages primary evidence but assumes such texts to be relative and highly subjective and therefore not of unassailable authority. Given Nijinsky's mental state at the time of writing and the various editorial interventions in the text, the *Diaries* stand as an obvious example of this type of subjective evidence. Given this assumption, the secondary texts and creative works (films, performance works,

study demonstrates that, however personal and emotionally involved the mentor-mentee relationship was between Diaghilev and Nijinksy, its primary nature was in fact professional and defined by the standard professional dynamics of a creative practice environment. These dynamics are certainly highly complex and this complexity can be read in part as an outcome of the intervention of personal issues. More generally however, such emotional and personal factors seem to stand more firmly as metaphors for the extremities of creative energy and ambition exercised in performing arts production. These factors are testament not so much to the commitment of mentor and mentee to each other, but to the strength of commitment to their vocation and their own professional and creative ideals and ambitions. This is the reason they make good subjects for film and dance works (*The Red Shoes*, 1948; *Black Swan*, 2010) and why such narrative fictions can be useful in understanding these emotional complexities. In the case of Diaghilev and Nijinsky, two passionate people never needed each other more nor had as much to give one another. Whatever the level of emotional commitment that each of them made to the relationship and whatever complexities this brought about, as mentor and mentee their *liaison* was, in the final analysis, about work not love.

WHEN AN UNSTOPPABLE FORCE MEETS AN IMMOVABLE OBJECT

The company that came to be known as Diaghilev's Ballets Russes emerged as the primary practical application of the critical work of the artist-writers circled around Diaghilev and his magazine, *Mir Iskusstva / The World of Art* (1899-1904). This group, which included artists Leon Bakst (1866-1924), Alexandre Benois (1870-1960), the writer Walter Nouvel (1871-1949), and company *régisseur* Sergei Grigoriev

---

artworks) are read alongside the primary accounts as similarly compromised but equally informative pieces of evidence. Looking at these texts together does not seek to create a definitive history of the performing arts event. In an industry saturated in fiction and creative logic, however, it does provide compelling insights into its operations which cannot be ignored.

(1889-1972), gradually coalesced with dancers and choreographers from the St Petersburg's Mariinsky Theatre, particularly Mikhail Fokine (1880-1942), Nijinsky and Tamara Karsavina (1885-1978). Following Diaghilev's successful Paris exhibitions of Russian painting, concert music and opera between 1906 and 1908, ballet emerged as his premier expression with a season of dance works staged at the Théâtre du Châtelet in May and June of 1909. Dancing key roles in *Le Pavillon d'Armide*, *Les Sylphides* and *Cléopâtre* that season, Nijinsky became a sensation in Paris. This success marked the beginning of his ultimately exclusive commitment to Diaghilev, as dancer and later choreographer, which lasted until Nijinksy's marriage to Romola de Pulzsky in September 1913 and his subsequent dismissal from the company. Most notable amongst this work were Nijinsky's performances as a dancer in *Schéhérazade*, *Giselle* (both 1910), *Le Spectre de la Rose*, Stravinsky's *Petrushka* (both 1911), Debussy's *L'Après-Midi d'un Faune* (1912) and *Jeux* (1913), both of which he also choreographed. Ultimately it was his revolutionary choreography for *Le Sacre du Printemps* (1913), in which he did not appear at all, that not only stamped Nijinsky's renown forever, but also that of Diaghilev and the Ballets Russes.

Nijinsky and Diaghilev had become lovers by the autumn of 1908, having met a year or so previously[3]. In March 1908 Diaghilev turned thirty-six and Nijinsky nineteen. Their expectations for what their relationship was, and what it might hold in store, must have been radically different. Evidence for the beginnings of this relationship as a case of 'love at first sight' is scant if not non-existent. Nevertheless, Nijinsky's sister, Bronislava Nijinska (1891-1972), also a member of the company, observes that early in their association her brother was significantly impressed with and somewhat excited by Diaghilev, and venerated a full set of *The World of Art* which Diaghilev had given him as a gift in 1907[4]. According to Nouvel, Diaghilev's attitude towards Nijinsky that year was reserved, although by December it appears that he had begun to think highly enough of Nijinsky to ask a mutual friend for advice about his relations with the younger man (Scheijen, 2009, p. 162-163).

3 Sjeng Scheijen, *Diaghilev: A Life*, Oxford and New York, Oxford University Press, 2009, p. 169.

4 Bronislava Nijinska, *Bronislava Nijinska: Early Memoirs*, Durham and London, Duke University Press, 1992, p. 253.

Whatever feelings they possessed for each other at the start or the end of their relationship, reading the primary accounts of their colleagues and friends, it is evident that the beginning, middle and end of their *liaison* were significantly dominated by professional rather than strictly personal concerns. In this their intentions ran parallel and the feeling was mutual. Consistent with the inevitable necessities of their vocations and their ages, Nijinsky revealed many of the characteristics of the chancer and Diaghilev clearly knew a good thing when he saw it. Nijinsky's *Diaries* are an essential source for the chancer nuance implicit in their arrangement. Coating the pursuit of his ambitions with a notion of physical and emotional sacrifice, as well as financial necessity, Nijinsky is explicit about his motivations for enduring, as he accounts for it, Diaghilev's attentions:

> I did not like Diaghilev, but lived with him; I hated Diaghilev from the first days of our acquaintance, because I knew his power. I was poor and 65 rubles were not enough to keep my mother and myself from starvation[5].
>
> [Lvov][6] introduced me to Diaghilev, who asked me to come to the Hotel Europe, where he lived. I disliked him for his too self-assured voice, but went to seek my luck. I found my luck. At once I allowed him to make love to me. I trembled like a leaf. I hated him, but pretended, because I knew my mother and I would die of hunger otherwise. I understood Diaghilev from the first moment and pretended to agree with him at once. One had to live, and therefore it was all the same to me what sort of sacrifice I had to make. I worked hard at my dancing and was always tired. But I pretended not to be tired at all in order that Diaghilev should not be bored with me. (*Ibid.*, p. 49).

The idea that Nijinsky and family were facing starvation is absurd[7]. In relative terms, however, we see in the *Diaries* how Nijinsky employs the poverty scenario to admit to a certain utilitarianism at the origins of his relationship with Diaghilev. This is the very same emotion that earlier in the *Diaries* he criticises in a certain friend of Diaghilev, "Z", possibly Igor Stravinsky (1882-1971), who "wants to become rich and learn everything that Diaghilev knows" (Nijinksy, 1968, p. 19). Beyond the *Diaries*'s potent

5 Vaslav Nijinksy, *The Diaries of Vaslav Nijinsky*, Berkeley and Los Angeles, University of California Press, 1968, p. 46-47.

6 The text is printed as "Ivor", but I have replaced with "Lvov", i.e. Prince Pavel Lvov, the former being generally agreed to be a misprint.

7 Richard Buckle, *Diaghilev*, London, Weidenfeld, 1993, p. 126.

melodrama of poverty, power and sexual seduction, this latter accusation, pointing to Diaghilev's educative powers as a mentor, comes closest to what appears to be the basis of Nijinsky's motivation. Diaghilev's biographer Sjeng Scheijen, drawing heavily upon Nouvel's private writings, puts it best when he writes, "Nijinsky's interest in Diaghilev seems to be a classic case of a young person taking an older lover to further his career, intellectual growth and social development", (Scheijen, 2009, p. 163). Nouvel was close to both men and, indeed, to Nijinsky's protector at the time, Prince Pavel Lvov, referred to in the *Diaries* entry quoted above. Lvov was wealthy and Diaghilev was not. For all the financial incentives for Nijinsky to remain close to his admiring Prince, Lvov could not give him the opportunity for success as a premiere dancer in a great company that Diaghilev promised after his successful first Paris season (*ibid.*, p. 161-163; p. 169).

As for Diaghilev's motivations, in planning a second Paris season what he wanted more than anything was star dancers. Given the fame and pre-eminence of Mathilde Kschessinska (1872-1971), Anna Pavlova (1881-1931) and the growing celebrity of Tamara Karsavina, as well as the established priority of female dancers in the ballet pantheon of the day, for all his developing repute in the environs of the Mariinsky Theatre, this did not necessarily mean Nijinsky. Like Fokine, Diaghilev's theatrical inclinations towards leading male dancers and his vision for a taste for leading males in the eyes of the public did, however, require someone like Nijinsky[8]. Clearly Nijinsky came to understand this and wrote in his *Diaries* of the extent to which Diaghilev understood his worth (Nijinksy, 1968, p. 133-134). In 1908, however, Benois had highlighted Nijinsky's promise to Diaghilev. Furthermore, the fact that Diaghilev and his committee had planned their 1909 production of *Les Sylphides* around Nijinsky as romantic lead – although he had only hitherto featured in secondary roles – indicates the extent to which his exceptional abilities were obvious[9]. As in so many situations of creative endeavour, innovation is so often the offspring of practicality. Diaghilev's initiative in promoting male leads in ballet can easily be understood as the outcome of the availability of a dancer such as Nijinsky, not to mention his collaboration with a male dancer/choreographer such as Fokine.

8 Lucy Moore, *Nijinsky*, London, Profile Books, 2013, p. 48; Modris Eksteins, *Rites of Spring: The Great War and the Birth of the Modern Age*, Reading, Black Swan, 1990, p. 65.

9 Sergei Grigoriev, *The Diaghilev Ballet 1909-1929*, Hampshire, Dance Books, 2009, p. 3, p. 10.

THE IMPRESARIO AND HIS FAVOURITE SLAVE

Bronislava Nijinska relates that her brother co-opted her in the creation of his first choreographic work for Diaghilev, *L'Après-Midi d'un Faune*, in late 1910 (Nijinska, 1992, p. 315-316). Prior to that period of higher responsibility and long after, the professional relationship between Diaghilev and Nijinsky was largely that of a proprietor and his star attraction. This was the essential and enduring context of their work together. Nijinsky provided his substantial labour, commitment and talent as well as frequently deferring the salary and other expenses owed him by Diaghilev (*ibid.*, p. 278, p. 486-487, p. 507; Nijinsky p. 89, 108). Most importantly, as Bronislava Nijinska makes clear, Nijinsky had a very strong desire to subordinate himself to Diaghilev's genius. Gaining Diaghilev's approval was evidently very important to Nijinsky (Nijinska, 1992, p. 258, p. 429; Scheijen, 2009, p. 169). Like everyone else, Nijinsky was impressed by Diaghilev's wide-ranging talent and his air of power and authority. He reflects this in the *Diaries* by way of direct compliment and, indeed, heart-felt complaints about Diaghilev, comparing him to Lloyd George as eagles always ready to prevent smaller birds from living (Nijinsky, 1968, p. 16, p. 52, p. 71, p. 130). The deeply pitiful expressions of Nijinsky's love for Diaghilev in the *Diaries* (*ibid.*, p. 49, p. 70-72) bear further and potent testament to the extent to which Nijinsky was in awe of Diaghilev and therefore willing to give himself, and his art, to him whole-heartedly. Writing of Diaghilev as the eagle, Nijinsky expresses both the fear and the fascination, as well as the demand for priority that such potentates attract: "An eagle must not interfere with the smaller birds and must therefore be given enough to eat in order not to attack them", (*Ibid.*, p. 16)

For his part, Diaghilev educated his young and seemingly docile and puppet-like pupil[10]. He took control over every detail of his performing career and his life generally, even down to the micro-details of his personal grooming and general health[11]. There is a thesis of his manufacturing the excuse for Nijinsky's resignation from the Mariinsky Theatre, over

10 Alexandre Benois, *Reminiscences of the Russian Ballet*, London, Putnam, 1945, p. 289-290, p. 318. See also: Grigoriev, 2009, p. 64; Nijinska, 1992, p. 306, p. 314.

11 Igor Stravinsky and Robert Craft, *Memories and Commentaries*, London, Faber and Faber, 2002, p. 94-101, p. 142.

the apparent scandal caused by the revealing Benois-designed tunic which he wore in front of the Russian royal family while dancing *Giselle*. This appears to be little more than a fabrication (Benois, 1945, p. 318; Scheijen, 2009, p. 217-218). Like other Diaghilev-induced scandals of similarly questionable authenticity, however, the fabrication of this part of the Ballet Russes myth tells us a great deal about the situation[12]. In particular the *Giselle* story highlights the extent to which Diaghilev's, no doubt frequently beneficial, control of Nijinsky's life and career also lead to an emotionally manipulative (Nijinska, 1992, p. 339) and utilitarian/dependent 'handling' of his prize 'property' that was odious for Nijinsky (*ibid.*, p. 322, p. 327-328, p. 382-384; Stravinsky and Craft, 2002, p. 94-101; Nijinsky, 1968, p. 20, p. 39, p. 133-139). It also stands as evidence of the side-show promoter inclinations, which Nijinsky tells us were so opposed to Diaghilev's own view of his vocation as 'God of Art', and which he vigorously denied (*ibid.*, p. 19, p. 51-53, p. 71, p. 142). In this context and given Diaghilev's early tendency to cast Nijinsky in the role of 'favourite slave', as in *Schéhérazade* and *Cléopâtre*, Walter Nouvel light-heartedly expressed the hope that Nijinsky might one day secure his 'release' from Diaghilev (Grigoriev, 2009, p. 32; Scheijen, 2009, p. 200). In the broader context of their work together, this was clearly reference to a very real master/slave dynamic obviously operating between Diaghilev and Nijinsky in the early years of the relationship.

« *LE DERNIER CRI* »

The reasons for Diaghilev wanting Nijinsky as choreographer tells us something about the nature of their relationship. For all the control and subordination that marked their arrangement as proprietor and dancer, new dynamics necessarily became important once Nijinsky took a greater role in the artistic affairs of the Ballets Russes as choreographer. Nevertheless the settings of the original mentor-mentee dynamic

12 The most notable of such scandals is the moment of masturbation, simulated or otherwise, staged by Nijinsky at the end of his performance of *L'Après-Midi d'un Faune*, which Stravinsky considers as an example of pure Diaghilev calculation and forethought (Stravinsky and Craft, 2002, p. 96).

remained in place and undiminished by the fact that this period roughly corresponds with the time that they stopped sleeping together. Whatever the emotional situation between them and however the basis of authority in their relationship changed, we see very little movement in the business-like imperatives and professional ambitions of either party.

The obvious potential publicity triumph in making a choreographer of Nijinsky was too great to be shunned. There were, however, plenty of reasons for Diaghilev to be cautious about this new enterprise. Benois, Stravinsky and Fokine all had reservations about Nijinsky's capacity to be a choreographer[13]. There is ample evidence from Nijinsky's most loyal friends that, once he had begun his work taking over from Fokine as principal choreographer, his ability to communicate his ideas was clearly deficient[14]. Diaghilev had doubts too. Only Leon Bakst's enthusiastic approval of Nijinsky's exhaustive and time-consuming labour on *L'Après-Midi d'un Faune* persuaded Diaghilev against making his *protégé* re-choreograph the entire work before it opened (Nijinska, 1992, p. 429). The fact that the Dalcroze-trained Marie Rambert (1888-1982) was brought in to assist Nijinsky on *Le Sacre du Printemps* demonstrated that, at the very least, Diaghilev's confidence in Nijinsky's abilities had not increased in the intervening period (*ibid.*, p. 455). In the end, the experience of *Le Sacre du Printemps* did not do anything to assuage Diaghilev's obvious suspicions. With the completion of this third ballet, the year-long public experiment of turning his star dancer into a choreographer was over.

Given these obvious potential pitfalls of the project, Diaghilev's motivations represent the complex mixture of his personal and professional character. One inescapable conclusion to be drawn is that the appointment of Nijinsky as choreographer had nothing, or at least very little, to do with Nijinsky at all. Much has been made of Diaghilev's sense of Fokine's fatigue and the idea that the established choreographer's ballets were, in 1911, no longer progressive or interesting. In *Nijinsky* Sergei puts it thus:

13 Michel Fokine, *Fokine: Memoirs of a Ballet Master*, London, Constable and Company, 1961, p. 132, p. 186, p. 194. See also: Benois, 1945, p. 290, p. 338; Stravinsky and Craft, 2002, p. 97.

14 Karsavina Tamara, *Theatre Street: The Reminiscences of Tamara Karsavina*, London, Columbus Books, 1948, p. 220, p. 237. See also: Marie Rambert, *Quicksilver*, London: Macmillan, 1972, p. 69; Nijinska, 1992, p. 405.

> Do you know the one tragic fact about a creative artist? Most have only so much to give the world. Sooner or later they reach their limits and every new ballet is just an old ballet with a new hat on. It's beginning to happen to Mikhail Fokine, I've seen it for some time now. So, if he goes, he goes. Sad of course. But I have always made it a cardinal rule of this company that no one person is indispensable. Moreover, there can be no room for sentiment or misplaced loyalty to yesterday's heroes. My eye must always be on the future – which, thank Heaven, in this case is Nijinsky[15].

The idea that Diaghilev wanted to move him on, however, does not account for the fact that Fokine was planning to set up his own company and that this would have almost certainly brought about a split in the Ballets Russes. In the cultivation of Nijinsky as a choreographer, therefore, we cannot forget Diaghilev's most basic motivating anxieties that he might one day need one. At least he might need a choreographer who was more malleable to his wishes than Fokine had proven (Scheijen, 2009, p. 211, p. 233; Karsavina, 1948, p. 285-286). Diaghilev was nothing if not pragmatic and his arrogance, despotism and his need to exercise these sentimental, selfish and sometimes judgement-lacking qualities was clearly part of his motivation in this important matter (Benois, 1945, p. 127, p. 165-167, p. 169, p. 205, p. 290, p. 301, p. 319; Fokine, 1961, p. 217).

Benois criticises Diaghilev for his slavish attachment to the latest fashion or sensation, *le dernier cri* (Benois, 1945, p. 375-376), but this undoubted tendency in Diaghilev accounts for his endorsement of Nijinsky in this key role. In his defence, Diaghilev was obviously preeminent in talent spotting, indeed Benois is one of the first to say so (*ibid.*, p. 305, p. 385; Karsavina, 1948, p. 211, Scheijen, 2009, p. 233). His cultivation of Nijinsky as a dancer, as with Stravinsky as a ballet composer, made this clear. Following the early seasons of the Ballets Russes in Paris and elsewhere, *le denier cri* was quite obviously Nijinsky and no impresario serious about his business would have failed to capitalise on this by pushing his creation forward wherever possible. In this too Diaghilev was demonstrating his well-recognised creative individualism, his anti-establishment credentials in the creation of art outside the constraints of hide-bound opposition (Karsavina, 1948, p. 211; Grigoriev, 2009, p. 9-10). His reputation to date suggested Diaghilev himself, and others, had every right to back

15 Herbert Ross, *Nijinsky*, Paramount Pictures, 1980.

his judgement in this. His personal relationship to Nijinsky may have played a role in this but there is no more likelihood of this than in his championing of a range of other emerging and unconventional talents, such as Bonislava, the dancer Ida Rubenstein, the dancer and founder/director of the Ballet Rambert, Marie Rambert, and Stravinsky himself, who earned his interest even if they had, hitherto, failed to impress the art world generally.

For all the doubts of his colleagues about his prospects as a choreographer, Nijinsky had none. His own account of his preparations for *L'Après-Midi d'un Faune*, his confidence in his own abilities and, above all, his creative independence and isolation in this work, demonstrate not only his willingness but his clear sense of vocational compulsion (Nijinsky, 1968, p. 115-116, p. 137-140). This point is also asserted by Bronislava Nijinska, emphasising her brother's resistance to the creative suggestions and even the basic interpretations of his colleagues dancing with him in *L'Après-Midi d'un Faune* (Nijinska, 1992, p. 427-429; Rambert, 1972, p. 61-62). Nor was such resistance limited to company inferiors. Even the great Tamara Karsavina, his senior and superior in every sense, was regularly subject to Nijinsky's arrogance and insults over choreographic decisions which he claimed for himself, whether choreographer or not (Karsavina, 1948, p. 220, p. 237; Rambert, 1972, p. 69). Given that for Nijinsky, in his unwillingness and apparent incapacity, there was no real sense of collaboration with other dancers, we can deduce the same in his working relationship with Diaghilev. Certainly, as Bronislava Nijinska makes clear, Nijinsky had great need for Diaghilev's approval and recognition (Nijinska, 1992, p. 429), but he also clearly resented Diaghilev for the same reason, as is patently obvious throughout the *Diaries*, and did much to exclude Diaghilev from his choreographic work:

> I practiced my dances and composed ballets alone. Diaghilev did not like this. He did not want me to do things alone, but I could not agree with him. We often quarrelled. I used to lock my door – our rooms were communicating – and would let in no one. I was afraid of him. I knew that all my life was in his hands. (Nijinsky, 1968, p. 46).

Certainty of his own abilities, opinions and artistic ambitions, rather than any professional or emotional collaborative spirit inclined towards working with Diaghilev, were the basis of Nijinsky's desire to take up choreography. The attitude expressed in his *Diaries* about his work on *L'Après-Midi d'un Faune* indicates the arrogant extent of his sense of his own independence and, indeed, his own vocational obsession and isolation:

> I created the whole ballet alone. I also gave the idea for the scenery, but Leon Bakst did not understand what I wanted. The creation of this ballet took a long time but I worked well, feeling the presence of God. I loved this ballet and therefore I made the public love it too. (*Ibid.*, p. 137)[16].

Quite simply, Nijinsky's view can well be summarised by his assertion, "The *Faun* is me" (*ibid.*, p. 140).

MENTORSHIP AND COLLABORATION

Ordinarily in the operations of his Ballets Russes, Diaghilev was nothing if not intensely involved. From Grigoriev's account we can summarise Diaghilev's Herculean interventions in the work of his company as follows: naming ballets (Grigoriev, 2009, p. 7)[17], musical direction (*ibid.*), editing (*ibid.*, p. 33) and commissioning scores (*ibid.*, p. 47), choreographic plot (*ibid.*, p. 7)[18], set (*ibid.*, p. 8)[19], costume and make up design (*ibid.*, p. 17, p. 75), set change plot (*ibid.*, p. 53), lighting design and operation (*ibid.*, p. 38)[20], casting and contract nego-

16 Contrary to the notion of Nijinsky's total control and his sole authorship of *L'Après-Midi d'un Faune*, Stravinsky writes of how Leon Bakst dominated the production, saying "he inspired the choreography even to the slightest movements", (Igor Stravinsky, *Chronicle of My Life*, London, V. Gollancz, 1936, p. 64). Bronislava Nijinska herself emphasizes the importance of Bakst to the work. When all around Nijinsky were getting nervous and Diaghilev wanted Nijinsky to re-do the whole thing, it was Bakst who insisted it was a work of genius and that it should be performed as rehearsed (Nijinska, 1992, p. 431). In addition, Grigoriev writes of the influence of Dalcroze on Diaghilev's idea to create the work (Grigoriev, 2009, p. 61-62).

17 Diaghilev renamed *Chopiniana* as *Les Sylphides*.

18 Fokine writes that "cuts were his specialty, his weakness and his prerogative", Fokine, 1961, p. 229.

19 Fokine points this out in relation to *Firebird* (*ibid.*, p. 174).

20 See also Leonide Massine, *My Life in Ballet*, London, Macmillan, St. Martin's Press, 1968, p. 81.

tiation (*ibid.*, p. 9-10), attending the company's morning classes (*ibid.*, p. 49), attending rehearsals (*ibid.*, p. 66), talent handling (*ibid.*, p. 46), the cultivation of patronage and other financial support (*ibid.*, p. 11), publicity (*ibid.*, p. 35) and even attending to theatre auditorium décor, seating and stage re-modelling (*ibid.*, p. 18). Diaghilev undertook all these activities in relation to Nijinsky's *L'Après-Midi d'un Faune*, *Jeux* and *Sacre*, but it is useful to consider whether the mentor-mentee aspect of his relationship with Nijinsky allowed for any degree of extraordinary collaboration between them, particularly once Nijinsky became choreographer.

Being present in many rehearsals, Diaghilev was obviously not reticent in intervening in the working process of his *protégé*. Bronislava Nijinska speaks of Diaghilev calming Nijinsky when, during the creation of *Sacre*, her brother became enraged at his fellow dancers' inability to understand his instructions (Nijinska, 1992, p. 460). Rambert writes of Diaghilev mounting a stinging verbal attack on Nijinsky who had insulted Karsavina for similar reasons (Rambert, 1972, p. 69). Both examples demonstrate Diaghilev's capacity for intervention in Nijinsky's process of creating the choreography and his willingness to show his disapproval with Nijinsky's failings in public. These interventions did not involve detailed advice or correction in relation to the specifics of Nijinksy's choreography. Diaghilev, however, clearly claimed the right to control the choreography of his mentee in general terms. Diaghilev's threats to cancel *L'Après-Midi d'un Faune* at the eleventh hour when Nijinsky refused to make significant choreographic changes is a case in point (Nijinska, 1992, p. 428-431). Diaghilev's imposition of Rambert's assistance on the production of *Sacre* is another (*ibid.*, p. 450-455; Grigoriev, 2009, p. 61)[21].

Clearly Nijinsky relied heavily on Diaghilev and came to understand his 'handling' and public interventions as a necessary part of the elder man's expertise (Nijinska, 1992, p. 429, p. 509; Karsavina, 1948, p. 151). For all this and despite the level of their essential interaction

21 Emile Jaques-Dalcroze (1865-1950) and his musical education system 'Eurhythmics' influenced Diaghilev in his plans and preparations for *Le Sacre du Printemps*. After visiting Dalcroze at his institute in Hellerau outside Dresden with Nijinsky and Bronislava Nijinska, Diaghilev arranged for Dalcroze's star pupil, Marie Rambert, to join the Ballets Russes and teach the company Eurythmics – unsuccessfully as it turned out (Nijinska, 1992, p. 450-452; Rambert, 1972, p. 54).

as producer and choreographer, there seems little to suggest that the partnership ever became truly collaborative. Indeed, there is much to suggest that, even once Nijinsky took higher duties in the company, Diaghilev jealously guarded his mentor's prerogative and Nijinsky never fully gained the freedom Nouvel hoped for him, until he took it by way of his unexpected marriage. The growing distance between them, as evidenced by Bronislava Nijinska's increasing role as 'buffer' for Diaghilev between himself and her brother (Nijinska, 1992, p. 472-473, p. 454), represents the impossibility of any truly collaborative idea to their professional relationship. Given the extent to which we read Diaghilev's need for Bronislava Nijinska to play this buffer role as an expression of his desperation to preserve his authority rather than reveal his weakness – we also derive a sense of Diaghilev's own jealously guarded sense of a mentor's priority in the face of his mentee's extreme value and necessity to the entire enterprise.

Taking all this into account, we may conclude that if the mentor-mentee dynamic between them had any effect on their creative collaboration, it was, in fact, to diminish the balance of authority that might be expected between producer and choreographer. From all the evidence, this balance was certainly much more in place with Diaghilev and Fokine, despite their myriad difficulties, than it ever was between Diaghilev and Nijinsky.

THE END OF A LOVE AFFAIR

Contrary to the truism of civilian love affairs, between Diaghilev and Nijinsky it was the sex that went first. Bronislava Nijinska comments that by the summer of 1913 "their close friendship had been over for some time" (Nijinska, 1992, p. 482), possibly since the end of 1911 when they were sleeping in separate rooms (Schijen, 2009, p. 238, p. 278). In professional terms, at this point in their *liaison*, given that the premieres of *L'Après-Midi d'un Faune*, *Jeux* and *Sacre* were still ahead of them, the end of their physical relationship seems to have been of little consequence for their work. With, what has become known as, the "showmance" the sex may come and go, but it is only when the audience subsides and the show closes that the affair inevitably comes to its end. Clearly Nijinsky's unexpected marriage played some role in the severing of relations between the two men. His substantial professional redundancy to Diaghilev, however, came with his failure, in Diaghilev's final estimation, as a choreographer (Grigoriev, 2009, p. 87, p. 91; Nijinska, 1992, p. 482). This failure resulted in the need to re-engage the formerly rejected Fokine, the terms of whose agreement required Nijinksy's dismissal from the company both as a choreographer and a dancer (Nijinska, 2009, p. 484). To whatever extent Diaghilev, his company, his preferred theatres and their audience still demanded the presence of Nijinsky, *Dieu de la danse*, Fokine's participation made Nijinsky's impossible and Nijinsky was dismissed from the Ballets Russes in November 1913.

There is evidence of the personal slight Diaghilev felt over Nijinsky's marriage to Romola de Pulzsky. Misia Sert (1872-1950), a friend and patron, was with him in Venice when he received the news by telegram. Diaghilev's immediate hysterical performance of "extreme sobbing and shouting… grief and rage" was still working itself through by the time his group of friends had removed him "to Naples, where he launched himself on a frantic bacchanalia" (Scheijen, 2009, p. 279). Benois says he had it from the horse's mouth that Diaghilev "nearly lost his reason" at that time (Benois, 1945, p. 352). Bronislava Nijinska reports sightings by friends and some personal experience of Diaghilev's hurt feelings and general gloominess (Nijinska, 2009, p. 489-490). In the same context, however, both Bronislava Nijinska and Benois make it clear that whatever was personal about his reaction to Nijinsky's behaviour, the major significance for Diaghilev was related to his own professional concerns rather than any romantic feeling for Nijinsky. Given the fact that the marriage had provided an excuse to assist him on a course he had already planned (to replace Nijinsky at least as choreographer), he might well have welcomed the news. If there was anything genuine about his response it is more likely to have come from the blow to his professional ego and the realisation, as Benois points out, "that he had been tricked and deceived" (Benois, 1945, p. 352). Grigoriev makes the point that in Diaghilev's mind there may well have been a power struggle going on over control of his 'favourite slave'. He writes:

> Having no mind of his own, Nijinsky would certainly fall entirely under the influence of his wife; and I could not imagine that would suit Diaghilev for a moment. (Grigoriev, 2009, p. 87).

Given his almost total doubts about Nijinsky's future as choreographer, the final threat to his control over Nijinsky with the advent of the marriage may well account for his reactions: "He [Diaghilev] was not a man to depend on other people, however necessary to him they might appear to be", (*Ibid.*, p. 90). Thus, if there was 'violence' in Diaghilev's response to the marriage news, as Grigoriev indicates (91), it was at the final loss of the continuing prospects of Nijinsky as, what Benois called, his "creative agent" (Benois, 1945, p. 290) rather than as his lover or friend. Whatever the extent of Diaghilev's rage, Scheijen demonstrates that the fatal telegram dismissing Nijinsky, which he insisted Grigoriev sign, was not sent until late November – two months after Diaghilev had news of the marriage. Not only did this give him ample time to calm down and avoid an impulsive emotional response to the marriage news but, as Scheijen points out, it gave him time to secure the hard-won and prickly agreement of Fokine to re-join the company. Whatever was in Diaghilev's heart, it was only once the matter of his choreography had been solved that he could finally break with Nijinsky (Scheijen, 2009, p. 282).

HISTORIES OF LOVE

Standing aside from the primary accounts of the Diaghilev/Nijinsky encounter, I turn now to *Nijinsky* and *Petrushka* as fictional representations of this mentor-mentee relationship. My intention is not to expose their historiographical shortcomings or exaggerations, but to read them as alternative pieces of evidence which inform us about some of the complex emotional, often unspoken or undocumented, aspects of such relationships. These films are created by artists within a similar context to the subject they describe. In the case of the original *Petrushka*, this is the very same context. Accordingly these narratives claim an authority as evidence for the passion play aspect of creative endeavour which is not far removed from the primary accounts I have considered hitherto.

In *Nijinsky* Sergei Diaghilev, the 'Old Monster' of the film, is a complex and sympathetic figure. He genuinely loves Vaslav Nijinsky and his enduring faith in his talent is only outdone by his utter conviction of Vaslav's genius. Restraining Sergei somewhat in his personal and emotional commitment to Vaslav, however, is his own rhetoric of a rational commitment to 'the good of the company'. Sergei's story is seemingly a melodrama and a love story of sorts, played out in relation to these increasingly competing commitments. In the creative and publicity triumphs of his dancing and then in the similar success of his performance and choreography for *L'Après-Midi d'un Faune*, Vaslav offers Sergei his longed-for paradise of art. Once apparently attained, however, this paradise soon becomes lost in the obscurity of Vaslav's work on Debussy's *Jeux* and in the disaster, as Sergei calls it in the film, of *Le Sacre du Printemps*. Vaslav, as the harbinger and agent of paradise, is then lost to Sergei, sacrificed, according to the familiar narrative conventions of the male melodrama, on the cross of his own genius which here takes the form of mental illness. According to the logic of Sergei's 'for the good of the company' rhetoric following his marriage, Vaslav is dismissed from the company, and left to decline into insanity. Leonide Massine is engaged to replace Vaslav as premier dancer and *protégé*, Fokine is recalled to the role of choreographer and the company goes on.

Despite the extent to which Sergei loves Vaslav, adores his genius and laments his growing mental illness, in dismissing him from the Ballets Russes it is the rhetoric of 'the good of the company' which prevails over these personal feelings. In this regard, the film appeals to the enduring myth of Ballets Russes ensemble creativity and *Gesamtkunstwerk* (Nicholls, 2017, p. 437-439). The expression of the idea that 'no one in the Ballets Russes is indispensable', as well as the fact that Sergei stands willing to sacrifice any one of his artists/friends to these principles, including Fokine and Stravinsky, indicates that the work, and the collective efforts of the company to realise it, is apparently all that matters. What this rhetoric occludes, however, is the reality that 'the good of the company' is really what is good for none other than Sergei. One person is indispensable from the Ballets Russes and personal sensitivities and emotions do play a role in the company, so long as that person is Sergei and those sensitivities are his own. *Nijinsky* may then be read not so much a melodrama about the competing factors of Sergei's feelings for Vaslav set against the ideals of Ballets Russes ensemble production, but as struggle in Sergei's mind between the Ballets Russes as his own personal expression of ego against its nature as something beyond him and beyond the ego of any individual. This is a struggle over the strength of the rhetoric of his own creative dedication and professionalism.

In Alan Bates' expression and performance as Sergei there is a strong note of insecurity about the impact of this internal struggle. This is particularly evident in the private conversations Sergei has with his servant Vasilli (Colin Blakely) and their discussion which I quote at the beginning of this essay. This note of insecurity can reasonably be read as an expression of love for Vaslav. Equally, however, it can be read as Sergei's overwhelming realisation of his own tendency and capacity to allow his personal feelings to complicate his professional agenda. That there is an emotional dimension to his professional dreams and that, as a result, there is no or little distinction between *the* company and *his* company.

The fragility of Sergei's rhetoric is even more apparent in the fact that its ideal of company professionalism and individual indispensability is Sergei's rhetoric alone and he soon contradicts it. Sergei has no time for either Fokine's or Stravinsky's reasonable criticism of Vaslav's abilities, their apparent concern for the company or, indeed, their genuine concern for Vaslav. Vaslav himself articulates serious concerns that Sergei's professional dedication to him is waning. Both men obviously become highly conscious that Vaslav's work in the company is becoming synonymous with failure and scandal. Despite this, however, up until to the point of Vaslav's surprise marriage, Sergei shows no sign of abandoning his plans to work with Vaslav as dancer or choreographer.

The essential point is that although the film makes much of Sergei's concern for Vaslav's choreographic 'failures', Sergei dismisses him, in effect, on a highly personal basis at the point of his own apparent rejection. This looks like the act of a jilted lover and, in part, it is. In a subsequent discussion with Romola de Pulzsky, however, we understand that there is a further dimension to it. Just as he championed Vaslav according to his instincts, Sergei dismisses him in the film for very similar personal and even more selfish concerns. Again, citing the rhetoric of 'the good of the company' to Romola, he explains his refusal to take Vaslav back by expressing his fears about discipline, factionalism and gossip within the company.

He may be unwilling to express the extent of his feelings for Vaslav in front of the young woman for whom he was jilted, but Sergei's concerns expressed here are not for his love of Vaslav but for his performance of personal authority in front of the company. Sacking Vaslav out of love and wounded pride would have been one thing. Refusing to take him back into the company in the face of a perceived compromised authority is taking the intervention of emotional factors to another level altogether. The idea of it leaves 'the good of the company' rhetoric in tatters In representing Sergei as a romantic figure, conflicted by a rhetorical expression of corporate responsibility but largely subject to the weaknesses, insecurities and the folly of ego, *Nijinksy* asserts the idea of the mentor's priority in Sergei's ultimate claims to authority. The Ballets Russes, we understand from this, will stand or fall not by a collective company sublimation to the religion of art supported by a rhetoric of ensemble, corporate professionalism and *Gesamtkunstwerk*, but by the romantic and purely egotistic inclinations of the 'Old Monster' at its helm.

Nijinsky begins and ends with Vaslav in a straitjacket on the floor of an empty room, presumably in a mental asylum. Apparently vanquished at the hands of Sergei, accompanied by passages from Stravinsky's score, there is little other possibility of reading these scenes as alluding to anything but *Petrushka.* The film contains only one actual scene from the ballet itself, the pathetic, lonely complaint of its hero against his mistreatments by his impresario. This directly associates Sergei and Vaslav with their obvious counterparts in the ballet, the Conjuror/Showman and the eponymous Petrushka. Accordingly, with very little explicit presence, we see how *Petrushka* haunts *Nijinsky.* Considering its dynamics in relation to Diaghilev and Nijinsky as we have considered them above, I now outline the ways in which *Petrushka* tells us a great deal about the Ballets Russes and the conflicts of private passions and corporate responsibilities that are potentially involved in the mentoring partnership.

Petrushka was first performed during Diaghilev's third Paris ballet season on the 13th of June 1911 at the Théâtre du Châtelet. Alexandre Benois and Igor Stravinsky co-wrote the libretto, Stranvinsky composed the score, Benois created the décor, Michel Fokine the choreography, Pierre Monteux was conductor and the principal roles were danced by Nijinsky (Petrushka), Karsavina (Ballerina), Alexander Orlov (Moor) and Enrico Cecchetti (Charlatan/Showman) (Grigoriev, 2009, p. 264). The ballet is set in Admiralty Square, St Petersburg in the 1830s during the Shrovetide Fair. In 'Scene 1'[22] the Conjuror/Showman hypnotises the fairground audience into entering the space before his little theatre and "charms the three puppets [Petrushka, a Ballerina, a Moor] into life with his flute"[23]. The puppets dance first in the theatre but then break from its confines to dance among the audience. In 'Scene 2' the Showman thrusts Petrushka into a cell where the Showman's own 'scowling' image is hung from the wall. Here Petrushka contemplates his fate, his oppression by the Showman and his hopelessly unrequited love for the Ballerina. At one point she is, herself, thrust into the cell only to be scared off by Petrushka's amorous excitement and his 'uncouth antics'. In 'Scene 3' the thuggish Moor is successfully seducing the Ballerina when Petrushka interrupts them in a jealous rage. There is an ensuing fight between Petrushka and the Moor which ends with Petrushka's ejection. In 'Scene 4' the characters spill out again to the fairground and the Moor kills Petrushka with his scimitar. The Showman is then called for to "reassure the bystanders that [the now dead] Petrushka is nothing more than a puppet" (*ibid.*). When the crowd have dispersed, he then drags Petrushka's lifeless body away only to be confronted by Petrushka's ghost appearing on the roof of the little theatre "jeering and mocking at everyone whom the Showman has fooled" (*ibid.*)[24].

In the television film version of *Petrushka*, which forms part of *Nureyev and the Joffrey Ballet / In Tribute to Nijinsky* (Ardolino, 1981), Nureyev shuns the thick paint as mask make-up and does a great deal in his portrayal to emphasise Petrushka as a human being rather than as a puppet. In the final scene, when Petrushka appears on the roof of the little theatre, Nureyev simply stands up on his mark, more like an actor calmly making his own way on stage than as a puppet unwillingly thrust into the scene as we often see him through the ballet. Very

22 Stravinsky's score refers to these four scenes as four '*tableaux*'.

23 Eric Walter White, *Stravinsky: The Composer and His Music*, London and Berkeley, University of California Press, 1966, p. 158-159.

24 This summary is derived from Eric Walter White's "conflation of the outline synopsis and general note that are printed in the 1911 score" (White, 1966, p. 158-159).

brightly lit, his cheeky grin and laugh directed towards the Showman (Gary Chryst), he stands energetic and erect, only bending to make his mocking gestures, which receive great prominence in this production. As the Showman scurries off in horror, Petrushka stands tall and gestures in triumph like a sporting hero celebrating victory from a balcony in a stadium. Only once the Showman has escaped do we see any fatigue or anything other than mocking triumph, in Nureyev's Petrushka. When he does finally give way to fatigue, once the Showman has left the scene, his collapse indicates, not a loose ragdoll-like body but a presence of corporal substance. He hangs over the theatre's proscenium arch, not like a stuffing-drained soft toy, but like a strong and powerful body, finally given way to extreme exhaustion. His body slams down on the proscenium arch, but does not come to rest. As the lights go down Petrushka is still moving, not a shadowy ghost figure, nor an apparition of the Showman's distracted mind, but a powerful and physically imposing presence dominating the scene.

Petrushka, itself based on a folk narrative of some antiquity, is the most frequently revived of the original Ballets Russes productions and there are a variety of approaches taken with its hero. Nureyev's is one interpretation that clearly asserts Petrushka's power extending beyond the plot of the narrative and more than matching that of his Showman-controller. To the extent that all interpretations of Petrushka relate back to Nijinsky, his creator, Nureyev's sad clown demonstrates that both are more than merely the hapless victim of an evil overlord. Petrushka's final, mocking assertion of his endurance, fame and popular attraction shows that he does not send the Showman off in terror simply because the latter believes that his defunct creation has come to life again. The Showman's horror is also located in the first realisation that 'his' Petrushka is an entity independent of him and fully aware of his own power and popular appeal – the impresario's worst nightmare. It is this thought that haunts the Showman, for all his confidence displayed when confronting the slain clown minutes earlier. His final departure in terror clearly implies the sleepless nights and distracted days that are to follow. No one who encounters Petrushka can fail to be impressed and bound up in feelings of enduring empathy. The Showman, more that anyone, knows Petrushka's full value. As we see in Gary Chryst's protective and jealous coveting of the lifeless clown once he has been killed, the

Showman readily confuses that valuation with feelings of love. It is for this confused combination of feelings of love and commercial valuation that the haunting will be endless.

AUTEUR OVER *ENSEMBLE*

As evidence related to the Diaghilev/Nijinsky mentorship case the narrative fictions of *Nijinsky* and *Petrushka* offer powerful and emotive representations of the individual claims and ambitions of both mentor and mentee. There is clearly a heavy note of company professionalism expressed in *Nijinsky*. Despite this, Sergei's performance of professional insecurity undercuts company rhetoric and asserts the mentor's ego and the strength of his personal priority as key factors in this example of mentorship practice. For all that such characteristics are represented in the Showman of *Petrushka*, we cannot escape the fact that the ballet is really all about its hero, Petrushka, and the strength of our emotional connections with this sad clown. As in *Nijinsky*, with *Petrushka* the personal makes a powerful intervention in the professional, even at the expense of the logical. Just as *Nijinsky* powerfully asserts the mentor's claim, *Petrushka* illustrates the overwhelming power of the mentee. This may seem to place the mentee in an apparently weaker, victim-like position. We see this with Vaslav institutionalised and in a straitjacket in *Nijinsky*, and with Petrushka slumped over and exhausted at the apparent conclusion to his story. But neither Vaslav nor Petrushka are finally defeated and *Nijinsky* asserts the point by concluding not with the straitjacket image, but with a short montage of stills of Vaslav, proud and dynamic, in his most memorable roles.

As two interventions in the voluminous Ballets Russes myth-scape, the mutual assertion of individual priority in each story echoes the accounts of the primary evidence, itself a part of that myth-scape, that I have considered here. From these we observe that despite the intervention of the emotional and the intimate in the Diaghilev/Nijinsky relationship, it is the professional, in this context considered as individualistic vocational drives, that dominate the mentorship dynamic.

Personal passions are very much at play, but they are directed towards the creative outcome, the work itself. For the creative artist this is, no doubt, a form of love (Nicholls, 2003; Nicholls, 2012). In terms of the emotions swapped between the creative arts mentor and mentee in pursuit of mutually desired outcomes, however, from the Diaghilev/Nijinsky example we can see that in the realm of inter-personal relationships this form of love counts for little more than a temporary *mariage de raison*. Within the mentorship dynamic of *auteur* over *ensemble*, this love story sits firmly within an enduring theatrical tradition commonly known, and sometimes deservedly derided, as little more than the showmance[25].

Mark NICHOLLS
The University of Melbourne
Australia

25 Thanks to Ali Wirtz for her contribution to this essay.

CONSTELLATION MENTORSHIP

In this essay, I discuss Marjorie Barstow's Alexander education as a constellation-mentorship. For the uninitiated, the Alexander Technique is a way of becoming consciously aware of our underlying coordination in activity. It was created by Frederick Mathias Alexander (1869-1955), an Australian actor whose recital career was hampered by the continual loss of his voice. After years of self-observation and reflection, Alexander observed that our coordination can be adversely affected *unconsciously* by our inner sense of striving and *consciously governed* by altering the quality of the relationship between our head and spine, what Alexander called "the primary control". It is a technique that has particular utility for performers, who need to operate psycho-physically at a heightened level in order to do what they do. One of his first trainees was his brother, Albert Redden, 'A.R.', (1873-1947), who became the only teacher in whom F.M. put his complete trust[1].

In 1933 Marjorie Barstow (1899-1995) was the first person to graduate from F.M. Alexander's inaugural three-year training course in London and was one of three Americans in that course. She was drawn to the Alexander Technique as a dancer and dance teacher. After training in the Alexander Technique, Barstow stopped teaching dance in Nebraska and taught from 1934 to 1942 as assistant to A.R. Alexander, who was teaching his brother's work in Boston and New York. By the 1940s, F.M. Alexander and his English protégés disapproved of Barstow's teaching. They showed their disapproval either by ceasing to answer her correspondence, or writing to others about how she had gone "clean off the rails"[2]. In the 1970s criticism of her was more widespread, and by the 1980s a heated debate had sprung up about whether she

1 In this essay, the name 'Alexander' on its own refers to F.M. When referring to his brother, A.R., I will use his initials to clarify.

2 Walter Carrington, *A Time to Remember: A Personal Diary of Teaching the F.M. Alexander Technique in 1946*, London, Sheildrake Press, 1996, p. 26.

was teaching the Alexander Technique at all. By the early 1990s the English school had turned against her altogether[3]. Many of Barstow's long-term students have since become world-renowned teachers, despite being unrecognized by Alexander 'Societies' as certified teachers.

Barstow's unique Alexander education occurred through what I call a constellation mentorship. The mentors included F.M. Alexander himself, A.R. Alexander, with whom Barstow worked for many years, and John Dewey (1859-1952), the American philosophical pragmatist who studied with both Alexander brothers. I aim to show that Barstow's output (teaching, training, mentoring) showed the influence of that mentorship. I then consider her as an Alexander mentor rather than (or as well as) an Alexander teacher, asking whether her methods may have been more widely accepted if her teaching had been labelled *mentorship*, rather than *teaching*.

I argue that Barstow's relative obscurity and controversial status is partly due to the fact that she did not publish any of her arguments or experiments. I suggest that this lack was related to her deep commitment to the experimental, ever-unfinished nature of her work. Her willingness to embrace its constant 'becoming' quality is what makes her a true philosophical pragmatist in the tradition of the thought of the philosopher John Dewey. I illustrate the details of her work through references to her mentorship – by correspondence – with the Alexander teacher, Frank Pierce Jones (1905-1976). Jones was one of the few teachers to train with the Alexanders in the United States, where they had retreated during the second world war. As Professor of Classics at Brown University, he was an unlikely candidate for the role of scientific researcher, which he ultimately became at Dewey's urging. He remains the most universally recognised American writer on the Alexander Technique, his *Body Awareness in Action* (1976) still ranking as one of the key texts for Alexander students today.

3 See Jeremy Chance, « Editorial », *Direction Journal*, 1991, vol. 1, n° 8, p. 4; Michael Frederick, « Interview with Michael Frederick by Barbara and Bill Conable », Barbara Conable, ed., (Festschrift) *Marjorie Barstow: Her Teaching and Training. A 90th Birthday Offering*, Columbus, Andover Road Press, 1989, p. 46-53.

CONSTELLATION

The 'constellation' that constituted Barstow's education as an Alexander teacher consisted of people whose work brought her in line with many of the ideas of philosophical pragmatism. Much of Alexander's earlier work, for example, showed parallels with the scientific process. His brother (A.R.), under whose guidance Barstow spent her formative years as an Alexander Technique teacher, could be said to have *emphasised* the pragmatic aspects of Alexander's work in his teaching, while F.M. and his English disciples began to de-emphasise them. Barstow's training brought her into contact with scholars of Dewey, and also with Dewey himself, in person and through his books. These connections strengthened as she began her long correspondence with Jones on all aspects of the Alexander Technique, including Dewey's support of Jones's first forays into scientific research on the technique.

Barstow's Mentorship Model, as already foreshadowed, shows many parallels with the philosophy of Dewey. These parallels can be summarised as follows:

1. Barstow's practice of reconstructing Alexander's terminology and methods of teaching to make it accessible, getting rid of jargon and unhelpful words and practices. This aligns with Dewey's reconstruction of philosophy to make it relevant to everyday problems of everyday people.
2. Barstow's practice of teaching Alexander Technique in groups at *all* levels, including beginners and not just in teacher training programs, aligns with Dewey's belief in the importance of community in education and the impact of social intelligence on purpose. The connection Dewey makes between community and communication can also be seen in Barstow's teaching.
3. Barstow's insistence on *applying* the Alexander Technique to other disciplines. As she said, "if the Alexander work cannot be taught alongside other things then there is not much hope for it." (Letter, 19 June 1945)[4]. Barstow's practice aligns with Dewey's observation

4 *Correspondence with Frank Pierce Jones*, The F. M. Alexander-Frank Pierce Jones Archive, New York, Dimon Institute. All letters between Marjorie Barstow and Frank Pierce Jones quoted here refer to this publication.

that interest is required for real learning to take place and that desire is required for action. Her practice also satisfies Dewey's desire for the unity of theory and practice (in this case application) and for context in learning and teaching.

4. Barstow also brought theory and practice together in her method of training teachers. Beginner pupils and trainee teachers were taught in the same group to avoid what Dewey called the "split between the experience gained in more direct associations and what is acquired in school."[5]
5. Dewey's critical pragmatism, with its emphasis on experimentation and doing 'what works' shows up in Barstow's unwillingness to continue on in a way she believed could be improved upon by applying the very steps of the Alexander Technique, which represent the scientific process, as Dewey pointed out[6]. She lamented the fact that Alexander did not continue to apply his own critical pragmatism to his methods of teaching so that writers of influence, who took lessons from him for brief periods, could fully understand and further his work[7]. She was "not convinced" that his way of teaching showed "scientific value". (Letter, 29 April 1948). She also points out the irony of being rejected as an agent for change within a technique of change[8].

In the following sections, I will examine these parallels with Dewey in detail and go on to suggest that Barstow's style of teaching more closely resembles mentorship than traditional teaching.

5 John Dewey, *Democracy and Education*, Radford VA: Wilder publications, 2008, p. 14.

6 F. Matthias Alexander, *Constructive Conscious Control of the Individual*, Introduction by John Dewey, Foreword by Walter H.M. Carrington, ed. by Jean M.O. Fischer, 8th ed., London, Mouritz, 2004.

7 "I do not think any of those great men – Shaw, Huxley, Ludovici, etc., got the real significance of the work. I saw F.M. teaching some of them in the early days – they had lessons like I had, and I see now that I really found nothing of value with that kind of teaching." Letter, 13 January 1946.

8 "This isn't a complaint – it's statement of facts. I could have gone on a hundred years that way and gotten nowhere fast. I see it clearly now, that's why I continue to experiment, and that's why, as you have probably discovered, I'm the 'black sheep' or 'bad bandit.'" Letter, 13 January 1946.

RECONSTRUCTION

After working closely with A.R. Alexander for many years (1934 to 1942), Barstow began to reconstruct the teaching of the Alexander Technique. In truth, her reconstruction probably began to incubate during her long apprenticeship to A.R., since he was a very different teacher from his brother and asked questions of the technique and its assumptions about teaching[9]. Barstow remained convinced of Alexander's 'discovery' of the primary control but believed the teaching needed a significant review. During her lifetime she was careful not to say anything at all against Alexander publicly. But in letters to Jones she frequently revealed her private opinion. For example, she writes:

> You must remember he never has been interested in people who do any original thinking… He is not keen about progress in his own work. (Letter, 11 March 1947)
>
> FM is a genius and has made a marvellous discovery but I do not think he excels as a teacher. If he had, he would have well trained teachers all over the world by this time. The proof of the pudding is always in the eating of it. (Letter, 20 June 1948).

Jones expressed a similar view, describing himself to John Dewey as 'alarmed' at the (English) view that the teaching technique had been perfected (Letter, [no day] March 1947). "This is by no means my opinion", he went on to say. "I think the whole thing is in an experimental stage." Barstow even believed that a general separation between Alexander's 'technique' and 'discovery' should be made. She began to call Alexander's teaching methods 'his technique', while the fundamental principle, that of primary control[10], she called 'his discovery'. In the

9 Despite this, F.M. "never lost faith or trust in A.R. and his work," while he expressed reservations about all of the teachers who remained in London. Donald L. Weed, « Our Debt to A.R. Alexander », *Interactive Teaching Method: A revolutionary approach to the Alexander Technique*, 2012, web.

10 Alexander called the mechanism of changing the relationship between head and spine 'the primary control', which, he observed, had an effect on the overall functioning of the body. For a discussion on this term and how Marjorie Barstow clarified it and changed its name, see Amanda Cole, *Marjorie Barstow and the Alexander Technique: Critical Thinking in Performing Arts Pedagogy*, Palgrave Macmillan, 2022.

same letter, she noted: "Somewhere in *Universal Constant*[11] he calls it 'a technique of inhibition'. That seems a perfect definition of it, but I am more interested in constructive activity than 'learning how to stop.' It makes more sense to me." (Letter, 20 April 1948).

Inhibition has indeed become one of the defining features of the Alexander Technique as taught in the English paradigm. Barstow's teaching was – and still is – criticised for not including it. And yet, many of her students saw that she taught nothing *but* inhibition, only reframing it as *replacing* a non-constructive plan with a constructive one, so that students stayed in action and in thought, or as Dewey described it, 'thinking in activity', Barstow saw students who were intent on inhibiting as 'stiff,' 'set' or holding positions, as described by one of her long-term students (or mentees), John Wynhausen. He points to her fluidity and flexibility of approach and way of moving, noting, as many others have, the stiffness of some teachers of the other schools. He observed a major difference between Barstow's interpretation and the way his teachers before her had discussed it: "Marj describes the work in terms of taking actions. You move your head, you let your body follow. The traditional view is: first you refuse to do anything, that is, you 'inhibit' your impulse to move. Small wonder so many Alexander teachers look stiff, almost paralysed, in their movements."[12]

This was one of the keys to Barstow's teaching that marked it out as being at variance to the English way. She said: "In my early teaching I used it as it had been taught to me as inhibition, but I soon realized it was not getting the kind of results I wanted." (Letter, 17 November 1947); "I do not want people to think the principles of primary control are some form of hocus-pocus, that you sit in a chair looking stiff and blank and automatically repeat formulas and everything will be O.K. (Now, how is that for a description?)" (Letter, 19 August 1946).

Like Barstow, Jones did not use the 'directions' or 'orders' as Alexander had coined them, being more interested in "being able to apply the work to what you already did in a more efficient way."[13] Jones and Dewey also

11 Alexander's fourth and final book, first published in 1941: F. Matthias Alexander, *The Universal Constant in Living*, 3rd ed., London, Chaterson, 1986.

12 John Wynhausen, « From Portland to Lincoln: From Chiropractic College to the World of the Alexander Technique », Barbara Conable, ed., (Festschrift) *Marjorie Barstow: Her Teaching and Training. A 90th Birthday Offering*, Columbus, Andover Road Press, 1989, p. 133.

13 Robert Rickover, « The Teaching of Frank Pierce Jones: Robert Rickover Talks to Tommy Thompson », *Body Learning 2014*, MP3 file, web.

discussed Alexander's terms and their shortcomings, seeming to be in alignment with what I call 'Barstow's reconstruction of the Alexander Technique'. Jones writes that the Alexanders both left him somewhat bewildered and that he had been "forced to work the thing out" for himself (Letter, [no day] March 1947). "In that task" he tells Dewey, "I found your phrase 'thinking in activity' more useful than anything else. It is a unified concept and seems to me more suited to describe the experience than F.M.'s 'inhibition' and 'orders,' both of which terms I consider misleading." When Dewey was asked for pre-publication advice on one of Alexander's books, Dewey even made a special trip to warn Alexander that the word 'inhibition' would cause confusion in the climate of psychoanalytic opinion[14].

Barstow constantly reviewed and revised her own teaching methods as well as Alexander's, noting in 1948 that she would not teach groups the way she had in 1944 (Letter, 16 May 1948). To show her commitment to this process of self-review, she said: "I would never blame *the pupil* who was thinking and ordering for a year and was still stiff. Of course, that's the easiest way out." (Letter, 29 April 1948, emphasis added).

GROUP TEACHING

The group situation is one of the aspects of Barstow's teaching that most made it resemble mentorship. She would hold weekly classes for those who had moved to Nebraska to study with her. These would be supplemented by summer and winter workshops of several weeks' duration, which attracted students from all over the world. Such an approach to teaching fulfils Plutarch's requirement, that of igniting wood and no more, then motivating the mentee towards originality and instilling the desire for truth. Barstow's method satisfies the requirement in two ways. First, the group situation allowed for time in the hot seat, as well as time watching what is these days called 'side-door coaching' whereby students learn by watching others' significant learning moments.

14 Carrington, 1996, p. 12; Edward Maisel, ed., *The Resurrection of the Body: The Essential Writings of F. Matthias Alexander*, 1st Shambala ed., Boston, Shambala, 1986, p. XXXVI.

Second, Barstow allowed time between workshops and between weekly classes for the students to move towards originality. This model is in stark contrast to the English model of training teachers, where trainees must attend full-time study for three years: 3-4 hours daily, five days a week, engendering exhaustion, staleness and no time for individual reflection or direction. One of my early teachers did describe her training in this paradigm as exhausting, recounting, tongue-in-cheek, the kind of conversation she and her colleagues would have at home after a hard day's training[15]. Walter Carrington and Alison Grant-Morris report the same phenomenon, and Barstow was highly critical of this kind of training[16]. The English immersion model also makes it very difficult to pursue any other interests, thus consolidating the end-in-itself approach.

While group teaching was not something Barstow invented altogether in Alexander studies, her innovation was to teach it to 'pupils' as well as 'students'. I am adopting Alexander's terminology here: students were training to teach the Alexander Technique; pupils were merely learning the technique. By extending the group format to all her teaching Barstow also did away with Alexander's artificial separation between pupils and students. The effect was multi-level teaching, which benefited not only beginners and intermediate students, who could see the technique being applied (and taught) at a range of levels, but also those wishing to teach, as their 'turns' in class could be teaching students at various levels, rather than only their relatively advanced colleagues. Whether or not Barstow foresaw this, her method was a way of taking the Alexander Technique to the masses, because she instilled at all levels the ability to communicate clearly what the Alexander process was, even to newcomers. This was something Alexander had struggled with, and may be one reason the Alexander Technique is still relatively obscure today. One of Alexander's English graduates said it was common for beginners to say: "I can't understand a word (F.M.) says!" He defended Alexander, saying:

> And it was rather like that. People *didn't* understand a word he said. And he didn't even explain to people at all reasonably *why* they couldn't understand

15 Trainee: "I'm *so* tired", – Partner/spouse/flatmate: "What did you do today?" – Trainee: "Oh, got in and out of a chair a few times and lay on my back for a long time."

16 Carrington mentions it repeatedly in *A Time to Remember*, while Grant-Morris wrote to Barstow about it, who then commented upon it to Jones (Letter, 11 November 1947).

> what he said. Because you mustn't *expect* to understand what an Alexander teacher tells you straight away. (Macdonald, "In the 80s", at 23m 37s).

This was unacceptable to Barstow: "I believe that bad teaching is the cause of pupils not being able to talk simply and easily about their lessons. As teaching methods improve I am sure many of our problems will diminish." (Letter, 10 September 1947).

Clear communication became another hallmark of Barstow's teaching. If, during a turn in class, a student could not clearly articulate what s/he saw to the rest of the class without tightening (or what my teacher, who trained with Barstow, calls "going out of coordination"), Barstow would ask the student to sit down and think about what had just passed[17]. She used the group format to emphasise communication. Even as early as 1947, Barstow had understood that teaching constructive thinking was more important than what teachers could do with their hands, and that the use of the hands in teaching often took a student past the point to which they could follow with their thinking and certainly past the point from which they could continue on their own between lessons.

This point marked a major change in how Barstow proceeded to teach (Letter, 10 September 1947). It also aligned with pragmatism's premium on making ideas clear. This was one of the hallmarks of philosophical pragmatism: a way of doing philosophy that made ideas clear, rather than as a place to look for ideas themselves. Barstow also emphasised the *how* of the Alexander Technique over the *what.* A fundamental part of her reconstruction was to make the process of the work as clear and understandable as possible.

In a book of collected essays written by Barstow's long-term students about her teaching, community is another of the over-riding themes that emerge, alongside communication (see Barbara Conable, *Festschrift*[18]). The words 'community' and 'communication' are etymologically linked, which is something Dewey discusses at length and which Barstow understood either from her education or her experimental methods, the results of which she closely observed. Barstow had observed that "young people do not, as a rule, like to work alone, they want association and companionship, which is natural." (Undated letter). Barstow's new teaching format answered this need.

17 See Cathy Madden, *Teaching the Alexander Technique: Active Pathways to Integrative Practice*, London and Philadelphia, Singing Dragon, 2018, Kindle e-book edition.

18 Barbara Conable, ed., (Festschrift) *Marjorie Barstow: Her Teaching and Training. A 90th Birthday Offering*, Columbus, Andover Road Press, 1989.

Finally, Barstow's group model had another benefit. It allowed musicians and other performers to practise applying the technique in a performance situation, that is, the class group, which at times grew quite large. In the following paragraphs I discuss this application in detail.

APPLICATION

Barstow came to the Alexander Technique as a dancer. It followed that she would be interested in applying the technique to her art. During her London training, Barstow helped Irene Tasker in Alexander's "Little School" for children. Tasker was probably the first teacher to teach "mostly [...] application work"[19], and Barstow acknowledges the influence that Tasker's application work had on her: "I used to help her some in the school [...] and observing the children made me see how valuable our whole coordination is in relation to any of our activities."[20] Alexander had trained Tasker only 'informally' to do his 'application work'. Tasker consequently describes the application work as being somehow other (or less?) than the Alexander Technique *per se.* While teaching children to apply the Alexander Technique Tasker did not consider herself an Alexander teacher. In the 1980s Barstow wrote that she thought Irene Tasker had been of more value than they realised at the time of their training: "Now I appreciate what she did for me more and more."[21] And yet this apparent separation of theory and practice is not in alignment with critical pragmatism, and Barstow rejected it in her own teaching. This may be part of what she was referring to when she said later that Tasker had taught her many things she thought were fine then, but did "not agree with now." (Letter, 28 April 1947).

Irene Tasker had studied with Dewey at Columbia University. She certainly seems to have applied Dewey's philosophy that the educational process must begin with and build on the interests of the child, and that the teacher should be a guide and co-worker with pupils. During her life,

19 Irene Tasker, *Connecting Links*, London, The Sheildrake Press, 1978, p. 13.

20 Janet O'Brien Stillwell, « Marjorie Barstow: An Interview », *Somatics*, 1981, vol. 3, n° 3 (Autumn/Winter), p. 18.

21 Erika Whittaker, « The FM Alexander Memorial Lecture », delivered before the Society of Teachers of the Alexander Technique (STAT) on October 26, pamphlet, 1985, p. 14.

she published only one significant article about her work as an Alexander teacher[22]. She applied her writing skills to Alexander's books, rather than writing her own, providing another example of a woman behind the scenes and one whose contribution is largely forgotten. Barstow recalls seeing Tasker slave for "hours and hours over F.M.'s ideas getting them in book form" (Letter, 17 July 1948), and noting that Tasker did "a lot of F.M.'s writing but I don't suppose anyone will ever know it." (*Ibid.*).

Barstow's correspondence with Frank Jones tells of her many associations with university departments and academic colleagues. In 1944, she began teaching groups of students at the University of Nebraska (Letter, 19 June 1945) and, two years later, she had more than one senior academic there interested in experimenting with the Alexander Technique. From here, Barstow's associations with university departments grew, and she taught at an increasing number of tertiary institutions around the country, including Ohio State University, Washington University, and the Eastman School of Music.

Barstow's educational background and her continued affiliations with tertiary institutions was probably one of the factors that sustained her mission to *apply* the Alexander Technique to other disciplines. Alexander himself tended to get caught up in the technique as an end in itself, to the extent that Barstow's teaching came to be known as the Application Approach, even by her English colleagues, suggesting that Alexander's approach was somehow 'pure' or theoretical only. This apparent separation of theory and practice is one thing that still keeps the Alexander Technique relatively unknown today. Tertiary students and professionals want to know how it will help them in their own endeavours and often fail to see the relevance of a technique that centres around the chair and table. As Barstow observed, "you must remember the world is never going to stop and get itself all perfectly co-ordinated and then start on again. If the Alexander work cannot be taught alongside other things then there is not much hope for it. This winter I've proved that it can be – I've had four classes at the university – 15 students in the largest, 6 in the smallest." (Letter, 19 June 1945).

At the same time, Barstow had begun to teach groups of musicians. She took pleasure in their rapid progress and willingness to apply what they were learning. In 1948 she wrote encouragingly to Jones, "pleased

22 Tasker, 1978.

to hear of the success" of his music students in New York. "Yes," she agrees, "it is a pleasure to work with people who are neither sick nor neurotic. It is surprising what can be done in a short time and I find young people really enjoy making use of the freedom they acquire, in a simple straightforward way." (Letter, 20 June).

Like Dewey, for whom "neglect of context is the greatest single disaster which philosophic thinking can incur" (Dewey, 2008, p. 11), Barstow believed in the importance of context. Bruce Fertman (now a highly regarded teacher himself) recollects his first contact with Barstow, when he called to enquire about her winter workshop in 1976. Her questions show her conviction about context and that the Alexander Technique is not an end in itself.

> She said, "What do you do?" I said that I studied the Alexander Technique. "Is that all? What else do you do?" I was a little taken aback, but proceeded to tell her that I was a graduate in movement education, a professional modern dancer, and a martial artist. She said something like, "Come to my winter workshop. I think you might enjoy it." (Fertman, 1989, p. 66).

Throughout the duration of Barstow's correspondence with Jones, she mentions her constant work with orchestras, chamber groups, professional soloists, doctoral students in music, dance teachers and institutions who invited her to teach all over the country.

TRAINING TEACHERS

I have mentioned in the illustration of group teaching how Barstow trained teachers. In this section, I outline briefly how this evolved and how it more closely resembled mentorship than Alexander's intensive training course model.

In 1946, Barstow observed the shortcomings of Alexander's formal training course.

> I have been shocked at the conditions and lack of progress in the Alexander assistants and the students [...] They have all lost confidence in themselves, are unhappy, discontented and really worried about their lack of improvement.

> Their great problem can be summed up in a few words – we have finished the training course, three years of concentrated study, we are not prepared to teach, we do not know how to get what we need so where do we go from here? A rather pathetic and hopeless outlook is it not? (Letter, 19 August 1946).

Bruce Fertman describes how Barstow's method of certification was based on the quality of teaching rather than quantity of hours spent formally studying: "I remember someone once asking her how long it took to become a teacher of the Alexander Technique. She said: 'I don't know. It depends on the individual. It could take six months, six years, or it might take forever!'" (Fertman, 1989, p. 68). He also recalls how she changed her description of her teacher training over the years. Occasionally, at workshops, people would ask her if she trained teachers. Fertman remembers her replying for a number of years: "No, I help people to become sensitive and what they do with their sensitivity is their own business", Later, she used to reply, "No, I don't train teachers, but many of my students have gone on to become excellent teachers." (*Ibid.*).

William Conable (who studied with both Barstow and Jones) highlights Barstow's commitment to process, rather than to the result, or in Alexander's words, the "means-whereby" rather than "end-gaining":

> She has often been distressed to see graduates of other training courses who have learned 'Alexander teaching techniques' but who do not in her view really understand the core of Alexander's discovery… I believe that she has also been reluctant to concentrate her energies on setting up a structure, a curriculum, and a school. I don't think she is sure that is the best way to train Alexander teachers. I think that this is what she means when she says 'I do not train teachers' [because] in fact, she *does* train teachers[23].

In fact, this method of training was not so unusual. There were many examples of fine 'first generation teachers' whom Alexander had trained by the apprenticeship method, rather than by three-year training course, including his brother A.R., his sister Amy, Ethel Webb, Irene Tasker and Margaret Goldie. Frank Jones also claims that his training was a kind of apprenticeship, he being the only trainee in 1941, and the training being "conducted informally like a protracted private lesson in

23 William Conable, « Marjorie Barstow », Barbara Conable, ed., (Festschrift) *Marjorie Barstow: Her Teaching and Training. A 90th Birthday Offering*, Columbus, Andover Road Press, 1989, p. 26. Emphasis in original.

which one or more of F.M.'s assistants took part."[24] Despite these well known and respected teachers who had trained by apprenticeship, people claimed in the 1980s that Barstow could not be training teachers at all because she did not run a three-year training program[25].

Jones, like Barstow, did not run a formal training course and taught informally by apprenticeship. His training methods were similarly disregarded, as evidenced by one comment William Conable encountered when claiming to have done part of his teacher training under Jones (at Barstow's urging). "You can't have trained with Frank Jones", said one Alexander Technique teacher, "because he didn't train teachers". (Private Interview).

Further confirming their alignment of ideas and thinking, Barstow and Jones discussed creating a training course. In 1969, Barstow wrote to Jones about her requirement for her trainees to have another discipline to which to apply the Alexander Technique, and indicating that there was significant student interest in a training course[26]. Their formal training course did not come about, but they continued to teach each other's students and make appearances at each other's workshops and they both trained teachers informally.

As explained above, the apprenticeship model more closely satisfied Plutarch's definition of mentorship than it did teaching. One of Dewey's chief aims in philosophy was to mend the split between theory and practice. Similarly, I claim that Barstow repaired several splits that had begun to appear in the Alexander Technique. One of these was discussed above (between theory and practice, or 'pure' and applied). Another was the split between teaching and training. The repair of this split has the added benefit of teaching trainees how to teach beginners, something which would otherwise be left out of training courses. It was said of Barstow that she did not train teachers, but it could equally be argued that *all she did*

24 Frank Pierce Jones, *Body Awareness in Action: A Study of the Alexander Technique*, introduction by J. McVicker Hunt, New York NY, Schocken Books, 1979, p. 77.

25 Frank Ottiwell, « Let Us Now Praise Marjorie Barstow », Barbara Conable, ed., (Festschrift) *Marjorie Barstow: Her Teaching and Training. A 90th Birthday Offering*, Columbus, Andover Road Press, 1989, p. 3.

26 "There are several who have expressed an interest in becoming teachers and have asked about training. I told all that you and I had discussed starting a training course but had made no definite plans. I have also stressed that they should have a job of some kind or be interested in other things besides this training." (Undated Letter. Barstow mentions having just watched the second walk on the moon, so it was probably July 1969).

was train teachers, whether people went on to teach others or they simply learned to teach themselves. Furthermore, Barstow did this in a way that did not try to turn teachers into imitations of herself or the Alexanders, but that preserved their independence and honoured their individuality.

It was not until a political situation erupted that Barstow decided to clarify to the outside world what she was doing by way of teacher training. In 1986, when the North American Society (NASTAT) was forming[27], Barstow was approached by one of her students who was already an English-certified Alexander Technique teacher and therefore eligible for membership with NASTAT. He asked Barstow to write a letter to the society acknowledging and listing the people she recognized as teachers, assuring her that they would then be welcome to join. She wrote the letter, explaining that each of the people named had worked with her in "what can be considered an extended apprenticeship training program." Every one of the teachers named had studied with her for "over 1600 hours". They had assisted her at workshops as Alexander teachers, had been observed by her "at various times and under different situations", some having worked with her consistently since the early 1960s and moved to Lincoln, Nebraska, for various lengths of time to study with her, "some for up to six and seven years"[28]. There are 26 names in the letter. Barstow added that she fully supported the formation of NASTAT. The board gave Barstow a membership – something she had not asked for – but rejected her claim and her teachers. Barstow tore the membership certificate up. (Madden, Private Correspondence, 4 April 2015). Out of the political rubble, Alexander Technique International (ATI) was born, an association that embraced those trained by Barstow and Jones and that now embraces the next generation of teachers trained by her graduates to her standards.

ATI was formed in 1992 with 28 teachers as an open organisation. By 2004 it had twelve regional offices around the world serving over 300 teachers in nineteen countries. It accepts members of the Affiliated Societies and other Alexander Technique societies. ATI represents the legacy of Barstow's community and a school of thought that places a high value on Barstow's pragmatic approach and qualitative evaluation

---

27 NASTAT was formed by teachers and teacher trainers no more qualified than Barstow to train teachers and, in many cases, far less experience than her.

28 Marjorie L. Barstow, « A Letter from Marjorie Barstow », *The Alexander Review*, 1986, vol. 1, n°1, p. 42-45.

(my description, not theirs). The other Alexander Technique societies do not reciprocate or recognize ATI members as Alexander teachers. Perhaps a next step could be for ATI to consider renaming or reframing their training processes as Alexander mentorship, to highlight the positive aspects of mentorship over traditional training.

COMMITMENT TO THE SCIENTIFIC PROCESS

One of Dewey's greatest compliments to Alexander was on his application of the scientific process in discovering what he called "the primary control". This was also one of the aspects of Alexander's work that Barstow most prized. Consequently, she wished to continue the process in pursuit of improving both the understanding and the teaching of Alexander Technique: "My interest in the work", she wrote, "is not to sit and give lessons year after year as the Alexanders have done, but to develop the work on an educational basis so it can be recognized and accepted as a *true* new field of science and education." She describes her work in this regard:

> To accomplish this will require an experimental research project of some kind, and that is what I have been working toward these last few years. My progress has been slow because first I had to learn by myself the practical meaning of the primary control and all it connotes. Second I had to find a way to pass such information on in as simplified a form as I realized I had acquired it. Working individually and also with groups gave me a variety of experiences (Letter, 19 August 1946).

MENTORSHIP BY CORRESPONDENCE

Frank Jones and Marjorie Barstow agreed on a large number of issues within the Alexander work. These included: an emphasis on the steps of the scientific process in Alexander's work, the importance of application, a creative and philosophically pragmatic approach to teaching, and the superiority of the apprenticeship model of teacher training. These confluences of their thought may be fairly easily observed.

Yet it was only recently, while reading their correspondence, that I had the first inkling of the existence of Barstow's mentorship of Jones. The extent, depth and breadth of this mentorship was astonishing, but perhaps not as astonishing as that fact that it is such a well-kept secret. Admittedly, this mentorship matured into something else over time, something which maybe resembled more of a mastermind of two experienced equals than a mentor-mentee relationship. This is suggested by their three decades of correspondence during which they shared many confidences about the direction of the technique in England and the United States. They also made a trip to England and Europe together, taught in each other's courses and had a life-long friendship which included Jones's wife and children as well. After Jones's death, Barstow wrote to his wife, Helen, describing what his loss would mean to her: "I have for so many years looked forward to my spring visit with both of you and a chat with him, his writings, and the future of the Alexander Technique. Our ideas were always so much alike on this. Now I must recognise that I am carrying on alone in this direction." (Letter, 7 November 1975).

Whatever it later became, the mentorship aspect of their relationship is an important and hitherto unknown part of Alexander history in America. Barstow not only mentored Jones in the things we might expect from her prior teaching experience, but in areas which, had Jones acknowledged her contribution, might have earned Barstow the respect she deserved. She mentored him not only in how to teach and build a business, but gave insightful feedback on his writing and conceptualisation of his research projects, which she also helped to finance.

As I hope I have already shown to some extent through my frequent references to their letters, this mentorship by correspondence reveals Barstow's depth of knowledge about and insight into a wide range of topics (body-mechanics, teaching, science, education and Alexander's work and limitations), the trajectory of her thought and experiments, and her influence on Frank Pierce Jones. Her generosity and championing of him to Alexander, even when she herself was *persona non grata* is remarkable: "I had told [Alexander] what a fine teacher you were becoming, that he could always be proud of whatever you would say or do with the work... but he brushes all of these aside." (Letter, 20 June 1950).

Furthermore, Barstow answered Jones's questions about teaching children and teaching in groups and offered significant help with a range of questions and issues, including finding his own way as a teacher, marketing, building up a business and how to set up and advertise a teaching practice. She also offered constructive criticism on his writing and his research project designs and questions. They swapped endless notes about the primary control, or Alexander 'mechanism', training teachers, the use of words, the use of hands and the extent to which a teacher should manipulate a pupil with their hands, amongst other things.

The first example to illustrate Barstow's mentorship is the way she guided Jones in his first experiments with teaching children, showing a distinct parallel with Dewey's ideas on child-centred education:

> I cannot tell you exactly what to do for I always start from what I see in the child… One thing, don't be too serious with them – have a bit of fun. When the child first came to you I would, if I were in your place, talk to her *first* about *her* interest, that is her music. Get some of her ideas about music and what she is doing, then gradually tell her the relation her own manner of use (or co-ordination or posture) has to her playing and gradually show her how it will be helpful in her interest of music. (Letter, 19 June 1945)

In 1946 Barstow encouraged Jones to venture into group teaching:

> If you have a chance to work with a small group of students I would suggest that you do so by all means. You will gain a great deal and find it valuable for later on in case you should have the opportunity to do a research problem. (Letter, 19 November 1946)

Two years later, Jones asked to see her notes on teaching groups. She invited him to come and stay (unable to leave her aging father) so that he could read her notes but was unwilling to send her vast store of notes through the mail (Letter, 16 May 1948). She also notes that it is "always more interesting" to work with a small group when teaching musicians (Letter, 2 February 1965).

Barstow believed that "everyone has to work out his own way of teaching" since "after a principle has been learned there are many ways of presenting it." (Letter, 19 June 1945). She was also very willing to guide him firmly, sometimes wondering if she had overstepped the mark. In an early letter, she wrote: "Now that I've read this over it sounds like 'grandmother's advice' – hope it has not been too severe for you. I'll be glad to help you any way I can." (*Ibid.*).

Barstow had many thoughts and ideas on ways to market the Alexander Technique and urged Jones not to wait until scientific research could back him up (although she was adamant that such an investigation was necessary for the future of the Alexander Technique). "Don't be too timid about working out a notice on your own experiences", she wrote. "Try and see what it is like, you need not print it… you need not wait for an investigation." (Letter, 19 November 1946). She also understood what would get people's attention and what might turn them off. She writes, for example:

> I think your opening paragraph should contain practical information instead of 'animals', 'subconscious level', 'mental' and 'physical'. I think you can also find a better way of expressing 'up to the level of consciousness' … You need more life, pep and practical interest to attract attention, and I think you can do a much better notice than this. Build it on your own experiences rather than on F.M.'s terminology. Hope I have not been too critical. (Letter, 11 November 1946)

Jones often made use of Barstow's clear thinking, asking her to comment on his articles before publication:

> Enclosed am returning your paper with a few suggestions. This is an improvement on what you sent before. It seems more impressive to me to leave out unnecessary words and phrases. I consider the places I marked unnecessary as they did nothing to the things you are talking about." (Letter, 17 July 1947).

Barstow was always aiming to get him to think in practical terms: "People liked your question and answer pamphlet – could you carry on the same idea into practical activities?" (Letter, 27 July 1948).

Her insights showed not only her experience of teaching musicians and her understanding of communication and writing and the Alexander Technique, but her ability to put herself in the shoes of her audience:

> None of the musicians I know would be interested in your first three paragraphs as a beginning to an article. It is too long a jump for them to take and they will never interpret 'essential relationships among the moving parts' as you expect. They have been taught a lot of stuff about muscular control and you have to go a long way around to show them they have a few wrong ideas on the subject. You want this article to attract people who are not coming

> to you, so you must show your interest in music and then lead them on into your field..." (Letter, 7 August 1948).

Barstow discussed her own research projects with Jones, for example, her first attempt with pictures and the need to clarify with scientific research the precise changes that are made through the Alexander Technique.

> I have done another series ... but have not seen the results. It will be necessary to learn to read them as a doctor learns to read x-ray. I see a great deal in them that the untrained eye does not see. I plan to do more of this during the summer and have some fine professional photographers working with me. Some day I am sure we will need this type of record because it does show change of relationship of parts to parts, the thing we talk about but is not clearly understood. (Letter, 8 April 1948).

She also answered many of Jones's questions about research projects, offering ideas and approaches to research design, and suggesting potential problems and bias, how to simplify the project and how to maximise the chances of accurate results (Letters: 8 January, 1949; 2 March 1954; 7 July 1954).

Thus the question remains why, given the significance of Barstow's mentorship of Jones, her influence and guidance remains such a secret. In the 1940s, when Barstow had been practising the Alexander Technique for two decades and teaching for more than one, Frank Pierce Jones asked her why she had not published anything about her own experiments. Her answer was this:

> You asked me why I do not write up and publish what I have learned in my recent teaching. I do not know enough yet to do that. I'm just in the process of learning many valuable things. (Letter, 2 August 1945).

It is a shame, however, that Jones was not more generous in his acknowledgement of what Barstow had shared with him. He has risen to the status of a serious teacher, thinker, researcher and writer, while she remains controversial, her contribution, expertise, intelligence and scientific approach overshadowed by politics and prejudice – a naughty girl, whose name Alexander linked with the 'vandalism' of his technique (Letters: 20 June 1950; 28 April 1947).

More than one American Alexander teacher has told me irrelevant and catty tales about Barstow in an attempt to make me think less of her. "She was no academic", "People really need to know who Marj was: she was a *Republican*!", "She used to sell creams that were carcinogenic", "If someone says they 'studied' with Marj for ten years, that has to be taken with a grain of salt", "Jones used to think well of her until he saw a late group class and told me it was a travesty of the technique". I have investigated all these comments and find them exaggerated, lacking context or lacking evidence. There is nothing in the correspondence to suggest any change in Jones's regard for Barstow, besides which, Jones died before Barstow could be said to be teaching late group classes.

William Conable observed that Barstow was 'interested' in Jones's scientific studies into the technique and postulated that Barstow may even have been one of his benefactors (Conable, Private Interview). Conable concedes that Barstow "was not an academic". "But," he adds, "she supported Frank's research and made financial contributions, I *think*… She could also to a certain extent follow what he was doing. But it wasn't where she lived. It *was* where he lived." (*Ibid.*).

Conable was correct in his postulation about Barstow's financial support of Jones's research. There is ample evidence of this in their correspondence. What Conable did not know, however, was the extent to which it *was* where she had lived for a significant period of time. While she did not spend her time writing up her results for publication, she was constantly writing to Jones about photographs and film she had taken of students, as a kind of documentation of their progress. Even if not in writing for publication, she was his equal in clear thinking, articulating the Alexander Technique and iterating approaches to scientific research, frequently commenting on his proposals and research questions, and offering thoughtful solutions to the many impediments to his research. How could it have happened that Barstow was seen by one of her champions as an 'almost follower' of Jones's lofty projects, when she had been the one to lead and guide Jones in so many areas?

Adding to the sidelining of Barstow and the promotion of Jones, Tommy Thomson, who trained unofficially with Jones from 1972, claims that "it was Frank who sent Marj to Southern Methodist." "I don't think anybody knows this", Thomson adds, saying that Jones was asked to "come out to Southern Methodist and give the workshop, but that's when he was stumbling so he called Marj and said, 'Why don't you go instead?' and that's when she started her career with all those workshops."[29] Barstow's correspondence shows that she had been teaching groups since the 1940s and professional musicians were referred to her as early as 1949. She was already frequently solicited by professional ensembles and institutions to teach groups and musicians in the 1960s. These had nothing to do with Jones and she certainly did not owe him anything for the escalation of her career. Perhaps even the contrary. If Jones had been more publicly supportive of her, the truth may have come out earlier.

Perhaps Barstow asked for obscurity and misunderstanding by not publishing. Or maybe she just did not see or guess how things would turn out. Maybe she did not care. As Sarah Barker observed of her teacher in a private interview with the author, Barstow did remain outwardly unaffected by the backlash against her. This backlash was something Jones seems never to have experienced. Was she the scapegoat that allowed their critically pragmatic views to be heard, as expressed only by Jones? It is certainly a pattern in the Alexander world that the male is heard and the female does the work behind the scenes. Alex Murray even wrote an article on this topic[30] in an attempt to recognise and acknowledge the important women in the history of the Alexander Technique, but there was no mention of Barstow. When I interviewed him, he was more interested in denigrating her than discussing the nature of her teaching.

Frank Pierce Jones appears to have missed an opportunity not only to support his great supporter, mentor and colleague publicly and in writing. Perhaps we will never know what his intentions were and how or whether they were hampered by his illness and later his death, both of which occurred as he was creating his now famous book, *Body Awareness in Action.* His wife, Helen, also an Alexander teacher, was responsible for the final draft and for getting it published. We cannot know the full extent of her role and decision making. The book barely mentions Barstow[31]. Helen was, however, also responsible for making the correspondence between Jones and Barstow available to the Alexander archive after her

29 Robert Rickover, « The Teaching of Frank Pierce Jones: Robert Rickover Talks to Tommy Thompson », *Body Learning* 2014, MP3 file, web.

30 Alexander D. Murray, « The Role of Women in the Growth of the Alexander Community », *American Society of Alexander Teachers* AGM, 2002.

31 It is not beyond the realms of possibility that Barstow suggested that Jones downplay her role because she cared about the future of the Alexander Technique more than receiving credit where it was due. She may have felt that his book would carry more sway if people saw his ideas and writing as entirely independent of her.

husband's death. She did this in consultation with Barstow, who gave permission but with the provision that it must not be copied or published, as she was sensitive – upon review of all her letters – to the fact that her freely expressed opinions of other teachers may be hurtful. Most of these teachers are no longer living, and I hope I have been discreet in making such references to others as diplomatic as possible.

CONCLUSION

If the 'constellation mentorship' of Barstow and her mentorship of Jones were more widely understood, then she would perhaps be recognised today as less of a heretic and at least the equal of Jones and the Alexanders themselves. The confluence of ideas, or philosophical constellation between Barstow, Dewey and Jones allowed the opportunity for Barstow to mentor Jones, with philosophical pragmatism holding their ideas together, though the term was not mentioned in their correspondence. This is, rather, the lens I have used as a researcher. Barstow's mentorship model seems to have come out of her deep commitment to philosophical pragmatism, although she did not name it as such. It arose from her dissatisfaction at Alexander's *lack* of pragmatism and what she saw as his failure either to teach successfully or foster and encourage new thinking and research into his work. This dissatisfaction she shared with Jones and Dewey.

Marjorie Barstow was a master of philosophical pragmatism. If her experimental method were better understood as resonating with two of the most esteemed writers on the Alexander Technique (Dewey and Jones), and her teaching recognised as an original model of mentorship rather than a poor imitation of Alexander's Technique, she would perhaps be more uniformly respected by the Alexander societies that shun her and her mentees. These latter continue to inspire performers around the world who are far more interested in a technique that can inform, enhance and sustain their art than one that most closely resembles a teaching technique that has changed little since Edwardian times.

The crucial ingredient in an informal mentoring partnership, such as that between Barstow and Jones, is trust. While Barstow certainly benefitted from the relationship in many ways, it seems that at some point this trust was put aside, and Jones – or perhaps his wife, Helen – missed a chance to acknowledge fully Barstow's contribution not just to his own formation and development as a teacher, but to Alexander Technique pedagogy in general. Ironically, and unfortunately for Barstow, who believed so fervently in this informal approach to the exchange of ideas and experiences, Jones's reluctance to defend and support her has helped to cast a shadow on her reputation and make professional life for her 'graduates' far more difficult than it needs to be.

Amanda Cole
Griffith University
Australia

THIRD PART

MENTORS IN CONTEMPORARY NOVELS

MENTORING SUBVERSIONS

An exploration of success and failure in two mentoring relationships in Marie NDiaye's *Mon cœur à l'étroit* and *Trois femmes puissantes*

In this essay I explore two mentoring relationships from the novels of the contemporary French writer Marie NDiaye. The purpose of a mentoring relationship is the development of a less experienced party, the mentee, by a more experienced party, the mentor. Mentoring relationships are of their very nature unequal relationships; the inequality consisting in the relative experience and wisdom, and thus the relative power, of the two parties to the relationships. Mentoring relationships have always occurred informally in a variety of work, social and family situations, but in recent years many organisations, including academic institutions, have set up formal schemes within which senior members of an organisation undertake to help junior members develop their knowledge and skills and their ability to operate successfully within the particular culture of an organisation. Not least because of the imbalance of experience, and often of real exercisable power, within a mentoring relationship, there is a need for an ethical framework within which mentoring relationships are begun, carried on, and brought to an end. While the mentoring relationship within a formal scheme is intended to be entirely beneficial, an insensitive or ill-informed mentor can easily damage a mentee[1].

The two mentoring relationships which I analyse from the novels of Marie NDiaye develop within an informal context. In both cases the intent of the mentor is to use his experience to help the mentee but

1 For an overview of the spread and practice of mentoring within organisations and the ethical questions it raises see Dennis J. Moberg and Manuel Velasquez, « The Ethics of Mentoring', *Business Ethics Quarterly* », 2004, vol. 14, n° 1 (January), p. 95-122.

the success or failure of the relationship is in each case arguable and its ethical foundations, whether read simply within the context of the diegetic text or against generally recognised contemporary mentoring 'best practice' is dubious. My reading of the novelistic relationships as subversions of mentoring will be seen to be revealing in two ways. It deepens our understanding of the text and it highlights some key issues which need to be both understood and addressed by those engaged in mentoring in the real world, whether as mentors or as mentees.

Mary NDiaye is a contemporary prize-winning French writer, born in 1967. She is primarily a novelist, but has also written plays, children's books, a screenplay and an operatic libretto. She was born of a white French mother and a black Senegalese father, and this mixed colour heritage is an increasingly overtly expressed theme in her writings, which belong assertively to the classic French literary tradition. The characters in her novels suffer from various degrees of social alienation and rarely feel themselves at home in the world in which they find themselves. Not a few of them, however, are focused on escaping from their background, whether by denying it, by physically fleeing it or by aiming to better themselves and their social standing through education and hard work. In this essay I am focussing on Nadia, from *Mon cœur à l'étroit*, and on Khady Demba from the final novella from *Trois femmes puissantes*[2]. Nadia has been making her way, through education and ambition, to membership of the bourgeoisie, determinedly escaping from and subsequently denying her lower class, immigrant origins. Khady Demba has been rejected by her family in (probably) Africa and has been put into the hands of people smugglers; an uninformed and uneducated refugee, she is on her way to Europe.

Before turning to the detail of my texts, however, it is appropriate to say something more about the nature of mentoring. A mentoring or quasi-mentoring relationship normally involves two players of whom one has a function that might be described as fatherly (or indeed, and perhaps better, motherly) who is the older, more knowledgeable, or more thoughtful or perspicacious, and who takes it upon himself or herself to develop the younger, less able or more inexperienced person into a greater degree of maturity and self-awareness, so that they can function

2 Marie NDiaye, *Mon cœur à l'étroit*, Paris, Gallimard, 2007; and *Trois femmes puissantes*, Paris, Gallimard, 2009.

as a mature adult in a complex world. Moberg and Velasquez summarise that the mentor provides three key benefits to the mentee – knowledge, wisdom and developmental support (Moberg and Velasquez, 2004, p. 99). In 2007 I acted as a mentor in a formal public sector mentoring scheme known as *Leaders Unlimited*, whose aim was to increase the presence in the UK Civil Service of women, people with a disability and people from ethnic minorities. You might say that the aim of the scheme was to make certain people, who might be in some way disadvantaged and whose talents might be ignored because of prejudice, visible and useful within the public sector of the UK. A mentor within this scheme was defined as:

> Someone, operating effectively and successfully in an organisation, who agrees to inspire another by providing the support, advice and the sharing of experience to enable them to learn and to grow into a higher level of personal and operational effectiveness.

Participation in the scheme was not imposed on either mentor or mentee. Help was given to mentees who wanted a mentor to find one. Training was given to both parties with the aim that both mentor and mentee should be clear as to the nature of their relationship and what each should expect from the other.

I turn now to *Mon cœur à l'étroit* which was published in 2007, the same year as that definition of a mentor was formulated. The novel is narrated in the first person and in the present tense by Nadia, and the reader is prompted towards interpretation by often enigmatic section headings and by passages in italics which suggest thoughts which Nadia does not quite admit to her consciousness. Nadia's history emerges largely through flashbacks and we have to seek a sort of objective reality through Nadia's narration, which not unnaturally puts her for the most part in the right, and from remarks she reports which are made by others; and these she often rejects, denies, or simply refuses to listen to.

We meet Nadia at a point in her life when her determined (un-mentored) efforts at self-improvement, which she firmly believes to have succeeded, have begun to fall apart. Born to immigrants, from an unspecified country, in an undesirable suburb of the French city of Bordeaux, Nadia has replaced her mother tongue with French and has trained and secured a position as an infant school teacher. Her second marriage, to a fellow teacher, Ange, is for her a further badge of success and they share a flat in a respectable quarter of Bordeaux. However, for reasons which are never quite explained, the couple have now become the focus of hatred and have been effectively ostracised from both their teaching and their neighbourhood communities. Ange suffers a mysterious and atrocious life-threatening wound which stinks and suppurates. The couple are guided back to a state of health and happiness by a neighbour, one Richard Victor Noget, a public intellectual, who ensures that Ange is cured of his wound and that Nadia leaves France to be re-united with her estranged son and reconciled with her parents, who have returned to live in their country of origin. The mentoring relationship between Noget and Nadia appears to succeed despite an inauspicious start and unorthodox methods.

At the heart of this novel lies a mysterious fault, committed by Nadia, and symbolised concretely by the disgusting wound inflicted on Ange[3]. Nadia's guilt is obvious to others whose attitude towards her varies from pity and compassion, through fear and hostility, to active aggression and insult[4]. This fault is never conclusively explicated in the text but its elements surface more or less distinctly from time to time. They include Nadia's entrapment of Ange in order to improve her own social status, her abandonment of her first husband for similar reasons, and her financial defrauding of him during their divorce, her neglect of her son in favour of her career, and her mistreatment of ethnic minority children in her class. She has denied her own origins, suppressed her mother tongue in favour of French, told others that her parents are dead, and cut off all contact with them, with no explanation, over a period of thirty-five years. Nadia's denials stem from a deep shame of her background, but she has come to see herself as a devoted teacher, eminently respectable and respected. Indeed she considers herself and her husband to be slightly superior to their neighbours, in their rejection of consumerism and their refusal to watch television. The crisis with which the novel is concerned is prompted, the reader slowly realises, by the birth of a daughter to her

3 Ange is not innocent. Noget insists that he be made to face up to the horrors of his wound and though Ange often appears close to death, he is quicker than Nadia to accept the ministrations of Noget as a necessary punishment and path to rehabilitation. This paper focuses on Nadia and largely ignores Ange but we should note that his rehabilitation appears complete while that of Nadia is more doubtful.

4 Not only people but the town of Bordeaux and its tramway conspire against her, and thick fog surrounds her movements as obfuscation surrounds her thoughts.

estranged son, Ralph. Nadia cannot bring herself to accept the name given to the child, Souhar, which suggests Nadia's origins and threatens to make the child herself one of those people now despised by Nadia for their race and colour. The name dooms the granddaughter to become, in the phrase people use of Nadia and always fail to define, one of those « *gens comme vous* » (NDiaye, 2007, p. 29, 211, 210).

Richard Victor Noget properly enters Nadia's life when she returns home from school followed by Ange, whose wound cannot be ignored, despite Nadia's attempts to minimise its seriousness. Noget, expressing pity for the couple, forces himself to her attention and into her house. He has been their neighbour for some time but the couple have made a point of rejecting, quite cruelly, any advances he has made towards them. As far as Nadia is concerned he is « *une parfaite nullité* », « *cet épouvantable voisin* », an unprepossessing, scruffy, and even dirty, individual, with a long matted grey beard (NDiaye, 2007, p. 39, 31, 33). Every description of him is consistent and appears to confirm this as his outward appearance[5]. Noget was the one neighbour not invited to a reception given by Nadia to celebrate the birth of her granddaughter. A section heading reminds us, by a reference to offending « *la vilaine fée* » of the dangers of not inviting the right people to a party (NDiaye, 2007, p. 91). Whereas, though, the fairy not invited to the birth of Sleeping Beauty takes her revenge by ensuring that the princess sleeps for a hundred years, Noget's revenge (if such it is) is to wake Nadia's unconscious from its sleep. The hallmarks of Nadia's psyche are the suppression of guilt, memory and conscience, the repression of anything that threatens the view she has chosen to take of the world or of herself, and the desire to control the lives and thoughts of others. Ange's wound represents Nadia's guilt which she needs to recognise if it is to heal[6]. Nadia does not recognise that she needs help but Noget appoints himself her mentor and his goal will be to reveal Nadia to herself[7].

5 Even allowing for the prejudices of Nadia as the narrating voice, Noget certainly seems to have unsocial habits – smoking in Nadia's bedroom in a household which he is told is non-smoking, and dealing with an unexpected sneeze by blowing his nose on a paper tissue and kicking it unceremoniously under the sick man's bed.

6 Ange's daughters and others make it quite clear that Ange must not be seen by the doctor or taken to the hospital. Arguably this is because this would remove the responsibility from Nadia.

7 NDiaye has expressed her admiration for the work of Franz Kafka and indeed this is a Kafkaesque plot, as Nadia stands accused of a crime which she does not know she has committed but must ultimately come to recognise her guilt. In this it also echoes the

To achieve this Noget must enter into a relationship with Nadia. How, outside the world of the novel, do mentor and mentee meet? In formal organisational schemes it is usual for some sort of matching process to take place – volunteers are sought to mentor and are hopefully given some training and others are asked if they would like a mentor. Generally, there is a mutual acceptance of the arrangement. Moberg and Velasquez do not see the mentoring relationship as a contractual one, because they believe this would suggest that the parties bargain as equals. Nor do they see the relationship as personal friendship, because it is essentially one-directional, in that the mentor seeks to develop the mentee but not vice versa. Arguably the mentor might be seen as a gift-giver, but within an organisation the role will generally be formally assigned and so be part of the mentor's organisational role. They accept however that mentor and mentee should establish beforehand what each expects from the other (Moberg and Velasquez, 2004, p. 98-99). Within a formal scheme, an initial meeting between the two parties usually involves some mutual self-disclosure, a commitment to honesty and a discussion of aims and motivations on the part at least of the mentee, who generally wants to improve performance and their future career path. The motivations of mentors are harder to pin down, ranging from a vague desire to 'give something back', a sense of responsibility connected to one's position in an organisation or profession, and a less easily admitted need for some self-valorisation, in which a feeling of superiority and power may play a part. Moberg and Velasquez note that while mentors have more power within the relationship than the mentee, there is another inherent inequality within the relationship in that the mentor provides significant benefits to the mentee while the mentee provides few comparable benefits to the mentor. (*Ibid.*, p. 98)

The initial meeting between Noget and Nadia sees Nadia and Ange arriving home and Noget expressing pity for them. Nadia resents this especially, as the reasons for the pity are not explained. Noget subsequently makes his way into their house when Nadia is absent. He makes the age-old gesture of friendship and openness in offering food and drink to share – ham, bread and a good bottle of wine from his own part of the world. In an organisational context a mentor might well

development of *Oedipos Tyrannos* with Noget as a willing Tiresias, whose bisexuality he appears to share.

inaugurate a relationship by inviting a prospective mentee to lunch. Noget identifies himself as the only person who nourishes friendly feelings towards the couple and explains his understanding of their position and his agenda. They are suffering a disaster – no-one has ever sunk so low. He attempts to express empathy by explaining that he has also been a teacher and could have had the bad luck to find himself in a similar situation. More ambivalently, he expresses his knowledge of and admiration for Ange whose excellent academic papers he has read and admired. Neither Nadia nor the reader is aware at this point that Ange's published papers have plagiarised Noget's work. Noget is a television celebrity in the field of education, his name and fame recognised by everyone except Nadia, who refuses to acknowledge that he has a reputation of which she is ignorant. She completely rejects his offer of help, accuses him of lying about having been a teacher and drives him out of her house. And as if to finally confirm that no positive relationship can ever exist between them she rejects his one concrete piece of advice, that she should not attend her school the next day (NDiaye, 2007, p. 15, 31-49).

It is interesting that here Noget has attempted to enter a relationship with Nadia by offering first gifts and then friendship, neither of which, in the view of Moberg and Velasquez, as we have seen, can define mentoring. It is clear, however, that Nadia needs help to come to terms with her situation and that Noget wants to provide this. A clear ethical issue emerges here. If one person sees that another needs help which they are capable of providing, how can or should they give that help if the person in need denies the need and/or refuses the help? And indeed, what might make one person want to impose their assistance on another? In the diegetic situation Noget's motivation is not clear. He expresses himself wounded, when Nadia offers him money to go away and which he refuses (mentors are not paid for mentoring) and his initial pity is contaminated by his hurt admission that Ange has never deigned to say hello to him in a natural way (*ibid.*, p. 35, 39). Noget also knows that Ange has stolen his ideas. His motives may thus not be entirely pure, but they do appear to stem from a strong sense of duty. He grips the sides of his seat hard so that he cannot be dislodged. To Nadia this body language says: « *Mon devoir je l'accomplirai jusqu'au bout* » and Noget has said aloud «*J'ai compris que je devais vous soutenir envers et contre tout* ». (*Ibid.*, p. 33, 32). A sense of duty determines his persistence with the relationship, but it may be that Nadia's hostility and rudeness damages the purity of his altruism.

The key to the relationship that subsequently develops between Noget and Nadia is food, which Noget uses calculatedly and manipulatively to get under Nadia's 'radar' and subject her to his influence despite her unambiguously expressed resistance. He aims to force her to recognise her suppressed guilt and rid herself of the attitudes and motivations that gave rise to it. In the absence of her consent, this is an ethically dubious project, akin to a psychotherapeutic rape. Noget usurps Nadia's kitchen and prepares rich and aggressively traditional French dishes for her. She finds them irresistible, despite her dislike and mistrust of Noget, and despite the fact that his food makes her slightly nauseous and causes her to gain a great deal of weight. Noget's food is described in such a way as to make the reader, like Nadia, salivate. Noget details the time and care involved in its preparation, and asserts that the food is homemade, or from a source in the part of France he comes from, or from a supplier well known to him. The food is wholesome, but rich, and there is far too much of it. Nadia never accepts the food willingly and complains about the amount of fat Noget's dishes contain. On one occasion, when she expresses the desire for a roast, Noget explains he has prepared some 'croque-monsieur'. Here is his recipe:

> [...] *je fabrique mon propre pain de mie, je le coupe en tranches épaisses que je fais rissoler dans le beurre, puis je garnis le pain du meilleur comté que je connaisse et d'un beau morceau de jambon à l'os, et sur la tranche supérieure, juste sous le fromage, savez-vous ce que je mets pour le moelleux de l'ensemble? Une fine couche de sauce béchamel, voilà.* (*Ibid.*, p. 130)

Nadia's salivation as he goes to the kitchen to put his creations in the oven is accompanied by « *un élan de gratitude* ». Yet at the same time she is persuaded that « *sa bonté est empoisonnée et sa cuisine, d'une certaine façon, infectée* ». (*Ibid.*, p. 132). And in a sense Nadia is right. While Noget apparently plays a nurturing, mothering role, acting with a mentor's benevolence to look after her body in order to gain the confidence of her mind, this may not be what he is really about. His attitude is initially described as « *soucieux* » and « *plein d'inquiétude* ». (*Ibid.*, p. 45, 46). But in their ongoing relationship, although he manifests delight and gaiety in his cooking activities, Nadia describes his eyes as cold, inquisitorial and devoid of sympathy and his gentleness as forced (*ibid.*, p. 65, 77, 78, 100, 102). However, his attentions are gradually shaking her view of the world and disturbing her:

> *Je me sens oppressée, mécontente, comme chaque fois que je parle avec* Noget. *Il m'embrouille l'esprit, en cherchant à m'attirer sur le terrain bourbeux, où lui-même évolue avec une répugnante délectation.* (*Ibid.*, p. 100-101)

Noget is gradually stirring Nadia's subconscious and his food is drawing her into dark, previously unadmitted places. Nadia gets fatter and fatter as despite herself she eats more and more of Noget's rich food; her periods stop and she begins to look as if she is pregnant. She insists to those who enquire that she is entering upon the menopause, but Noget's feeding of her has in fact induced a different sort of change of life. Nadia is beginning to review her past life and motivations, so that finally, through empathy with the tragedy of another, she realises the extent of her wrongdoing:

> *Le mépris pour mon propre caractère me submerge, l'horreur de ce que je suis et ne peux m'empêcher d'être, à tel point que dans une fulgurance de compréhension presque cosmique* [...] *je conçois enfin et approuve et ratifie les raisons de notre martyre, Ange et moi* [...] (*Ibid.*, p. 201)

The impact of Noget's food, which has brought her to this point, evolves further through the food provided to her by her son whom she visits in the country of origin to which her parents have returned. She dislikes it but eats it to please him and notes the childish pleasure on his face when she claims to enjoy it. We come to realise that her son has struggled to valorise himself aside from his mother's control. When Nadia then meets her mother again and once again eats her mother's simple and spicy food, symbolic of all she has repressed, she gives birth to the fruit of her relationship with Noget. A black slimy, eel-like creature leaves her body and she wipes away all traces of its path on the floor. When she meets Noget not long afterwards he asks her if she has given birth to his child. In a sense she has (*ibid.*, p. 252-253, 293, 295).

Noget's feeding of Nadia has concentrated in one black mass all that she has suppressed and repressed in her past – the real blackness of her character. She has had to realise that her construction of a certain

French cultural identity had gone too far, did not represent her real self. Michael Sheringham summarises the position well in describing the dishes prepared by Noget as « *nourritures caricaturalement françaises […] parodie grotesque de l'assimilation culturelle et sociale qu'elle a tant convoitée, et dont il faudra maintenant qu'elle comprenne le côté factice*[8] ». This unadmitted core of falseness, deception and ambition departs from her when her re-encounter with her son and her consumption of the uncongenial food he has prepared makes her finally re-envisage her relationship with him and her own deficiencies as a mother. Reviving the relationship with her own mother and returning to the natural food of her childhood enables her to expel the past and enter again a state of something approaching innocence and freedom[9].

Noget has thus led Nadia into a better awareness of herself. Aiding a mentee to confront the reality of their situation and helping them form realistic plans and expectations is certainly one of the legitimate goals of a mentor. However, as I have suggested, there are ethical questions about Noget's motivations (an unadmitted desire for revenge, perhaps) and about his methods (he uses spells and traps to overcome Nadia's refusal of consent to their relationship). Whereas the novel closes with Ange restored to health, happy in a new reciprocated love, and re-instated in his teaching position, Nadia has been thrust back to her origins, to the country, the home and the company of her parents, whom she had previously seen as at fault for wanting to keep her « *dans la médiocrité d'une existence tout enclose par les bornes d'un quartier* ». (NDiaye, 2007, p. 220). She may now have a good relationship with her parents in their sunny village by the sea and may be enjoying her role as a grandmother, but everything she has attempted to build through her own efforts has been shown to have rested on immoral foundations and thus to have been rightfully discarded. Yet Nadia still cannot bear to watch mindless programmes on the television as her parents do. She no longer expresses her contempt for them but it is clearly the case that she has been educated into a different culture from that of her parents, and it seems unlikely that life with them will satisfy her, surely legitimate, ambitions in the longer term. Noget has not and will not help her

8 Michael Sheringham, « *Mon cœur à l'étroit*: espace et éthique », Andrew Asibong and Shirley Jordan, eds, *Marie NDiaye: l'étrangeté à l'œuvre*, Villeneuve d'Ascq, Presses Universitaires du Septentrion, 2009, p. 182.

9 The final section of the novel is headed *Tous guéris*.

to draw up a route map for the future and his role as mentor is thus incomplete and arguably abusive. He has used the magical temptation of food to exert a transformational power over Nadia, but he does not help her to use her new found self and moral awareness to create a new life. One truly ethical responsibility of a mentor is to assure an ending of the relationship which leaves the mentee, not abandoned, but ready to face the world independently, rather as a parent should encourage, acknowledge and support the independence of a child. Despite the general air of lightness, release and gaiety which informs the last few pages of NDiaye's novel, this is not a happy ending, nor is it a healthy prescription for a mentor/mentee relationship.

I now turn to the third novella in NDiaye's 2009 work *Trois femmes puissantes*[10] which was inspired by real life stories of the attempts of Africans to reach Europe in the hope of escaping poverty and abuse and securing a better life. Its central character is Khady Demba. When her young husband dies suddenly and unexpectedly, she loses the drinks stall business they carried on together and is forced to go to live with her husband's family. They do not want her, especially as she has never produced a child (despite, as we learn, being obsessed with becoming pregnant). They decide to get rid of the ongoing burden of housing her by sending her to Europe. They arrange her journey through people smugglers. Khady understands little of what is proposed for her. She is told to pack her almost non-existent belongings one evening and is bundled out of the house the next day, led by an uncommunicative and nervous man. Her husband's family provide her with a bundle of money but she has little idea who she is to pay and when.

At this early stage in the novella Khady is represented as a young woman with no will of her own. Her abiding obsession in life has been to have a child and with the death of her husband and the death for ever of this hope she has become, in her own mind, a nonentity and in her relationships with others an elective mute. She is in a mental state of total apathy, with no sense of agency and with all her emotions suppressed. We would recognise this as a deep depression (NDiaye, 2009,

10 The work is described as a *roman* but consists of three self-standing stories, linked only by the transitory presence of a character, or a character's name, in more than one story. Khady Demba, the principal character in the novella I am discussing appears as a housemaid/nanny in the first novella. In her own story she is advised that when she reaches Europe she should contact Fanta, a character in the second novella.

p. 252, 253, 255). The shock of her enforced departure does however stir Khady into life. Her deep and bitter distress at not having produced a child reawakens in her, she sees her former life in the shape of another young woman opening a drinks stall, and is then reminded of herself as a young girl. Realising that she and her childhood self are the same person delivers to her a sudden sense of her own identity, always solitary, especially in the presence of others. This consciousness of her own subjectivity is expressed to herself in the simple words "Hello Khady", as she becomes happily conscious of the sun warming her body, and it will stay with her until the end. She now misses her husband, suddenly and, for the first time, for himself and not as the instrument of her longed-for pregnancy. It is as if the realisation of her own subjectivity has enabled her, too late, to be aware of his. The pity she now feels for her husband, however, wakens in her a sense of her own good fortune and strengthens her appreciation of her own aliveness. She begins to think and to try to work out what is happening. After more waiting, and more journeys by bus and on foot, Khady finds herself and her meagre belongings being pushed on to a boat. She becomes more and more frightened and suddenly, in an unexplained act of self-determination, she leaps from the boat and runs away, filled with a fierce joy that she has accomplished an act which stems only from her own resolution (*ibid.*, p. 262-266, 282-283).

However, having taken control of her own life Khady must now do something with it and it is evident to the reader at this point that she will need help – she has learned nothing at school, and has only hazy recollections of what her husband's family told her they had planned for her; nor does she know where she is. But what wakes her in the morning is the sense of a gaze; although her eyes are closed, she becomes aware that someone is looking at her and this tells us that she exists now not just in her own consciousness but in the eyes of others. Watching her is a young man and in the relationship they develop the potential complexities of what at first seems like a straightforward mentoring partnership are explored.

The young man, Lamine, seems to Khady to be younger than her and his voice is almost childlike. Khady sees his nervous tension, his thinness, his suppression of the privations he has suffered and the sacrifices he has made, and for the first time ever, comparing her own life to that of another person, she sees herself as the luckier. But Lamine is not asking for her help. He is possessed of knowledge and experience that Khady needs. His goal is to get to Europe, and he will pursue this even at the cost of his life. When Khady hears this, she feels that he has done no more than make her own life project explicit to her. At this point she decides to accompany him (*Ibid.*, p. 284-286).

The stage is set for the commencement of a mentoring relationship, and the disadvantaged state of both its potential parties does nothing to belie this. Khady is newly self-aware, has a goal (to reach Europe), even if it is not a well understood one, is in possession of some resources (the money given to her by her husband's family) and has a clear sense that she needs help. Lamine is experienced in the difficulties of emigration. He has tried before and has failed but believes he has learned from this and now has all the knowledge necessary to succeed. Interestingly, we are told that Lamine did not embark the day before because of « *le délabrement de la barque* », something that Khady perhaps intuited but did not recognise as a rational choice. Lamine made the judgement based on his experience. He has identified Khady as someone he can help and wants to help. From this first moment their destinies are bound together (*ibid.*, p. 287).

There is reason, however, to pause for thought. A piece of practical advice given in formal mentoring schemes is that there should be a clear understanding between mentor and mentee so that each understands what is required from them in the relationship and what they might expect from it. Moberg and Velasquez note that the practitioner literature sees the specification of expectations as the role of the mentor (Moberg and Velasquez, 2004, p. 104). In the initiation of the relationship between Khady and Lamine it is, on the contrary Khady, whom Lamine has adopted as mentee, who, despite her lack of experience, is quite clear what she expects from Lamine:

> *Khady reconnut tout simplement qu'il était au courant de choses qu'elle ne pouvait pas même se représenter et qu'en demeurant avec lui elle profiterait et s'emplirait de ces connaissances, au lieu de parcourir par ses propres moyens l'inconcevable chemin jusqu'à celles-ci.* (NDiaye, 2009, p. 287)

She is also sufficiently self-aware to note that she is not simply going with him because she can do nothing else. She recognises, as something remarkable for herself, that « *elle eût pensé tirer profit de cette association* » (*Ibid.*, p. 287).

Khady is thus quite clear that she intends to exploit Lamine. There is no suggestion that she will see herself obliged to give him anything in return. This raises again the question of what mentors, as opposed to mentees, expect to get from the mentoring relationship, given that its premise is the exploitation of their knowledge, experience and contacts. The narration never explains directly what impulse moves Lamine to offer himself as a mentor and guide to Khady. As the story develops, however, some of his needs mistily emerge, and the relationship, whose mutuality and reciprocity has been dubious from the start, becomes increasingly problematic. Khady is greedy for information, but extremely wary of revealing to Lamine the extent of her own lack of knowledge.

> *Il semblait à Khady qu'il lui était accordé un suspens afin qu'elle pût s'imprégner d'une quantité d'informations telle qu'elle n'en avait jamais assimilé en vingt-cinq ans d'existence, et cela discrètement, sans avoir pratiquement l'air de rien apprendre, une prudence instinctive la retenant de montrer à Lamine l'étendue de son ignorance.* (*Ibid.*, p. 288)

Despite the fact that Lamine supplies her with food without ever asking her for payment, she gives only brief replies to any questions he puts to her, while she questions him avidly about the journey to Europe and how it might be achieved. At the same time, in a deliberate act of deception, she tries to cover her insistent thirst for knowledge with « *quelque chose de morne, de contraint, d'ennuyé* ». Khady does not offer payment to Lamine for anything that he does for her. She consciously hides the fact that she has monetary resources, and rationalises this on the basis that as Lamine does not raise the question of money, nor need she (*ibid.*, p. 288).

Formal mentoring relationships tend to begin with a degree of mutual disclosure on both sides. The mentor will explain the path that has brought them to their present position of seniority and experience; the mentee will similarly disclose their background and their aims for the future. In a normal mentoring relationship, one would expect most of the questions to come from the mentor, and these would be posed with the intent of raising the mentee's self-awareness and helping them think their way through the problems and/or opportunities with which they are faced. Moberg and Velasquez see mentees as having a duty of veracity to their mentors. They should be honest with their mentors so that the advice and support they receive from them is built upon accurate premises (Moberg and Velasquez, 2004, p. 114). The lack of honesty in Khady's approach to the relationship she has actively decided to enter and her determination to reveal as little as possible of herself and of the important resources available to her would thus make the role of a mentor in a formal relationship difficult. But how true a mentor is Lamine?

Lamine does talk to Khady. He explains his previous attempts to reach Europe, the unforeseen circumstances which have prevented him succeeding and his conviction that he now has all the knowledge necessary to succeed – and he seems to prove these credentials, in due course, by acquiring for Khady a passport, for which, again, he requests no payment. In these actions he performs as one would expect of a mentor. He explains his own path to knowledge and gives practical help to his mentee in achieving her own aims. Perhaps too he would have been able to help Khady develop some thoughts of her own about how they might progress their joint objective, had she been willing to answer his questions (the nature of which we are left to guess, but which, in view of what he chooses to reveal about himself, we might imagine to have concerned her personal history). Lamine shares with Khady some of his personal traumas. His mother died and he was beaten brutally by his stepmother – he shows Khady the scars; he went to the *lycée*, but failed the *baccalauréat* twice. Khady tries hard not to listen to these disclosures, partly because they might sadden or embarrass her, and partly because they might revive her own memories. Such memories might, she feels, actually hinder her own personal development, in that they « *risquaient seulement de freiner ou de dévier le développement encore jeune, incertain de ses pensées en y insinuant des éléments de trouble, d'incontrôlable souffrance* ». (NDiaye, 2009, p. 290). Whereas Khady does not want to involve another in her path to personal development Lamine is certainly in need of help himself – he needs a counsellor, he needs someone to recognise and admire his experience and, perhaps even more, he needs a mother, a role which he might perhaps have hoped the older Khady might fulfil – and indeed in her own frustrated childlessness that she might have been expected to want to. But her selfishness in her newfound sense of identity cannot answer Lamine's unadmitted neediness. In his self-imposed role of mentor Lamine probably seeks self-valorisation and to construct an identity.

The high point of Lamine's performance as mentor comes when he succeeds in obtaining a passport for Khady. He gives it to her with « *un air de fierté, de triomphe et d'assurance* ». At this point, perhaps for the first time in his life, he sees himself as a success, as existing powerfully in the eyes of another. The effect on Khady is indeed to make her fearful. She recognises that she is tempted by a return to her previous state of subordination and dependence on others. In thanking him with a nod of the head, without offering to pay him, she both resists the return to this former state and refuses to acknowledge (as a mother would) his achievement. Importantly, she also maintains her fundamental dishonesty within their relationship, which, ultimately, destroys the relationship and, in a sense, Khady herself (*ibid.*, p. 291).

Their relationship is effectively closed down at a border crossing. Lamine offers the border guards money and, because it is not enough, or because of pure caprice, a guard strikes Lamine down and brutally cuts open the soles of both his feet. At this point Khady, frightened, but thinking clearly (« *l'esprit limpide* ») draws out her money and delicately and respectfully hands it to the guard commander, making it clear by another gesture that she and Lamine are together (*ibid.*, p. 298-299). Although they subsequently continue as a couple, stranded by their lack of means to move on, Lamine has now changed. He never speaks of the pain of his wounds (in contrast to his previous willingness to expose his scars), and Khady understands that he is totally and irrevocably humiliated by this failure to secure for them both this journey, all of whose dangers and obstacles he had assured her he was familiar with. His humiliation is redoubled by his foreknowledge of, and subsequent inevitable acceptance of, the fact that their only means of survival and their only chance of escape and moving on, is for Khady to secure their joint livelihood by her acceptance of prostitution. She is first forced to sell her body to pay for food they have both eaten. She manages thereafter to keep them both and to save some money, but after some months of a wretched existence she awakes one morning to find Lamine and all her savings gone. He has robbed her and deserted her without an explanation (*ibid.*, p. 301, 307).

Lamine thus finishes by ruthlessly exploiting Khady as she had deliberately exploited him. He has ceased to perceive himself as her mentor because he has nothing more to offer. This is not of course how mentoring relationships should be brought to an end yet here is an odd commentary on the fact that when formal relationships do end, mentees may sometimes feel abandoned, a sense of abandon here made concrete

Lamine's theft reveals not only an apparent reversal of power in the relationship but the very shaky foundation on which Lamine's self-prized role as mentor was built. Resources were available to Khady which she hid from her mentor but which might, had they been shared earlier, have augmented the value of Lamine's experience and enabled them to make the journey as a relatively equal partnership. In fact, with the aid of her money, Lamine does indeed make it to France. Khady dies attempting to scale a border fence with other would-be migrants. Whereas Lamine must have seen himself as the senior figure in the partnership, this was not the case. He met Khady's needs for food and guidance – she refused to meet his for understanding, counselling and mothering, and she withheld her vital resource of money deliberately until it was too late. She did not match Lamine's transparency with her own.

NDiaye's works are never schematic and of course I do not argue that she has set out in this novel to provide a guide on how and how not to mentor. She has set out to present us with a relationship and because it is not uncommon for her later works at least to conclude with a 'happy ending' which is in some sense reconciliatory, I need to append some concluding remarks on what her narration tells us about events after Lamine has brought their relationship to an end by his cruel flight. Khady forgets Lamine quickly, indeed almost immediately he has gone, remembering neither his name nor his face and bearing no grudge. She remembers his betrayal as a blow from fate (*ibid.*, p. 308). The concluding words of the text tell us that Lamine, safely arrived and working in France, remembers her every time he is paid for the work he has done. He begs her to forgive him rather than curse him, without being clear which she is doing. In fact by this time she is dead and has perhaps become a bird. Sometimes Lamine senses the bird's wings overshadowing him, and talks to Khady, gently telling her what has happened to him, and giving thanks to her. I am reminded of the formal mentoring scheme, *Leaders Unlimited*, to which I referred earlier.

Mentors were expected to "act as a strategic guide to the mentee [...] especially towards the end of the programme *and beyond*"(my italics). In the realm of the au-delà Khady in fact demonstrates her power in this reversal of their relationship; she lives on in his memory as his protector and mentor.

Commentators have indeed discussed, and have come to different conclusions, about what makes Khady one of the three powerful women. Shirley Jordan suggests that the reader's empathy with Khady raises ethical questions about our responsibility for the plight of those like her – turning her into a literary creation makes her and those like her visible to us as real human individuals[11]. Christophe Ippolito sees in the character of Lamine a threatened masculinity which is opposed to the power of certain feminine characters[12]. I believe that my analysis, which is focused on the mentoring nature of the relationship between Khady and Lamine, suggests not only that the real power in the relationship lies with her but also, oddly, that her power lies in her inability to relate to other people. While the narration encourages us to see her as a victim who nonetheless maintains a sense of self-identity throughout all her horrendous experiences, the text reveals that in her relations with her husband she never enjoyed sex because she was obsessed with becoming pregnant and that her first reaction on finding her husband dead was to ask who might replace him to help her achieve pregnancy (he inconsiderately died on a morning when she believed she was ovulating). She makes no attempt to build relations with her husband's family, instead retreating into depression, blankness and muteness, makes no attempt to forge relationships with other refugees, presenting to them a face which is « *neutre, froid, privé du moindre encouragement à lui adresser la parole* » (NDiaye, 2009, p. 291), and, most significantly, as we have seen, refuses to Lamine, for her own reasons, the sympathetic ear he is so clearly seeking. At root, it seems, she is self-obsessed and selfish and it is that unattractive power which enables her to survive until the final crisis which leads to her death. She is flawed as well as tragic. Her

11 Shirley Jordan, « La puissance de Khady Demba », *Une femme puissante: L'œuvre de Marie NDiaye*, ed. by Daniel Bengsch and Cornelia Ruhe, Amsterdam, Rodopi, 2013, p. 263-283, p. 280-281.

12 Christophe Hippolito, « Trois contes, Trois femmes puissantes: le puzzle et l'oiseau migrateur », *Une femme puissante: L'œuvre de Marie NDiaye*, ed. by Daniel Bengsch and Cornelia Ruhe, Amsterdam, Rodopi, 2013, p. 305-318, p. 312.

betrayal of Lamine, by her false representation of her real power, leads to her betrayal and abandonment by him.

The two texts I have commented show us a determinedly unwilling mentee and an apparently willing mentee. In neither case does the mentoring relationship achieve for the mentee a truly satisfactory result – Nadia loses her place in French society and Khady loses her life. What emerges very clearly from both texts is the unequal nature of the mentoring relationship and its inherent temptation towards the abuse of power. Both texts leave us somewhat mystified as to the motivations of mentors, although Lamine's need for self-valorisation and friendship is more attractive than Noget's cold sense of duty, which is at root also aimed at securing recognition from the superior couple who thought he was not worthy of an invitation to their party. The issue of power in mentoring relationships is an important one. It does not always lie where we might expect and the roles of mentor and mentee may be reversed unexpectedly. Mentors have needs, albeit difficult ones to identify. It is perhaps incumbent on mentees to recognise that, to be transparent in their disclosures, and to attempt to meet those needs where they can.

Pauline EATON
London

INFORMAL FEMALE MENTORSHIP IN FATOU DIOME'S *CELLES QUI ATTENDENT* (WOMEN WHO WAIT)

The increasingly popular Franco-Senegalese author Fatou Diome secured her place in the French and African literary canons with the publication of her first novel in 2003[1]. An instant success, *Le Ventre de l'Atlantique* recounts the plight of its female protagonist Salie as she attempts to dissuade her younger brother from immigrating to France as a young, uneducated Senegalese man who dreams of integrating a professional football team[2]. A migrant living in France herself, Salie does this by exposing her brother (and the reader) to the fallaciously embellished narratives of other former African migrants thereby, undermining a well-entrenched myth on African soil of European Eldorado. She also provides her brother with the financial means to initiate a professional project in his community of origin.

Diome has since published five more novels which all, with one notable exception[3], take up the issue of contemporary African immigration to Europe. Not surprisingly, critical commentary on Diome's corpus remains primarily focused on this particular literary theme and especially so in *Le Ventre de l'Atlantique*, the only one of her texts to have been translated, among other languages, into English under the title *The Belly of the Atlantic*[4]. Other themes that resurface incessantly across Diome's *œuvre* have found themselves somewhat neglected as a result of this immigration fixation. One of these, I believe, is mentorship which, incidentally, plays a crucial role in whether Diome's fictional characters

1 All translations from French to English are those of the article's author unless explicitly stated.

2 Fatou Diome, *Le Ventre de l'Atlantique*, Paris, Éditions Anne Carrière, 2003.

3 Only Diome's third novel, *Inassouvies nos vies*, parts with the migratory theme: Fatou Diome, *Inassouvies nos vies*, Paris, Flammarion, 2008.

4 F. Diome, *The Belly of the Atlantic*, trans. by L. Norman & R. Schwartz, London, Serpent's Tail, 2006.

migrate or not and whether their decision to stay or leave results in personal fulfillment or failure.

As David Lazar has noted, mentorship "as a topic for literary discussion, is, surprisingly, somewhat rare."[5] This is indeed remarkable as the mentorship process has existed for centuries[6]. Moreover, mentor and mentee figures abound in diverse forms in both life and literature. In the Western tradition, the study of mentorship is generally restricted to that which occurs in formal, institutionalised contexts (namely academic and other professional spheres). In these settings, mentorship is rather coded and inflexible pertaining to an asymmetrical relationship axed on the transmission of knowledge and know-how from a more experienced or learned individual to another[7]. It is a relationship based on and expressed through an imbalance of power between a superior and an inferior, a dominant and a dominated party (*ibid.*, p. 90). These relationships tend to be not only hierarchical but also highly masculinized (Lazar, 1991, p. 25; Waquet, 2008, p. 301, 305). They are prone to excluding both "women and people of color" (Moberg and Velasquez, 2004, p. 96) by staging mentors as male and superior in terms of a very specific form of knowledge or wisdom, often Western.

The mentoring relationships that emerge across *Le Ventre de l'Atlantique* correspond to this classic 'master-mentor' narrative suggesting primacy of the mentor and his institutionalised experience (Lazar, 1991, p. 25, 31). In *Le Ventre de l'Atlantique*, Salie's former school teacher, Ndétare, is a key example of such a mentor. Ndétare is first and foremost an intellectual mentor figure for Salie who credits him and his "immense teacher's knowledge"[8] obtained in the West with providing her with "everything" – literacy, numeracy, "the key to the world" (Diome, 2003, p. 66) – enabling her to leave her conservative island environment and start afresh afar. Ndétare also positions himself as a mentor for the island's young men through his role as coach of the local football team. He, like Salie, attempts to discourage the players from migrating

5 David Lazar, « On Mentorship », *The Ohio Review*, 1991, n° 51, p. 28.

6 Dennis Moberg and Manuel Velasquez, « The Ethics of Mentoring », *Business Ethics Quarterly*, 2004, vol. 14, n° 1, p. 95.

7 Françoise Waquet, *Les enfants de Socrate. Filiation intellectuelle et transmission du savoir* XVII*e*-XXI*e* *siècle*, Paris, Albin Michel, 2008, p. 14, 17.

8 R. Haskell, « Plotting *Migritude*: Variations of the *Bildungsroman* in Fatou Diome's *Les ventre de l'Atlantique* and *Celles qui attendent* », *South Atlantic Review*, vol. 81, n° 1, 2016, p. 141.

to Europe by instead promoting Niodior Island, and by extension the African continent, as a place for viable and fulfilling life on the condition that certain outdated and detrimental practices be abandoned[9]. Yet Ndétare's impact on the island's male youth remains questionable as he is undermined by the very factors that made him a mentor for protagonist Salie, namely his outsider and intellectual status. In the eyes of many, he is seen to be a "learned parrot, paid [...] to instill the language, the customs of white people, [...] [a] colonist mask." (*Ibid.*, p. 124). Ndétare's mentoring abilities, which correspond closely to those of classical male mentor narratives, are ultimately sapped by his would-be mentees' unwillingness to accord him or his advice any merit. The main master-mentor relationship in *Le Ventre de l'Atlantique* is not invariably successful. Its fictional depiction in this novel accentuates the multitude of lived-world factors that determine the realisation of beneficial mentorships for both mentors and mentees.

In recent times, mentoring narratives have emerged that challenge the traditional master-mentor model. They shed light on forms of mentorship occurring outside of the classical mentoring environments of the educational institution (namely the university) or the workplace. These include models of female and non-Western mentorship which add depth and nuance to the "more obvious examples of institutional mentorhood" (Lazar, 1991, p. 26) framed around masculinity and formal (Western) education. In this essay, I will focus on informal and intergenerational female mentorship in Diome's fourth novel, *Celles qui attendent* [Women who wait], published in 2010[10]. *Women Who Wait* has been the subject of substantially less critical attention than Diome's first novel and is useful for our analysis of alternative mentorship expressions that deviate from the master-model displayed in *Le Ventre de l'Atlantique* as this text focuses almost exclusively on the lives of non-formally educated female characters living in a non-institutionalised setting. The novel recounts the everyday lives of Arame, Bougna, Coumba and Daba – the mothers and wives of clandestine migrant men having attempted the dangerous journey to Europe to better their own lives and those of their families left behind in Senegal. Left to fend for themselves during the men's

9 Namely polygamy and exaggerated childbearing.

10 Fatou Diome, *Celles qui attendent*, Paris, Flammarion, 2010. Winner of the Prix Solidarité in 2012. The English translation of the title is the author's own.

long absence, the women battle daily for their survival and dignity in a community governed by patriarchal codes and characterised by very tangible poverty. In the absence of male mentor figures, the women develop their own codes of informal mentorship, aligned with their particular circumstances, with varying degrees of success. They redefine in doing so the contours of traditional conceptions of mentoring partnerships whilst bringing into question what it means to 'grow' both intellectually and emotionally. I will begin my analysis by examining Diome's literary portrayal of multidirectional and symmetrical mentor-friendship between women as an alternative to the traditional male master-mentor model. I will then turn to intergenerational mentorship between family members (specifically between mothers- and daughters-in-law) analysing in particular the factors determining successful and unsuccessful mentor-mentee partnerships in informal contexts. This discussion will enable us to arrive at a judgement as to which model, the master-mentor or mentor-friendship, is granted greater credence by Diome in this text.

We have thus far established that typical mentorship models are hierarchical and one-directional staging the superiority of the mentor-master over that of the mentee-apprentice (Waquet, 2008, p. 90). As restricted for the most part to professional and academic contexts, these relationships appear to leave little room for the development of emotional connections between parties. The one-directional aspect of mentoring is a further distinguishing trait of mentorship as, unlike friendship characterised by mutual giving, in orthodox mentoring the mentor "is concerned about the development of the protégé but not vice-versa." (Moberg and Velasquez, 2004, p. 98). Yet, as indicated above, mentorship theorists and practitioners have begun to challenge this traditional view to highlight the essential role in mentorship of affective transactions whose transmission, unlike that of formal knowledge, is reciprocal. Late Italian novelist, literary critic and philosopher Umberto Eco went as far as to suggest that mentoring relationships should be based on "love, reciprocal trust and exchange"[11]. In this view the mutual exchange of emotions becomes a staple constituent of a relationship that is still, fundamentally, axed on the transfer of knowledge for the purpose of

11 Alberto Stabile, *I buoni maestri: chi sono, che cosa ci hanno insegnato sedici protagonisti della nostra cultura*, Milan, Mondadori, 1988, p. 83, 84 (in Waquet, 2008, p. 137).

personal and collective betterment. However, as these sentiments are no longer the unique domain of the mentor, the relationship becomes more symmetrical and the lines between traditional mentorship and friendship become blurred.

It is precisely this friendship-mentorship dynamic that manifests across Diome's *Women Who Wait*, a novel in which there is no clear-cut (nor masculinised) master-mentor figure. Mentors and mentees in this text do not inhabit strict categories – no one character is fully mentor nor mentee, all characters oscillate between roles as both givers and receivers of counsel and comfort. This is notably the case for Arame and Bougna, the mothers of the young male migrants that have left for Europe. If friendship is characterised by the mutual exchange of aid, advice and affection, in what manner can the relationship between these women be conceived of as both one of mentorship and friendship? Lazar defines the process of mentoring and being mentored as "the use of the experience of experience, in whatever form it takes." (Lazar, 1994, p. 32). As such, many friendships can concurrently be considered mentorships as they drift incessantly, according to the immediate circumstances, into the overlapping territories of both relational forms. I would argue that this is specifically true of friendships resulting in the emotional and intellectual growth of participants, something that, as we will see in *Women Who Wait*, is not invariably achieved in all friendships nor for all parties.

Like *Le Ventre de l'Atlantique* published before it and *Impossible de grandir* published after it[12], *Women Who Wait* uses the island of Niodior as its main fictional setting[13]. Niodior is, by all Western standards, an oppressive place for women who are unfailingly hindered by the patriarchal codes that govern the mostly poor and conservative community members. Polygamy and forced marriage are commonplace with each of the four protagonists falling victim to at least one of these practices. The first of the Niodior women to have her literary portrait sketched by the third-person omniscient narrator is Arame. In her late forties, Arame is married to Koromâk, a man as old as her father, whom her parents forced her to marry when she was just 18 years old. Despite being one of the rare women in this "stronghold of polygamy" (Diome, 2010, p. 14) to benefit from the enviable

12 Fatou Diome, *Impossible de grandir*, Paris, Flammarion, 2013.

13 A real island in Senegal's Sine-Saloum Delta and actual birthplace of Diome.

status of first and only wife, Arame's marriage is an unremitting source of misery and resentment. Not only has she come to abhor the man she was forcibly married to and who, furthermore, degrades her and *her* offspring incessantly, but ailing Koromâk is also largely bedridden and unable to work. To make matters considerably worse, Arame has recently lost her eldest son in a fishing accident becoming the sole carer and provider for the latter's seven children. Though she is weary of living, Arame continues her laborious quest as the survival of those who depend on her has become her spiritual "vocation". (*Ibid.*, p. 16). Impoverished, uneducated and seemingly without prospects, all her hopes for a brighter future for both herself and her grandchildren are pinned on the hypothetical success of Lamine, her second son and only remaining child.

Whereas Arame's marital union was forced upon her, her friend Bougna married a man of her choice electing to become the second wife of Wagane, a man Bougna thought, at the time of her marriage, enjoyed a comfortable financial situation. Despite learning the truth about Wagane's economic precarity shortly after their union, Bougna lived happily with her husband for many years giving birth to four daughters and two sons. Yet her husband eventually turned his attention back to the first wife – a "safe bet" as the mother of five grown sons capable of "guaranteeing his bread during his retirement." (*Ibid.*, p. 45). Despite her fury at having been forsaken for the first wife, subsequently reinforced by Wagane's decision to welcome a third wife, divorce is inconceivable for Bougna for many reasons. These include her economic dependence on her husband and, more precisely, on the money sent by the first wife's offspring. As the narrator pertinently asks and leaves the reader to ponder: "Where would she go with her abundant progeny?" (*ibid.*, p. 46), Bougna is also desperate to avoid the "unflattering" (*ibid.*) situation reserved for women her age who leave their husbands in conservative and patriarchal Niodior. Languishing in a polygamous household governed by competition and jealousy between co-wives and their offspring, Bougna too begins to ponder a solution to lift her family from poverty, secure a future for her children and, in doing so, preserve her honour, for according to the island's teaching "a mother's successes are rendered evident through those of her son." (*Ibid.*, p. 51).

For Nigerian women's, African and francophone literary academic Obioma Nnaemeka, it is "through friendship, sisterhood, and solidarity" that African "[w]omen appropriate and refashion oppressive spaces" reinventing themselves in the process[14]. Indeed, female friendship in patriarchal Sub-Saharan contexts such as Niodior goes well beyond personal fulfilment impacting saliently on entire communities, their concrete advancement and ultimate survival. When their husbands fail to provide the basic necessities that Arame and Bougna need to run and feed their households, it is towards each other that the friends and neighbours naturally turn. When Bougna arrives in a flurry at Arame's house to ask her if she can give her some soap for clothes washing, Arame apologises explaining that she has just purchased a bar of soap on credit from the local shopkeeper and therefore has none to spare (Diome, 2010, p. 33). Bougna is naturally understanding and respectful of her friend as she is aware of the deep shame Arame feels when forced to extend the long list of items purchased on credit from the local store with only hypothetical promises of one day being able to reimburse the debt. In the place of soap, Arame offers Bougna the remaining charcoal that she has managed to put aside sharing what she can with her friend with whom she is united in facing the daily horrors of abject poverty. Solidarity between women, as demonstrated by Arame and Bougna, takes on increasing importance in this environment where "reliable and durable friendships are the most lucrative of investments." (*Ibid.*, p. 34). The two friends are indeed conscious of the value of their "exceptional" bond (*ibid.*, p. 57). Diome employs vocabulary typically evoked to describe the experience of eating pleasurably and copiously, to describe the women's friendship, a "delicious complicity" that Arame and Bougna "relish in" (*ibid.*, p. 55). This choice of vocabulary serves to highlight the relative rarity of such friendships on the island, an occurrence as infrequent and as exceptional as the experience of eating well to one's fill. The women are willing to go to great lengths to protect this friendship and even defy "old tribal laws" (*ibid.*, p. 42). Arame is ready to come to Bougna's defense when the latter is implicated for an umpteenth time in a row with her younger co-wife, a far-removed member of former's family, despite Arame recognising her friend's noted tendency to be "provocative" and "cunning" towards her husband's other spouses (*ibid.*).

14 Obioma Nnaemeka, « Introduction: Imag(in)ing Knowledge, Power, and Subversion in the Margins », *The Politics of (M)othering: Womanhood, Identity, and Resistance in African Literature*, London, Routledge, p. 19.

For Arame, friendship with Bougna is "worth more than the couple of genes shared with this removed cousin." (*Ibid.*)

It is in each other's company that the two friends chose to accomplish the many physical chores that punctuate their arduous daily routines as they continuously lug water from the well, scour the rock pools for shellfish to embellish their meagre meals and cut wood in the mangrove to feed the kitchen stove. Yet, more importantly, their time spent together represents an opportunity to share their inner-most thoughts, to support and counsel each other regarding possible means through which to improve their respective circumstances. Both have lessons to give based on their individual experiences, their fields of (non-formal) expertise and both women recognise the importance of learning from the experiences of the other for their own self-development, whatever form this may take. These lessons vary yet are all related in one way or another to the women's domestic sphere. They include relationship advice designed to ease the burden of their equally unsatisfactory marriages and counsel concerning the type of life education that the mothers wish to impart to their respective children in order to improve the latter's future prospects to which their own are closely tethered. Most importantly, Arame and Bougna share economic advice and elaborate strategies that are designed to provide the women with greater financial independence. For instance, their friendship merges at one point in narration into a commercial partnership as the women begin to sell their excess stocks of shellfish and firewood together. Arame and Bougna even establish a small store preparing and selling doughnuts and peanuts, a commercial venture that, although not revolutionary, enables them to "improve the ordinary" (*ibid.*, p. 181). Shifting incessantly between the roles of the counsellor and the counselled, the carer and the cared for, the dynamic between Arame and Bougna reveals a multidirectional and non-hierarchical mentor-friendship based on Eco's principles of "love, reciprocal trust and exchange"[15].

Though it is Bougna who initially comes up with the idea of sending their children to Europe, it is together that the friends refine the plan that eventually sees Issa and Lamine embark for Spain. As mothers, Bougna and Arame are naturally anxious concerning the potential danger of their clandestine immigratory project. Yet the friends remain convinced that the destinies of their sons to which their own are inseparably linked

15 Stabile, 1988, p. 83, 84 (in Waquet, p. 137).

will not improve if the latter remain in Senegal. It is again in each other's company that the mothers search for and find solace regarding the conflicting feelings of wanting to protect their sons while concurrently ascribing wholeheartedly to the belief that their only hope for a better life requires that they be put in harm's way. After unveiling her idea to her friend, Bougna's "fear and guilt" are somewhat soothed by the serious and sincere consideration Arame accords her proposition for, as the narrator remarks, "another mother was ready, as was she, to send her son to the galleys" (Diome, 2010, p. 63) in order to guarantee his future. Arame, having already lost a child to the sea, is more hesitant yet allows herself to be convinced by her friend. With Issa and Lamine relieved to learn that their mothers have come to the same conclusion as themselves regarding their *need* to reach Europe, the two friends redouble their efforts in order to amass the sum of money needed to pay for their sons' passage across the Atlantic. United anew in this novel endeavor, the relationship between Arame and Bougna in *Women Who Wait* continues to be one in which mentorship and friendship are not easily disentangled from each other remaining, rather, in a state of constant overlap.

Women Who Wait, like Diome's other texts, employs narrative techniques and styles inspired or directly sourced from Serer mythology and Sub-Saharan oral cultures more broadly often in the form of tales, adages, maxims and proverbs. Drawing on her Serer roots, it is through recourse to the legends of the pre-colonial Guelwaar dynasty that Diome chooses to convey the strength of the family-focused and ambitious Niodiorois woman embodied by a specific recurrent figure – that of the female warrior. It is in reference to this particular image, accompanied by its corollaries of sacrifice and bravery, that Arame qualifies her friend Bougna: this "tenacious" woman whose "obstinacy" to see both their sons reach Europe at whatever cost reminds Arame of the legend of Queen Diâhère Tèw No Mâd – one of many Guelwaar women warriors reputed for "placing the honor and happiness of their sons above everything." (*Ibid.*, p. 81). For the legend sung by the griots and inserted into the storyline of *Women Who Wait* recounts that Queen Diâhère Tèw No Mâd did not hesitate to sacrifice her own life in order to "save the throne of her beloved husband"[16] and, in doing so,

16 *Ibid.*, p. 85. A 'griot' is a West African storyteller, praise-singer, historian, musician or poet. Griots are central to Sub-Saharan oral tradition and singularly to the transmission of collective memory and history.

secure the future of her son. In the contemporary context of large numbers of Sub-Saharan migrant deaths at sea, attributing the term "modern-day warriors" or "heroines" (*ibid.*, p. 100) to mothers prepared to send their sons on a dangerous journey which may very well result in death is controversial. Yet such an attribution needs to be placed in the socio-cultural context of contemporary Senegal and other Sub-Saharan regions where immigration to Europe by any means is considered a concrete solution to the endemic poverty and other disadvantageous factors that cumulate in the general perception, especially present among the youth, of an extremely limited number of opportunities for professional, economic and material ascent. As Rosia Beer notes in her article on *Le Ventre de l'Atlantique*, the French Eldorado myth entertained by Senegalese youth and maintained by the perception of relatively wealthier returning migrants is "inseparable from the realities of life in Senegal."[17] Accordingly, if it is accepted by these sea-farthing populations that the ocean will "take its tribute" in the form of human casualties during the treacherous ocean crossings, regrettable collateral damage in the name of a greater cause, the women who send their sons clandestinely, who "dare to brave administrative injustice", are nevertheless credited in their communities with attempting to "secure the future" (Diome, 2010, p. 100) of the region's children. Arame and Bougna are eventually successful in their efforts to get Lamine and Issa to Europe. The two young men survive the perilous trans-oceanic journey that, outside of fiction, claims the lives of so many in the contemporary era, and arrive in Spain where their long European trek commences.

We have seen that Bougna and Arame are open to giving and receiving advice from each other as they are both motivated by the desire to see their respective life conditions, as well as those of their sons, improved. Working within the restrictive limits of a patriarchal and impoverished setting providing little room for manœuvre, the advice offered is, at times and perhaps unsurprisingly, shortsighted and the means employed to put it into practice morally questionable. Yet it is almost always based on "the experience of experience" (Lazar, 1994, p. 32) and a true belief in the efficiency and veracity of the guidance given. For instance, Bougna counsels Arame to find a wife for Lamine as she has recently celebrated the marriage of her son Issa with her now

17 Rosia Beer, « Gesturing to an empty theatre? Author, Text and Audience in the Fiction of Fatou Diome and Aïssatou Diamanka-Besland », *RELIEF*, vol. 5, n° 5, 2011, p. 47.

daughter-in-law Coumba. The motivations behind Bougna's decision to marry Issa prior to his departure to Europe were not wholly honourable, nor were they without self-interest. In point of fact, Bougna was driven primarily by her jealously of the first co-wife's new-found freedom after celebrating the marriage of her own son whose new wife integrated her husband's household as dictated by tradition. If her motivations in regard to Issa's marriage were not entirely noble, Bougna's urging of Arame to follow in her footsteps is, fundamentally, well-intentioned. She wishes to see her friend in the company of a daughter-in-law, one who is additionally able to ease the heavy burden of running a household alone and, most crucially, likely to ensure her friend's son's eventual return to Niodior from Europe (Diome, 2010, p. 79-80). Acting upon the advice of her friend and her own desire to see Lamine returned to her, Arame devises (more so than organises) the marriage of her absentee son with Daba, the only girl on the island to have ever interested Lamine. Whereas Coumba married Bougna's son Issa for love, Daba's marriage to Arame's son Lamine was largely forced for Daba was engaged to another – Ansou, a local fisherman, for whom she had genuine feelings and to whom she falls pregnant during Lamine's long absence. Bougna and Arame armed with their expect knowledge of the island's marital practices and especially "the pressure that a young woman's entourage could put on her as soon as an immigrant showed interest in her" (*ibid.*, p. 172), manage to derail Daba and Ansou's engagement. Pressured by her family to espouse the perceived prospects that inevitably accompany European migration in rural postcolonial Senegal, Daba is married to Lamine while the latter is still in Europe and moves into the household of her new mother-in-law Arame. Thus begins Daba's long and anxious wait alongside Arame for Lamine mirrored by that, a few houses over, of Bougna and Coumba for Issa.

We will now turn to the issue of intergenerational female mentorship. The master-mentor model promotes the idea of a surrogate paternal figure (Lazar, 1994, p. 25). This knowledgeable master-mentor is expected to "feed, educate [and] protect" (Waquet, 2008, p. 175) the inexperienced apprentice-mentee, functions Françoise Waquet rightly associates with the family and specifically parent-children relations. In *Women Who Wait*, the surrogate parental figure is maternal and takes the form of mothers-in-law Arame and Bougna who (should) attempt to "train, guide and help" (*ibid.*) their new daughters-in-law in their new roles as women married to clandestine migrant men. As we will see, Arame and Bougna's mentor-friendship model is not necessarily replicated in the relationships they establish with their respective daughters-in-law Daba and Coumba. If Arame is able to draw on her own experiences to mentor Daba, while simultaneously recognising that she also has lessons to learn from her younger and less-experienced daughter-in-law, Bougna is not. This leads to two very different and highly unexpected outcomes for the Arame-Daba and Bougna-Coumba character duos. It similarly highlights the role to be played in patriarchal spaces by informal female mentorship, reconceptualised by Diome to include mentor-friendships built upon reciprocal exchanges of knowledge, counsel, respect and love which can ultimately lead to a greater chance of success for those who know how engage in them.

At the novel's conclusion, the reader is confronted by what appears to be an intergenerational reproduction of the individual itineraries of the four protagonists, an approximate duplication of their stories which clearly distinguishes two 'winners' in the collective European gamble – Arame and Daba, and two 'losers' – Bougna and Coumba. It is Arame and Daba who find themselves reunited with the men they love or have come to love. For Arame, this is both with her son Lamine and her first love, the father of her children, whom she is able to marry following Koromâk's death, becoming for the first time in her life a happily-wed woman. Daba is reunited with Lamine, the husband she thought would never accept her following her infidelity during his long European absence and whose acceptance of her and her young daughter generates in Daba genuine feelings of affection. Bougna and Coumba are, conversely, left bitterly disappointed. Bougna no longer recognises "the son" who left her side for Spain all those years ago, for Issa has turned into another, "the man" that she will henceforth only see for a month every year after having put everything in place to ensure his return (Diome, 2010, p. 238). Coumba, who like Bougna, married her husband for love, is now herself trapped in the snares of a polygamous union having lost the husband she waited so patiently for not so much to his second European wife but to Europe, this continent that she holds responsible for stealing him from her (*ibid.*).

I contend here that it is the establishment of non-hierarchical and symmetrical mentor-friendship between Arame and Daba characterised by emotional exchange, respect and a mutual willingness to learn from each other's experiences that plays a role in this duo's ultimate success. I am not alone in having come to this conclusion. Rosemary Haskell has also identified this character duo, and specifically Arame's character, as the site of "significant moral and spiritual and emotional change." (Haskell, 2016, p. 150). She is, in other terms, the fictional personification of the progress and personal development so central to the mentoring paradigm and process. Arame's and Daba's stories are mirror images of each other – both were forced into marriage with men that they did not love and both in their unhappiness fell into the arms of their respective childhood sweethearts, unions which produced children – Lamine and his older brother for Arame, and Daba's daughter fathered by her one-time fiancé Ansou. What is perhaps most curious for the reader is the fact that it is Arame, whose marital suffering is pushed to the forefront of narration until this point, who actively plays a part in this narrative doubling. Blinded by her desire to see her son return to Niodior and desperate to appease for the trauma she presumes was caused by her own confession concerning the real identity of his father, Arame prioritises what she believes is best for Lamine and herself in actively engineering her son's marriage. Ironically, or perhaps very understandably given the manner in which his own marriage came to be, it is Koromâk who cautions his wife against "forcing destiny" (Diome, 2010, p. 175) through the pressure placed on Daba's family, and therefore on the young woman herself, to annul her engagement with Ansou and marry Lamine. For the first time in the novel, it is Koromâk who endorses the voice of reason for he has experienced first-hand the tragic consequences that such unions can engender. Arame, a motherly figure normally so considerate of others, conversely fails to recognise that she is effectively recreating for the young Daba the same set of circumstances responsible for her own marital misery. Driven by shortsighted and at times egotistical desires, such as wanting to be able to "savour long hours of rest" (*ibid.*) freed from the bulk of her domestic chores like her friend Bougna, she pushes ahead with her project. It is only after becoming aware of Daba's pregnancy in the absence of Lamine, the very visual proof of her extra-marital relationship, that Arame comes to the realisation that she has exposed this young woman to the same pain that was once inflicted upon herself by others, not the least concerned for her own happiness in a "cruel repetition of fate, a terrible cycle." (*Ibid.*,

p. 228). A deep sense of guilt impinges upon her consciousness as she wonders if she will ever be able to "forgive herself" for potentially rendering her daughter-in-law "as unhappy as herself" (*ibid.*, p. 198). Arame has effectively broken the silent pact of female solidarity by sacrificing the well-being of her daughter-in-law in the pursuit of her own interests. She fails to learn from "the experience of experience" (Lazar, 1994, p. 32) and to provide her daughter-in-law with the mentorship Daba so desperately requires in her marital unhappiness.

Yet Arame does not remain insensitive to the misery and heartache that she has caused and eventually revisits her own experiences, in tandem with those of Daba, to learn and grow. In identifying in Daba's plight the shadows of the organised marriage that "devastated her own life" (Diome, 2010, p. 225), Arame decides to confess her faults (as well as those of her daughter-in-law) in a confessional letter to her son in which she reveals for the first time the truth concerning her own painful past. Her gesture is one of love for her son, for she understands his need to possess all the elements of the saga which unfolded during his long absence in order to make an informed choice. But it is also a gesture of love for her daughter-in-law whom she knows she has failed. Although Arame does not wish to interfere with the decision that her son alone must make, having witnessed the fateful consequences engendered by her meddling in his marriage, her resolution expresses strong solidarity with Daba. Not only does it denounce the many ills caused when young women and girls have little or no say in whom they marry, but, in relating her own experience, Arame draws a direct parallel between herself and her past actions and those of Daba through intense and constructive introspection. Wagering on the love and respect of her own son, as well as his intimate knowledge of his parents' disastrous relationship, her letter underscores the fact that Daba's behaviour was entirely comprehensible, indeed human, given the circumstances of her engagement and marriage and that Arame understands more than anyone the oppressive factors having driven her daughter-in-law into the arms of another. As such, she demonstrates loyalty towards Daba, an attribute that is central to the ethical tenets of mentor-mentee relationships according to Manuel Velasquez and Dennis Moberg (Moberg and Velasquez, 2004, p. 98). In admitting her fault, Arame moreover underscores the fallibility inherent in all human beings, including mentors, thereby challenging the master-mentee model based on an inflexible and irreversible power imbalance between superior and inferior parties (Waquet, 2008, p. 90). Arame and her newly reinstated mentoring qualities are portrayed as being exceptional in regard to the particular issue of female infidelity in patriarchal Niodior. Her demonstration of loyalty and solidarity towards Daba distinguishes her from the other women of the village, none of whom seek to understand the personal torment behind what they deem or, rather, feign to deem the most scandalous of acts with even the most "unvirtuous" among them intending to make Arame's daughter-in-law "their spittoon" (Diome, 2010, p. 218). None of them seek to gather the knowledge that would greatly enlighten their appreciation of Daba's actions. Instead, many of these women engage in vicious rumour-mongering and abasement of Daba – the same suffered by Arame – as agents of the patriarchal order uniquely concerned with their own reputations and low-minded self-elevation. Bougna is, unfortunately, not immune to this female *non*-solidarity. She too engages in the common practice of "indexing the expiatory victim and legitimising her collective repulsion", an "effective" yet "cowardly" way to avoid being accused of sanctioning the "undignified conduct of the young woman" (*ibid.*). The very hypocritical and misogynistic aspect of Niodior's social code is reinforced to the reader through the castigatory tone of both Bougna's and the other women's comments regarding Daba. For these constitute reproaches to which Issa and Lamine, by virtue of their male gender, will never be subjected to on behalf of the community at large despite the young men prostituting themselves throughout much of Western Europe[18].

In a further effort to reinstate the mentor-friendship she was responsible for neglecting, indeed sabotaging entirely, Arame apologises to Daba for her responsibility in what she now understands was the catalyst for her daughter-in-law's marital heartache. She stresses furthermore her profound desire to see Daba remain by her and her son's side. Drawing on the sea imagery so typical of Diome's fiction[19], Arame attempts to reassure her daughter-in-law who is, in her distressed state prior to Lamine's return, unsure as to what her destiny and that of her child holds and in need of guidance:

18 A-L, Toivanen, « Retour au local: *Celles qui attendent* et l'engagement diasporique de Fatou Diome », *RELIEF*, nº 1, 2011, p. 71-71.

19 As noted by Haskell (p. 143), the ocean is a "favorite Diome trope".

> I know why you are crying my dear. But don't worry. Nothing is happening that cannot be contained in a life. Continue to navigate your boat to the best of your ability, and don't be scared of the future. No sandbank awaits you on the horizon, only two arms of the sea: either Lamine forgives you and you stay here with us, this is what I hope for with all my heart, or he rejects you and Ansou will be ecstatic to get you and your daughter back. Whatever happens, your navigation will continue on near someone who loves you. Forgive me for making you the wife of an absentee because all your troubles stem from this. Forgive me my dear[20].

The effect of such a gesture is liberating for Daba who, though at this stage unaware of the parallelism linking her life story to that of her mother-in-law, is deeply touched by Arame's apology and her humble sharing of counsel, support and emotions. If, as Lazar has stated, mentorship "like gratitude is usually in the eyes of the beholden" (Lazar, 1994, p. 27), then Arame's re-enactment of mentor-friendship with her daughter-in-law is reflected in Daba's immense appreciation of her mother-in-law following her apology. For Daba, this is "a woman and a moment experienced together" that she will never forget "whatever her destiny holds" (Diome, 2010, p. 249). Mentor-friendship is symbolised concretely in *Women Who Wait* by Arame's implication in Daba's daughter's rearing. Previously uncertain as to how she should behave towards her daughter-in-law's child and now solicited by Daba for maternal advice, Arame is once again able to endorse the role which pleases her most and gives her life meaning – that of the mother. She is able to use her knowledge of child-raising to help new mother Daba hone her own skills in a non-institutional field of expertise, one that is no less important than any of the traditionally professional ones in which mentoring typically surfaces. The women's communal mothering serves to cement a relationship built on reciprocal exchange of knowledge, counsel, respect and love and suggests, for Daba's infant daughter, a promising future among two women open to both mentoring and being mentored in the name of self-and collective development. The women's enactment of mentor-friendship, coupled with

20 «*Je sais pourquoi tu pleures, ma grande. Mais ne t'en fais pas, il ne se passe rien qui ne puisse se tenir dans une vie. Continue à mener ta barque du mieux que tu peux, et n'aie pas peur de l'avenir. Aucun banc de sable ne t'attend à l'horizon, mais deux bras de mer: ou Lamine te pardonne et tu restes ici avec nous, ce que je souhaite de tout cœur, ou il te rejette et Ansou sera ravi de te récupérer, avec ta fille. Quoi qu'il advienne, ta navigation va se poursuivre auprès de quelqu'un qui t'adore. Pardonne-moi d'avoir fait de toi l'épouse d'un absent, car tous tes soucis découlent de là. Pardonne-moi, ma grande*», Diome, 2010, p. 248.

and complemented by Lamine's successful (in financial terms) migratory experience, therefore produces favourable consequences for this household. The "invisible mental and emotional work" accomplished by Arame in particular and to a lesser extent Daba, may very well be hidden for much of the novel "under the unforgiving concrete routine of daily household tasks." (Haskell, 2016, p. 147). Yet it eventually manages to pierce through at the novel's conclusion. It is furthermore rendered evident when compared to the fate Diome reserves for Bougna and her not so successful mentorship of daughter-in-law Coumba.

Just as Arame's and Daba's stories form mirror images of each other, so too do those of Bougna and her daughter-in-law Coumba. When Issa returns from Europe accompanied by his new European family, Coumba is devastated. She unwittingly finds herself ensnared in a polygamous union that she did not choose and cannot escape due to a lack of financial means much like her mother-in-law. If Bougna is offended by Issa's taking of a second European wife, it is not so much because she sympathises with the deep sense of betrayal and hurt felt by Coumba, after having herself lived through a very similar experience, but more so as she is concerned with the image his choice of wife presents to the community she is so eager to impress. Taking her son aside, she does not hesitate to reprimand Issa for his choice in companion, critiquing the European woman's attire that which she judges to be too revealing and her indiscrete manner of asking unbridled questions (Diome, 2010, p. 237). Not once does Bougna reproach Issa for his immense insensitivity vis-à-vis Coumba's love and devotion and subsequent heartbreak nor manifest any sense of solidarity in regard to these emotions that she would seemingly be well placed to comprehend. Bougna is, as Haskell states, "less reflective" and "inclined to self-examination" than her friend (Haskell, 2016, p. 148). She is unable (unlike Arame) to see that her "excessive ambition" (Diome, 2010, p. 147) for her son and her decision to marry him on the verge of his immigration are to blame for her daughter-in-law's marital misery. Bougna is similarly unable to draw on her own personal experiences of patriarchal oppression to bond with Coumba in a meaningful and productive manner as Arame and Daba were able to do. With her lack of maturity and self-awareness, she persists in believing that she has nothing to learn from both her own past and the experiences of her daughter-in-law. Whereas she engaged in open and reciprocal mentor-friendship with Arame, Bougna sees herself in relation to Coumba as the all-powerful and all-knowledgeable mentor, the giver of lessons with nothing to learn. She is, in *Women Who Wait*, the fictional embodiment of failed mentorship.

Fatou Diome's *Women Who Wait* is a complex and emotion-driven work focused on the experiences of Senegalese women in a distinctly patriarchal and impoverished environment. Reading this text invariably evokes issues of female oppression, empowerment and potential. Central to these concepts is the underlying framework of mentorship as a commonly invoked paradigm and process through which to better one's own circumstances as well as those of one's greater community. *Women Who Wait* does not conform to the traditional, masculinised master-mentee relationships that litter much of Western scholarship and that appear in past works of Diome's, notably in *Le Ventre de l'Atlantique*. It instead places at its heart the informal and intergenerational mentoring models of four non-educated female characters in a non-institutionalised setting. Yet these characters in their day-to-day lives which take place in contexts far removed from any orthodox arena of mentorship, such as university campuses or corporate offices, are no less in need of receiving counsel and comfort while having their own areas of non-formal expertise recognised by others. Successful transmission of knowledge and know-how is shown in this text to be dependent on multidirectional and symmetrical mentor-friendship between women facilitated through reciprocal emotional exchanges leading to greater self-awareness and subsequent self-development. The novel ultimately broadens the perceptions around what it means to mentor and be mentored while reinstating women at the heart of these processes. For mentorship touches human activities beyond the merely and narrowly intellectual revealing a connection that "signifies simultaneously authority and affection, sonship [or daughtership] and the continuity of generations, the gift of knowledge and the production of talent." (Waquet, 2008, p. 310).

Charlotte MACKAY
Monash University
Australia

THE ETHICS OF CARE IN A TRADITIONAL RURAL SOCIETY

Adopting a soul-child in Michela Murgia's Sardinian novel *Accabadora* (2009)

For Sunshine and Pasticcino.

Accabadora is the title of Michela Murgia's second novel published in 2009. Murgia is an Italian writer born in 1972 in Cabras, near Oristano, on the western coast of the Italian island of Sardinia. Her debut novel *Il mondo deve sapere. Romanzo tragicomico di una telefonista precaria* (The World Must Know. The Tragicomic Novel of a Call Centre Operator on a Casual Contract) appeared in 2006[1]. *Accabadora* followed three years later and was awarded numerous prizes, among which the prestigious Campiello literary prize in 2010. The novel quickly reached the status of a bestseller in Italy. It was later translated in more than thirty languages. The English translation by Silvester Mazzarella appeared in 2011. Following *Accabadora*, Murgia went on to publish other three novels, two short stories, nine non-fiction books, two of which as a co-author. She also contributed to the volume *Le nuove Eroidi*, a rewriting of *Heroides* by Latin poet Ovid, with a reworking of Helen's letter to Paris in a contemporary context[2].

1 In 2008 the novel became a successful film, *Tutta la vita davanti* (Her Whole Life Ahead), directed by Paolo Virzì. The movie won, amongst other prizes, the 2009 Golden Globe for best movie.

2 Michela Murgia, « Elena », *Le nuove Eroidi*, Milan, Harper Collins, 2019. Her other novels are: *L'incontro*, Turin, Einaudi, 2012; *Chirú*, Turin, Einaudi, 2015; *Noi siamo tempesta*, Milan, Salani, 2019. The short stories are: « L'aragosta », *Piciocas. Storie di ex bambine dell'isola che c'è*, Bologna and Naples, Caracò, 2012; and « L'eredità », *Sei per la Sardegna*, Turin,

This chapter focuses on the relationship between Maria Listru and Bonaria Urrai, the two main female protagonists of the novel *Accabadora.* At a young age, Maria Listru leaves her birth family to become Bonaria Urrai's 'soul-child' (*fill'e anima*). The term 'soul--child' indicates an unofficial form of adoption practiced in the Italian island of Sardinia until the Seventies. In this coming-of-age novel, the central theme of elective maternity intertwines with another unofficial and mostly undocumented social practice, embodied in the figure of the angel of mercy, present in rural areas and rooted in traditional customs. Maria will have to come to terms with the fact that her elective mother, Bonaria, is an *accabadora*, an angel of mercy: she is in charge of helping the dying to leave life behind. Maria and Bonaria are separated as a result of Maria's traumatic discovery of her elective mother's duties as the local *accabadora*. The novel takes us on a journey through the estrangement between the two women following Maria's discovery, as well as their final rapprochement, when Maria cares for her dying elective mother in the final part of the novel. My reading of the relationship between Maria and Bonaria focuses on the dynamics at play between the two women, which I analyse through the theoretical instruments offered by Adriana Cavarero's ethics of care, particularly as outlined in *Inclinations: A Critique of Rectitude* (2016) and « Inclining the subject: Ethics, alterity and natality » (2011), while also briefly referring to her earlier work *Horrorism: Naming Contemporary Violence* (2011). Central to my analysis remains the fact that the relationship between the two women can be construed as mentor-mentee partnership, especially due to the absence of a legislative framework legitimising this social practice as adoption. It remains, however, that the bond between the two women, albeit for its legal dimension, is much closer to the one formed through adoption.

Einaudi, 2014. The non-fiction books: *Viaggio in Sardegna. Undici percorsi nell'isola che non si vede*, Turin, Einaudi, 2008; *Ave Mary. E la chiesa inventò la donna*, Turin, Einaudi, 2011; *Futuro interiore*, Turin, Einaudi, 2016; *Persone che devi conoscere*, Padua, Messaggero di Sant'Antonio, 2018; *L'inferno è una buona memoria. Visioni da* Le nebbie di Avalon *di Marion Zimmer Bradley*, Venice, Marsilio, 2018; *Istruzioni per diventare fascisti*, Turin, Einaudi, 2018; and *Stai Zitta, e altre nove frasi che non vogliamo sentire più*, Turin, Einaudi, 2021. Finally the two publications as a co-author are: a non-fiction work co-written with radio presenter and writer Loredana Lipperini, *L'ho uccisa perché l'amavo (falso!)*, Rome and Bari, Laterza, 2013; and *Presente*, Bajani *et al.*, Turin, Einaudi, 2012.

Before moving on, I need to add here a necessary explanation: Murgia's 2015 novel *Chirú* deals, and explicitly so, with the theme of mentoring, yet this chapter focuses solely on *Accabadora*. There are several reasons for this exclusion. The first one lies in my interest in the theme of elective motherhood. In *Accabadora*, this specific narrative core is intertwined with a symbolism that elicits an analysis of the character of Bonaria as a manifestation of the Athena/Mentor of the *Odyssey*, as I will explain in more detail in the following section of this chapter. Furthermore, I have omitted *Chirú* due to the motives behind Eleonora's somewhat risky decision to take on the 18-year-old Chirú as a mentee, a thematic thread that diverges from my focus on the ethics of care that moves Bonaria to take Maria as a *fill'e anima*.

Eleonora's decision to take on her first mentee, Teo, is motivated by the fascination she feels for Fabrizio, her lover and friend, and can be viewed as a desire to emulate the person she admires, rather than a response to a request for help. When she meets Fabrizio after an audition, Eleonora finds out that the young actor who performed before her, Riccardo, is not Fabrizio's son as she imagined, rather his mentee. She is so initiated into the world of mentoring and becomes attracted and fascinated by its power dynamics[3]. Perhaps most significantly, the trajectory upon which Eleonora's relationships with her mentees is constructed, despite being predicated on a mother-son template (Eleonora, we know, is twenty years older than Chirú and she sets up her relationship with her mentees following the template offered by Fabrizio and Riccardo), presents a level of risk against which Fabrizio warns her, particularly when she takes on her last pupil, Chirú. There is an insistence, on Eleonora's part, on the matter of trust when she feels attacked by Fabrizio upon revealing to him the age of her new mentee (Murgia, 2015, p. 35-37). In this exchange, Fabrizio shuns trust altogether and instead highlights Chirú's age as the troubling factor:

> Trust is not the issue. How old was Teo, 15? And Alessandro? He was no more than 16. Nin was 17 and he already had you wrapped around his little

3 *"Per quella forma di contagio tra passioni che ammala certe coppie, fu durante la nostra relazione che presi il mio primo allievo"* (Murgia, 2015, p. 50); *"Due to the contagiousness of passions which afflicts some couples, I took on my first pupil during our relationship."* Two pages later, Eleonora reflects on this first experience referring to herself explicitly as a mentor: *"Feci da mentore a Teo per circa quattro anni"* (*ibid.*, p. 52) – "For about four years I was Teo's mentor." My translation. All translations are my own, unless taken from a translated volume included in the List of References.

> finger without you even realising it. What do you think you can get out of an 18-year-old? (*Ibid.*, p. 36)[4].

An explanation for Fabrizio's worries is not provided at this early stage and readers are left to their own conjectures as to what sort of risks Eleonora would face. However, as the novel reaches its final part, Eleonora falls in love and Chirú appears disturbed by her relationship with Martin. In one scene toward the end of the book, Chirú confronts her and asks if she loves him. Eleonora is taken aback and answers that this would be the first time Chirú sees her in love. Here Chirú rebuts that it would be the first time he sees her in love with someone other than himself, and proceeds to kiss her (*ibid.*, 176-182). This turn of events puts an end to the relationship between the two, with Eleonora highlighting that the condition of respect between them has been broken because "those who love guard their power to scare one another as a secret"[5] (*ibid.*, p. 182). Thus this relationship, initially presented by Eleonora as a mentoring one, is revealed as one moved by the predicament of reciprocal attraction, something that Eleonora recognises only after the scene described above and which clarifies the doubts instilled in the readers by Fabrizio's initial warning.

In short, while *Chirú* presents a suitable case-study to discuss the literary representation of the relationship between mentors and mentees, my specific interest in the theme of elective motherhood and the ensuing discussion of an ethics of care, which the relationship between Maria and Bonaria elicit, are the reasons why I decided to omit *Chirú* from my analysis. It is however important to note that, if we move away from the particulars of power dynamics related to the figure of the mother (with which I am concerned with in this chapter), *Chirú* remains a relevant novel to discuss the mentor-mentee binomial. It is indeed a text that presents a model of mentoring more in line with our current understanding of the term and its application to the dimension of day-to-day real life.

Now back to *Accabadora*. As mentioned in the opening paragraphs, there are two major thematic threads in this novel. The first one is that

4 "*La fiducia non c'entra. Quanti anni aveva Teo, quindici? E Alessandro quanti? Non più di sedici. Nin ne aveva diciassette e ti rigirava già attorno a un dito, anche se tu non te ne rendevi conto. Cosa pensi di ricavare da un diciottenne?*" (Murgia, 2015, p. 36).

5 "*Quelli che si amano mantengono segreto il potere di farsi paura a vicenda*" (Murgia, 2015, p. 182).

of the *fill'e anima*, a traditional social practice by which some Sardinian families, for a variety of reasons, decided to give up one or more of their children, generally the youngest one(s), and place them in the care of a trusted person, not necessarily a blood relative. The most common reason for this shift of care was a lack of financial capacity to duly support all the family's offspring.

The second theme is made explicit by the novel's title, which is a Sardinian term rooted in the Spanish verb *acabar*, meaning 'to finish, to terminate'. Neither the term itself nor the role it designates are fictional. The *accabadora* is the woman who ends someone's life. Rather than labelling a murderer, this denomination identifies a sort of angel of mercy, who helps the terminally ill to reach peace. Thus, within the Sardinian society, the *accabadora* fulfills a secretive, revered and feared role in the local communities within which she operates. On the publisher's website the novel is accompanied by a short introduction by Valeria Parrella, who writes:

> Michela Murgia, drawing upon the power of literature, transposes the current debate surrounding euthanasia and the matter of biological wills into a mythical dimension, thus gifting us with the opportunity to consider the question without shouting, with the required intensity and sensitivity[6].

The analysis I present in this chapter unearths the close connections between these two central themes. This interconnection unveils a complex and multilayered ethics of care, which I see as a core element of this novel. Despite its title, which seems to attribute a predominant role to the theme associated with the term *accabadora*, the narrative core of this novel is, in fact, only one and lies in "the hidden aspects of elective maternity". As Murgia explained in the book's catalogue record, formerly available on the publisher's website, she has always been "fascinated by those family relationships which do not have blood ties as their backbone". In these lines she also revealed that this topic sits deeply with her due to her own status as *fill'e anima*, a soul-child. She then adds that she

6 "*Michela Murgia, attingendo alla potenza della letteratura, traspone il dibattito attuale su testamento biologico ed eutanasia in un universo mitico, donandoci la possibilità di tornare a pensarvi senza urlare, con la giusta forza e delicatezza*", https://www.einaudi.it/catalogo-libri/narrativa-italiana-contemporanea/accabadora-michela-murgia-9788806221898.

> deliberately chose to narrate the story from the point of view of the adoptive mother, a woman for whom carrying people to the fulfilment of their destiny is only one of the many shades of maternity, possibly not even the darkest one[7].

Thus, the writer forewarns readers that the theme of euthanasia, encapsulated in the figure of the *accabadora*, is a sub-theme to the central theme of elective maternity, in that the *accabadora* Bonaria Urrai appears as the young Maria Listru's elective mother. This viewpoint is also introduced in the short blurb which presents the novel on the publisher's website:

> [T]he *accabadora* is she who terminates. To her community her actions are not those of a murderer, rather the merciful and loving ones of someone who helps destiny fulfil its course. She is the ultimate mother[8].

THE MENTORING DIMENSION
Bonaria as Athena/Mentor

Before delving into my discussion of the novel, I turn my attention to the term 'mentor', which sits as a premise to my discussion. Mentor is a character from Homer's *Odyssey*. He is a trusted friend of Odysseus and it is the latter who puts him in charge of his household and family, particularly of his young son Telemachus, after his departure to fight in the war for the conquest of Troy (Homer, II, v. 225-227)[9]. There are several passages in the *Odyssey* in which we witness the goddess Athena, disguised as Mentor, providing Telemachus with advice on

---

7 *"Il tema centrale per me resta quello dei lati nascosti della maternità elettiva; sono sempre stata affascinata dalle relazioni famigliari che non hanno il sangue come discriminante. Il tema della maternità elettiva mi appartiene profondamente, perché a mia volta sono fill'e anima; ma per non cadere nella trappola del parallelismo autobiografico, ho scelto volutamente di narrare il rapporto dal punto di vista della madre adottiva, una figura per la quale accompagnare i destini a compimento è solo una delle possibili sfumature della sua maternità, non necessariamente la più oscura."* Unfortunately, the page is no longer available. I last accessed it on 20th September 2016. htpp://www.einaudi.it/speciali/Murgia-Accabadora.

8 *"'[A]ccabadora' è colei che finisce. Agli occhi della comunità il suo non è il gesto di un'assassina, ma quello amorevole e pietoso di chi aiuta il destino a compiersi. Perché è lei l'ultima madre"*, https://www.einaudi.it/catalogo-libri/narrativa-italiana/narrativa-italiana-contemporanea/accabadora-michela-murgia-9788806221898.

9 Homer, *The Odyssey*, trans. by James Huddleston (The Chicago Homer).

what decisions to make and what actions to take[10]. From Book I, we know that the role of Athena, firstly disguised as Mentes, chief of the Taphians, is that of steering Telemachus to rein in Penelope's suitors and to convince him to set forth on a journey to find his father Odysseus and bring him home (*ibid.*, I, v. 80-95; v. 269-305). Upon meeting Telemachus as Mentes in Book I, the goddess infuses his spirit with courage and revives the memory of his father (*ibid.*, I, v. 320-322). In Book II, we then witness Mentor speaking to the men of Ithaca to convince them to free Odysseus' house from the suitors and to support Telemachus in his journey in search of his father. Soon after, Athena approaches Telemachus as Mentor and incites him to take the journey (*ibid.*, II, v. 229-241; v. 67-95).

Our knowledge of Athena's role in the *Odyssey* is an important premise to understand the dynamics at play in the relationship between Bonaria and Maria in *Accabadora*. In Greek mythology, the goddess, we know, represents wisdom, warfare, and handicraft. The fact that Bonaria is a seamstress echoes Athena's patronage of the crafts. Furthermore, in her village, Bonaria is known as a widow but she never married. Admittedly, this is a rather weak connection, as Bonaria was in love in her youth and lost her fiancée to the war. More significantly, villagers address her as *tzia*, which in Sardinian literally means 'lady'. The term is often used to address old women, frequently dressed in black, who are regarded as vessels of memories and old customs; wise women, in other words[11]. Bonaria is also surrounded by an aura of reverence; she is a somewhat feared figure, also by men, due to her duties as the local angel of mercy, a sentiment of which Bonaria is very aware. For instance,

10 See for instance Book III: "Astute Telemachus said back to her in turn: / 'Mentor, how should I go to him, how should I greet him? / I've never had any experience with cunning words, / and it's disgraceful for a young man to interrogate his elder.' / Bright-eyed goddess Athena said back to him: / 'Telemachus, you'll figure out some of this yourself, in your own mind, / and a divinity will advise you on the rest, for, no, I don't think / that you were born and raised against the will of the gods.' / So saying, Pallas Athena led / quickly, and he followed in the footsteps of the goddess." (Homer, III, vv. 21-30).

11 We know this is the way Bonaria dresses from passages in the novel, one of which contrasts the clothes of the teacher, the foreigner *maestra* Luciana, whose style is modern and urban, with the traditional clothes worn by Bonaria: "[T]he teacher in a blue tailor-made houndstooth suit of the kind women wore in the city, and the seamstress in her traditional long skirt with a black shawl round her shoulders." (Murgia, 2011a, p. 21) – "*[L]a maestra vestita con un piccolo tailleur blu pied-de-poule come usavano in città, e la sarta con la sua lunga gonna tradizionale e lo scialle nero sulle spalle.*" (Murgia, 2009, p. 20).

early in the novel, Maria notices the reserved behaviour male customers display when Bonaria takes their measures for a new garment: "[Men] are scared. They know what sort of a coat they might get from me." (Murgia, 2011a, p. 10)[12].

As I have already indicated, in her function as angel of mercy, Bonaria comes to clash with Maria, who confronts her upon finding out that she is an *accabadora* and that she helped Nicola Bastíu commit suicide. Maria accuses her to overstep into a role that is not hers: "If things have to happen, they will happen of themselves when the right time comes." (*Ibid.*, p. 124)[13]. For Maria, death is a matter better left to destiny, the kind of fate which desires that Odysseus' journey home should be long, perilous, and difficult. The gods do intervene to help their favourite champions, albeit within the limits imposed by fate. In Maria's eyes, this is the game Bonaria plays, not just in Nicola's case but in the very function she performs as *accabadora*. Thus, the rupture between the two women occurs when Maria unveils the truth and accuses her elective mother of interfering in those final encounters between life and death, contentions which are not for human beings to meddle with. Along the same line, a further connection to Athena comes shortly before the climax of this dénouement, when a vanquished Bonaria returns home after Nicola's death. Here we see the old woman transformed from an owl, a recurrent symbol of Athena, to a spider trapped in its own web, a sort of novel Arachne punished for her arrogance.

Another aspect to consider in this relationship is that Bonaria takes Maria into her house as a soul-child, a *fill'e anima* (short for *fillus de anima*). I explained that these are children voluntarily given up by the birth parents to be fostered by other adults, not necessarily belonging to the same family network but generally belonging to the same community[14].

---

12 *"Gli uomini hanno paura, non vergogna. Lo sanno loro qual è il cappotto che temono da me."* (Murgia, 2009, p. 10). Here the English translation loses the pun in the original Italian, in which the reader connects the reference to the coat to the expression *'fare il cappotto a qualcuno'*, literally 'making someone a coat', but figuratively 'to kill someone'.

13 *"Non sono io che ho fretta, anzi. Se le cose devono accadere, al momento giusto accadono da sole."* (Murgia, 2009, p. 116).

14 We have proven accounts of this custom from the first decades of the last century, but we know the practice continued until the Seventies. This means that he youngest *fill'e anima* we know of are today in their mid- to late forties. When the Italian government introduced a reform to the Family Law in 1975, this practice was still well rooted in the Sardinian territory.

Initially, Bonaria does not regard herself as Maria's mother, and Maria does not address her as such. The different dimension upon which the relationship between the two women is built is acknowledged by the young Maria:

> [...] [E]verything Tzia Bonaria said was God's law on earth. Yet in all the thirteen years they shared a home, Maria never once called her '*Mamma*', because mothers are something different. (*Ibid.*, 2011a, p. 8, italics in the original)[15].

When the bare word 'mother' appears in the dialogue between these two characters, it is used to refer to Maria's birth mother[16]. Maria's ties to her birth family are not severed: her birth mother calls upon her when help is needed and the girl fulfils to these requests with Bonaria's permission, with the only rule that Maria is not to miss school. Yet, as I discuss in the following section, the mentoring dimension I ascribed to the relationship between the two women is complex and evolving. In the years they spend together, they form a very close bond that brings the two to recognise one another as family. Thus, initially, in the premise set up by the use of the term *fill'e anima*, I argue we can still see a similarity with Mentor in the *Odyssey*, since the latter was "a noble comrade of Odysseus, / and to whom, when he went in his ships, he handed his entire house, / that it obey the old man and that Mentor preserve everything intact." (Homer, II, v. 225-227).

Finally, Bonaria's function is also somewhat comparable to that of Mentor in François Fénelon's *Les Aventures de Télémaque* (The Adventures of Telemachus)[17]. In this work, Mentor acquires a proper tutoring function, with emphasis added to his role of protector and counsellor. Our understanding of the term 'mentor' today has been shaped more strongly by the role played by this character (also a goddess in disguise, but this time latinised as Minerva), rather than the *Odyssey*'s Mentor[18].

15 "*[T]utto quello che diceva Tzia Bonaria era legge di Dio in terra. Eppure in tredici anni che visse con lei, nemmeno una volta Maria la chiamò mamma, che le madri sono una cosa diversa.*" (Murgia, 2009, p. 9).

16 I use the adjective 'bare' because there are instances, at the end on the novel, in which Murgia starts referring to Bonaria as Maria's 'adoptive mother'.

17 François de Salignac de la Mothe Fénelon, *Les Aventures de Télémaque suivies des aventures d'Aritonoüs*, La Haye, Adrian Metjens, 1701 [1699].

18 See, for instance, a short piece in the section 'Letters' of *Science* by Judith B. Klotz, Adjunct Associate Professor, UMDNJ School of Public Health, who, addressing the meaning of the term in today's world, reminds the reader of the origin story (i.e. the

In *Accabadora*, Bonaria's role in the opening of the novel is aligned with the protector figure impersonated by Fénelon's Mentor, something confirmed by the fact that Maria's sense of trust develops from the feeling of protection and safety that she soon starts to experience once under the care of Bonaria (Murgia, 2011a, p. 3). However, as we proceed with the reading, I argue that the character of Bonaria starts resembling more that of Athena, both for the role she plays, as well as due to the various facets she will come to show as her character develops.

ELECTIVE MOTHERHOOD
Adopting a *fill'e anima* or soul-child

If Mentor was originally the substitute for an absent father, in the novel I discuss here the young child, Maria, "a mistake after three things right" – her three older siblings (*ibid.*, p. 1), is given away by her birth mother and is consigned to the care of another woman. Thus, the theme of elective motherhood, as opposed to the centrality of the father-figure we recognise in the story of Telemachus and Mentor, is of particular significance.

In her discussion on the theme of care, the Italian philosopher Adriana Cavarero highlights how an ethics of care implies a movement outwards, towards the subject who is being cared for. In other words, the ethics of care can be spatially represented as the caregiver geometrically inclined on an axis moving away from its own vertical posture: it is a subject who shifts its internal barycentre towards an 'other', thereby putting its own physical stability, as well as its autonomy, at risk[19]. In a book

Odyssey) associated to this term and draws a distinction with Fénelon's Mentor (Judith B. Klotz, « Meetings with Mentor », *Science, New Series*, n° 308, 2005, p. 1112).

19 Adriana Cavarero, *Inclinations: A Critique of Rectitude*, trans. by Amanda Minervini and Adam Sitze, Stanford CA, Stanford University Press, 2016. The concept returns throughout the text: "As we might say with Arendt, the thrust of inclination knocks the I from its internal center of gravity and, by making it lean to the outside, 'be they objects or people,' undermines its stability. Besides posing a moral problem for the modern conception of the self, inclination is a matter of structural equilibrium and thus, in the end, becomes an ontological question as well. An inclined I, leaning towards the outside, is no longer straight: it leans forward with respect to the vertical line that

chapter on the same topic, turning to Hannah Arendt's *The Human Condition*[20], Cavarero observes that:

> Arendt regards natality as a fundamental aspect of our being human and therefore identifies it with the "naked fact of our original physical appearing", [...] This means [...] that each human being is, first of all, exposed to the mother. (Cavarero, 2011b, p. 199).

Cavarero goes on specifying that "[m]other [...] is thus above all the name of an inclination over the other; or, differently told, the function that evokes the figure of responsibility engendered on the inaugural scene of a human condition in which helplessness is the mark of the beginner." (*Ibid.*, p. 201).

In her discussion, Cavarero does not fail to point out that the inclination which we commonly refer to as 'maternal inclination' is not in itself an automatic response, rather a potential predisposition to respond:

> It is commonly understood that the maternal is, for women, an *inclination*. Which is plausible. Not, however, in the sense, usually invoke, that feminine nature is inclined to maternity; but rather in the sense, truer to the etymology of the term, that "every inclination turns outwards, it leans out of the self. (*Ibid.*, p. 197-198)[21].

In this sense the figure of the birth mother in the novel, Anna Teresa Listru, is an example of a woman who, for various reasons, we do not witness in an inclined position, bent over towards the infant Maria:

---

supports it and that, because it allows it to balance itself, makes it an autonomous and independent subject." (*Ibid.*, p. 6). In later passages, for instance in chapter 12 'Schemata for a Postural Ethics', Cavarero spells out the idea of inclination as connected to an act of self-exposure to vulnerability and also links it to the scene of maternity: "[T]he imaginary of maternity permits a shift of attention from a subject modeled on the idea of autonomy to a subjectivity structurally characterized by dependence and exposure, from the assertions of a self-consistent and partitioned subjectivity to a subjectivity that is open and relational. In this way, the free and rational subject's supposed integrity, free from all constraint, allows space for an originary and structural vulnerability, which is emphasized precisely in the fateful moment of beginning, when the new creature appears to the world and surrenders to another (who is, normally and in ordinary experience, the mother)." (*Ibid.*, p. 122). In the first extract, Cavarero quotes from Hannah Arendt's *Some Questions of Moral Philosophy* (Hannah Arendt, *Responsibility and Judgement*, New York, Shocken Books, 2003, p. 81).

20 Hannah Arendt, *The Human Condition*, Chicago, The University of Chicago Press, 1958.

21 Cavarero quotes again from Arendt's *Some Questions of Moral Philosophy* (Arendt, 2003, p. 82).

> Mother, [...] even if assumed as a name denoting an unbalanced inclination towards the other, does not coincide, necessarily, with the self-renouncing, oblative figure of the good mother. (*Ibid.*, p. 201).

Contrasting with Anna Teresa Listru, Bonaria, already predisposed to an ethics of care (she tends to another form of vulnerability and helplessness, namely the dying), responds to this call, and elects to care for Maria. Bonaria is aware that Maria is not getting the care she needs in order to flourish. This knowledge further reinforces the idea that Maria is better off under her care than living with her birth mother:

> [Bonaria] knew the world she was taking the girl from; in fact she knew it so well she had never felt any need to be aware of its every form. So she had not been surprised that Maria had never shown any obvious homesickness since deep down, in the privacy of her solitary infancy, the girl must always have known that her destiny did not lie in her old home. (Murgia, 2011a, p. 44)[22].

Here we can see the return of a reference to that 'destiny', which I linked to the role played by fate in governing the world of mythological gods and heroes in ancient Greek literature. Not only does Bonaria plays with matters of life and death, a realm traditionally viewed as one that lies beyond our (legitimate) control, here we see how she is inclined to think that Maria understood her destiny as that of joining *tzia*'s house, thus thriving in her care. In other words, we are called to reflect on how Bonaria's actions seem to be competing with the forces of destiny: Bonaria, elective mother to the vulnerable and helpless (the infant and the dying, to whom she is, as mentioned earlier, the ultimate mother), plays with and potentially alters the planned course of life.

Cavarero explicitly mentions this connotation of the child as the ultimate form of vulnerability:

> Vulnerable creature, the child is totally given to the action, benign or malign, of the one bending over him. In this sense, the infant embodies in an exemplary way the other as helpless. And in this sense, it is symptomatically indifferent whether the child in question is a boy or a girl. [...] His or her vulnerability,

22 "*[Bonaria] sapeva a quale mondo stava sottraendo la bambina, e per esserne certa non era stato necessario neppure averne visto tutti gli anfratti; per questo non si era stupita che Maria non avesse mai manifestato alcuna nostalgia evidente, come se in fondo, nell'immanenza propria delle infanzie solitarie, avesse sempre saputo che il suo destino non era lì.*" (Murgia, 2009, p. 40-41).

> as the primary mark of the human condition, [...] is regardless of gender. (Cavarero, 2011b, p. 200).

In an earlier work, *Horrorism*, Cavarero also remarked how that which is a condition in the child, helplessness, can return in the form of a circumstance for the adult and we know that Bonaria deals with the helpless in her role as *accabadora*[23]. These considerations help understand Murgia's identification of her novel's major theme as elective maternity.

On the theme of maternity, it is also significant that in *Accabadora* the figure leaning outwards from its own vertical axis, the caregiver, is a woman. The representation of the subject caring for a child as an inclined subject, Cavarero suggests, is "predictably gendered as female." We can easily see here that the attribution of a specific gender to this role seems to follow an Aristotelian dichotomy whereby men exist for themselves and the political community they contribute to create, and women exist for others. Yet, following Arendt's own argument, Cavarero highlights that, in the caring for the infant

> an *other* [...] is indeed always part of the picture and, even if substituted by someone else, she inhabits, under the name of 'mother', its imaginary. Generated by an infinite chain of other mothers that goes back to the beginning of time, she generates vulnerable beings and, above all, as well as beyond the act of procreation, she plays the role, never symbolically superseded, of the one who is responsible *for them.* [...] [T] he mother is a necessary part of the picture, but not due to the title she earns from the act of generation. Rather, she plays the role [...] of the one who, bending over the infant, is par excellence responsible for his vulnerability in the context of the relation. (Cavarero, 2011b, p. 200-201, emphasis in the original).

Anna Teresa Listru is a widow and is struggling to support her four children. Maria, her youngest daughter, is four years old at the time and has no father figure worthy of the name. Her birth mother decides to place her in the care of another old woman. Hence the young Maria does not gain a father figure in this exchange, something which occurred to Telemachus, but does move into a house where she will be properly

23 "Though she remains vulnerable as long as she lives, from the first to the last day of her singular existence, and adult falls back into defenselessness only in certain circumstances. She is always vulnerable but only sometimes helpless, as contingency dictates and with a variable degree of intensity." Adriana Cavarero, *Horrorism: Naming Contemporary Violence*, trans. by William McCuaig, New York, Columbia University Press, 2011, p. 31.

cared for by Bonaria. The villagers are surprised at this turn of events. They understand very well Anna Teresa Listru's decision to give up her youngest daughter, but they struggle to understand why Bonaria would want to take on a soul-child at her age:

> It was perfectly clear to the people of Soreni why Anna Teresa Listru had given her youngest daughter to the old woman. [...] Anna Teresa Listru loved to complain to her neighbours that her husband had been useless even in death since he had not even had the grace to snuff it in the war so as to leave her with a pension. [...] But now that Tzia Bonaria had asked if she could take Maria as her own daughter, it was almost beyond Anna Teresa's wildest dreams that she could add a couple of potatoes grown on the Urrai property to her soup every day. [...]
>
> But no-one had the slightest idea why Tzia Bonaria Urrai at her age should have wanted to take another woman's daughter into her home. (Murgia, 2011a: 4)[24].

From my earlier discussion, we know that Bonaria had no doubt Maria could not thrive in her birth mother's house, and that Maria did not initially regard her as a mother figure. The relationship between the two women changes quickly, as soon as Maria starts noticing how she is not treated as a nuisance in Bonaria's house:

> [...] Maria, arriving too late into her mother's womb, had always known she was the last concern in a family already weighed down with cares. But now, in the house of this woman, she began to experience the unfamiliar feeling that she mattered. She knew, when she set off for school in the morning, holding tight her textbook, that she had only to turn to see her benefactor standing watching her, leaning against the frame of the door as if holding it up. (*Ibid.*, p. 3)[25].

24 "*Perché Anna Teresa Listru avesse dato la figlia minore alla vecchia, a Soreni lo si capiva anche troppo bene. [...] Con le vicine, Anna Teresa Listru amava lagnarsi di come il marito non fosse riuscito a esserle utile nemmeno in morte, avendo magari la buona grazia di crepare in guerra per lasciarle una pensione. [...] Adesso che Tzia Bonaria aveva chiesto Maria in figlia, non le sembrava vero di poter infilare tutti i giorni nella minestra anche due patate dei terreni degli Urrai. [...] Perché invece Tzia Bonaria Urrai si fosse presa in casa la figlia di un'altra a quell'età, davvero non lo capiva nessuno.*" (Murgia, 2009, pp. 5-6).

25 "*Maria [...] era arrivata troppo tardi anche nel ventre di sua madre, e sin da subito aveva fatto l'abitudine a essere l'ultimo pensiero di una famiglia che ne aveva già troppi. Invece in casa di quella donna sperimentava l'insolita sensazione di essere diventata importante. Quando la mattina si lasciava alle spalle la porta e stringeva il sussidiario verso la scuola, aveva la certezza che se si fosse voltata l'avrebbe trovata lí a guardarla, appoggiata allo stipite come a reggerne i cardini.*" (Murgia, 2009, p. 5).

The unobtrusive attention Bonaria displays towards Maria establishes a foundation of mutual trust upon which the relationship between the two women grows.

The closeness and reciprocal fondness developed by these two characters is most noticeable in the episode in which Bonaria is summoned to school by Maria's teacher, the Piedmontese *maestra* Luciana. The status of foreigner inhabited by the teacher is initially highlighted by her modern clothes, which contrasts with the traditional long skirt and black shawl worn by Bonaria. But this externally visible difference marks a more significant cultural divide, which is articulated in the conversation that follows. After a brief exchange on Maria's achievements at school, Luciana Tellani's remarks veer towards the relationship between Maria and Bonaria:

> "It's strange, you know, this business of being a 'child of the soul'..."
> "What's strange about it? Bonaria's voice was expressionless.
> "Maria does not seem to have been affected by it. Does she often see her birth family?"
> "Yes, whenever she asks to. Why should she feel resentment?"
> [...] "Well, it seems to me rather strange that a little girl should be taken away... with consent, of course, but anyway, that she should be taken away from her family in this way, without showing any sign of trauma."
> "There's nothing strange about it [...]. "It's not strange at all."
> [...] The two women parted in a silence weighted with ambivalent tension: one sorry not to have said more at the exact point where the other was convinced she had heard more than enough. (*Ibid.*, 22-23)[26].

In the novel, the teacher's concerns over the practice of taking on a *fill'e anima* highlight her foreignness, even more markedly than her clothes do. We intuit she regards the practice as a sign of the backwardness of this rural and insular society. She is furthermore surprised that Maria does not seem to show signs of the trauma she must have suffered as a consequence of being relinquished to the care of the old woman. In fact,

26 "*– È strano sa, questa cosa del figlio d'anima... – Perché è strano? – il tono di Bonaria era inerspressivo. – Maria non sembra averne affatto risentito. Vede spesso la sua famiglia d'orgine? – Sí, ogni volta che lo chiede. Perché doveva risentirne? [...] – Be', è che mi sembra una cosa cosí insolita che una bambina venga sottratta... consensualmente, per carità, ma comunque che venga via dalla famiglia cosí, senza mostrare traumi... – Non è strano [...]. Non è strano. [...] Le due donne si separarono in un silenzio reso pesante da una tensione ambivalente: una di loro rimpiangeva di non aver detto abbastanza, proprio dove l'altra era convinta di aver sentito anche troppo.*" (Murgia, 2009, pp. 21-23).

she reveals that she is rather surprised that, when asked to draw a picture of her parents, it is Bonaria whom Maria portrays: "[...] Maria always draws you and not her real mother." (*Ibid.*)[27]. Soon after, when questioned about what she meant by 'real mother', the teacher is quick to clarify that she intended to refer to Maria's 'natural mother'. Disoriented by the clarification sought by Bonaria, she also adds that she has no intention of interfering in the relationship between the two women. In her characteristically sparingly bare manner, Bonaria closes this exchange by declaring that Maria's 'natural mother' in the one she draws when asked to do so.

When Bonaria returns home, Maria is eager and nervous to know what the teacher had to say about her. The conversation that follows takes on an interesting turn when, in the attempt to show Maria that learning standard Italian is important even in Soreni, where everyone uses Sardinian, the old woman leads Maria on a rather unexpected line of reasoning. After Bonaria underlined that Sardinia too is part of Italy, Maria affirms in a heightened tone that she saw the sea separating the island from the continent on a map.

> "Maria, whose daughter are you?"
> [...] "I'm the daughter of Anna Teresa Listru and Sisinniu Listru",
> "Quite right. And where do you live?"
> [...] "I live here with you, Tzia",
> "So you live separate from your mother, but you are still her daughter. Isn't that so? You don't live together, but you are still mother and daughter." (*Ibid.*, p. 25)[28].

In a cunning yet straightforward fashion, very much in line with her overall attitude and personality, Bonaria joins together the concept of the mother with that of language. However, she does so in a somewhat capsized perspective that may surprise the reader but not Maria, who quickly grasps where Bonaria is leading the encounter. Bonaria's metaphor implies the existence of two mothers: a birth mother (standard Italian / Anna Teresa Listru), and an elective mother (Sardinian/Bonaria).

Rather than reading this passage as a contradiction to the position she voiced in her exchange with the teacher, I argue that Bonaria is

27 "*– [...] Maria disegna lei e non la vera madre...*" (Murgia, 2009, p. 22).

28 "*– Maria, tu di chi sei figlia? [...] – Di Anna Teresa Listru e Sisinnio Listru... – Giusto. E però dove vivi? [...] – ... Vivo qui con voi, Tzia. – Quindi vivi staccata da tua madre, ma sei sempre sua figlia. È così? Non vivete insime, ma siete madre e figlia.*" (Murgia, 2009, pp. 24-25).

reinforcing the concept that, on a substantial level, family is associated with caregiving. Blood relations exist and have to be acknowledged but an ethics of care is never exclusively built upon genetic ties. Mother is she who cares and provides for the child. As Cavarero notices, maternal inclination is not, per se, an ever-present response to a call directed to the gendered female being[29]. The inclined subject is the one who poses her own balance at risk to lean outwards, towards the vulnerable and helpless:

> [T]he scene of the mother who bends over the infant, is not yet a response, but only a predisposition to respond. [...] [I]t is a leaning out over the helpless creature who [...] becomes himself a request. [...] [T]o hold oneself upright and turn around to go elsewhere, means to avoid, and escape from, the request [...]. It corresponds [...] to evil as expression of irresponsibility [...]. Feeding on the drama of this irresponsibility, the [...] narrative of the abandonment of the infant gives evidence precisely to this prejudicial form of violence, [...] ascribable to the actions of an inflexible and self-referential self standing on its vertical axis. Turned outwards, bending over, responsive, this alternative is typical of a self that leans out over the other, conspicuously abandoning its own balance. (Cavarero, 2011b, pp. 202-203).

Bonaria does not seek to replace Anna Teresa Listru; she does not need to do so. Following Arendt/Cavarero, on the scene of natality, the scene of our first appearance, Anna Teresa Listru is the (birth) mother, the one who generated Maria, the first human being Maria appeared to; yet it will take six years for Maria to find another mother figure (the elective mother) consciously ready to incline outwards to nurture her growth[30]. Maria arrives at this conclusion on her own after Bonaria brought her point home:

> We are mother and daughter, yes... but not really a family. If we'd been a family she would never have come to an arrangement with you... I mean, I think of you as my family. Because you and I are closer. (Murgia, 2011a, p. 27)[31].

29 "[I]n the maternal inclination, care is not an automatic or inevitable response." (Cavarero, 2011b, p. 203).

30 Significantly, acknowledging her own status of *fill'e anima*, Murgia dedicates the novel "[t]o my mother. Both of them" ("*A mia madre. Tutt'e due*").

31 "*– Siamo mamma e figlia, sí... ma non proprio una famiglia. Se eravamo una famiglia, non si metteva d'accordo con voi... cioè, io credo che voi siete la mia famiglia. Perché noi siamo piú vicine.*" (Murgia, 2009, p. 25).

We know Maria's position is shared by Bonaria, whose words seal Maria in the embrace of care:

> Instinctively [Bonaria] pressed the little girl's head against her lap as if to warm it. [...] "You became my daughter the very moment I first saw you, when you didn't even know who I was. (*Ibid.*, p. 26)[32].

ANGEL OF MERCY
The ultimate act of caring for the helpless

In this section, I start my analysis by considering Michela Murgia's reference to the "dark shades of maternity" I mentioned earlier. With this comment the writer hints at the fact that the elective mother, Bonaria, is known in the fictional community of Soreni as an *accabadora*. However, Maria initially only knows her as a seamstress, notwithstanding her feeling that there is something more to Bonaria, something that she cannot grasp. At the start of chapter two, we read that: "For some time Maria thought that Tzia Bonaria was a seamstress. She would spend hours at a time sewing, and one of the rooms was always full of remnants and pieces of cloth." (*Ibid.*, p. 10)[33].

Maria's discovery is paced throughout the pages of this novel. Two years after Maria left the house of her birth mother to live with Bonaria, the girl, now eight years old, notices for the first time that the old woman did not spend every night home. It is night-time and, after Bonaria has taken her to the bedroom for an early night, Maria hears a knock on the front door. Maria gets up from her bed, but she manages to catch just a glimpse of a male figure standing in the shadows of the hall when Bonaria and the visitor notice she is awake:

> "The child!" the man said in a low voice [...]. Tzia was instantly before her, black and severe in the long woollen shawl she only wore when she went

32 *"Con un gesto istintivo [Bonaria] prese la testa della ragazzina e se la strinse al grembo, come per scaldarla. [...] – Tu sei diventata mia figlia nel momento stesso in cui ti ho visto, e non sapevi ancora nemmeno chi ero."* (Murgia, 2009, pp. 25-26).

33 *"Per qualche tempo Maria pensò che Tzia Bonaria facesse la sarta. Cuciva per molte ore di seguito, e una stanza della casa era sempre piena di scampoli e stoffe."* (Murgia, 2009, p. 9).

> out to keep appointments. The shawl enclosed her lean body as tightly as a jewel-case, concealing both her figure and her intentions, whatever they may have been.
>
> "Go back to your room",
>
> Maria could not see her face, perhaps the reason she had the courage to ask questions.
>
> "Where are you going Tzia? What's happening?"
>
> "I'll be back soon. But you go to your room." (*Ibid.*, p. 12)[34]

The reader senses that the man has come to ask for the *accabadora*'s services. The aura of mystery and fearful reverence surrounding Bonaria in this specific scene, which happens early only in the novel, is a mechanism used by Murgia to allow readers to experience first-hand Maria's feelings of confusion at the realisation that there is a secretive, uncanny dimension to Bonaria's life. Yet the relationship between Maria and Bonaria is presented, as we have seen, in a positive light: the two women have formed a bond of reciprocal trust and love; they sincerely care for one another. Murgia is careful to portray this reciprocity as a welcomed exception and a rather unusual reality when compared to the other less fortunate children of Soreni, who do not generally experience this level of care and respect within their own birth families.

I argue that in this relatively short nocturnal scene, we can start appreciating the intertwined nature of the two major themes upon which the novel is constructed, elective maternity and euthanasia, of which the latter is only a shade of the former, as Murgia pointed out. In this novel, both images (the elective mother and the angel of mercy) sprout from the same seed, that of providing for the vulnerable and helpless, be it in the form of nurturing growth, Maria's material and personal growth, or helping the dying embrace death in peace. In the years Maria spends in the house of Bonaria as a soul-child, she collects a series of isolated episodes that only later is she able to piece together to come to the truth about her elective mother's mysterious duties. The discovery, facilitated by her close friend Andría's revelation, shatters Maria's world:

34 "*– La bambina! – ammoní a mezza voce l'uomo [...]. Tzia le fu subito innanzi, nera e severa nel lungo scialle di lana che usava solo quando usciva per le feste comandate. Lo teneva chiuso come uno scrigno intorno al corpo magro, celando in quel modo le forme e l'intento, quale che fosse. – Torna in camera tua. Maria non le vedeva il viso, e forse fu per questo che osò replicare. – Dove andate, Tzia? Cosa succede? – Torno presto. Tu però vai in camera tua.*" (Murgia, 2009, p. 13).

> "But I [...] had a brother! He said angrily. Then he added maliciously: "And now Bonaria Urrai has killed him [for me]",
>
> Maria looked at him in astonishment; with his twisted face and reddened eyes Andría seemed to her to have taken leave of his senses.
>
> [...] "Andrí, you have no idea what you're talking about," she said, taking back the towel and beginning to fold it.
>
> "No, I mean it. She killed him." (*Ibid.*, p. 111)[35]

Andría's dramatic and angry revelation followed Maria's refusal to marry him, a proposal that comes to Maria suddenly and unexpectedly from a close friend, one she held as dear as a brother, after he experienced the premature death of his brother, Nicola. Nicola's death did indeed happen with the intervention of the *accabadora* on the night of All Saints. Yet Nicola was not dying. Bonaria's decision to help Nicola achieve what he wants, what we would call assisted suicide nowadays, is a central node in the internal development of Bonaria as a character.

The young man was shot in the leg upon setting fire to Manuele Porresu's property, in a war about the border between the two adjacent properties that went back four years. He had to have his leg amputated, something he views as a death sentence. When Bonaria pays him a visit, Nicola asks her to help him kill himself.

> Bonaria suddenly sprang out of her chair as if she had been scalded, took several steps towards the window as to have her back to Nicola, and when she turned around again the expression in her eyes was one he had never seen before.
>
> "You're talking about things that have nothing to do with you, and Santino is wrong to do the same. And whatever he said, the two cases have nothing in common. Giacomo Littorra was dying",
>
> "And I'm already dead but they can't bury me."
>
> [...] "Do you really think my job is to kill people who haven't the courage to face their problems?"
>
> "No, I believe it's to help those who can't bear to suffer any more",

35 "*– Io lo avevo [...] un fratello! – urlò lui rabbiosamente. Poi aggiunse con cattiveria: – E Bonaria Urrai me l'ha ucciso. Maria lo guardò stupita, ma con il viso stravolto e gli occhi arrossati Andría le apparve come privo di senno. [...] – Andrí, non sai quello che dici, – mormorò recuperando l'asciugamano e cominciando a piegarlo. – Invece lo so. Lo ha ucciso lei.*" (Murgia, 2009, p. 103). Here I would like to add a comment to the English translation of this passage. When Andría accuses Bonaria for the first time, his line should read simply "[a]nd now Bonaria Urrai has killed him", Mazzarella's translation, with a "for me" at the end of Andría's line, misleads the reader and fails to capture the function of the personal pronoun in the original Italian, "*me* l'ha ucciso", which is a signal of emphasis.

> "That's Our Lord's job, not mine. Doing what is right has never mattered to you, so are you now trying to get me to do what is wrong?" (*Ibid.*, p. 71)[36].

Despite Bonaria's categorical refusal, Nicola continues to wait and hope for her help. Bonaria and Maria visit Nicola's house every day and, on one of these occasions, Nicola has an opportunity to face her with his request once more while they are alone. At the end of this exchange, Nicola threatens to act on his own if Bonaria continues to reject his pleading.

The words used by Nicola and his threat to kill himself on his own bring Bonaria back to a distant day of her youth, before her fiancée, Raffaele Zincu, left for the Great War. Without having got the call yet, Raffaele mentioned to her the possibility he would not return or would return severely injured. His words echoed those pronounced by Nicola:

> Maybe you can imagine having me back as a worm, but I'd rather die full of life ten times over than have to live ten years like a dead man. If that happens to me I shall do what Barranca did and shoot myself. (*Ibid.*, p. 91)[37].

On the night of All Saints, when traditionally the main door is left open for the dead souls' dinner, Bonaria sneaks into the house and through the door of Nicola's room, left ajar for her. She finally answers his plea. Andría is keeping vigil, keen to catch a glimpse of the dead souls who at night will visit his house to consume their dinner. He follows the black shadow and witnesses the events in Nicola's room, initially convinced he is observing a dead soul taking his brother's life, attracted by the open door of Nicola's room. But when Bonaria is leaving the house, moonlight shines, and Andría recognises her crying face. When home, Bonaria sits in front of the fire where Maria,

36 "*Con uno scatto improvviso Bonaria si alzò dalla sedia come se scottasse; fece qualche passo verso la finestra facendo in modo di dargli le spalle, e quando si voltò aveva negli occhi un'espressione che Nicola non le aveva mai visto. – Stai parlando di cose che non ti spettano, e Santino ha sbagliato a fare lo stesso. In ogni caso, qualunque cosa ti abbia detto, non sono casi nemmeno vicini. Giacomo Littorra stava morendo. – E io sono morto già, ma non mi possono sotterrare. [...] – Credi davvero che il mio compito sia ammazzare chi non ha il coraggio di affrontare le difficoltà? – No, credo sia aiutare chi lo vuole a smettere di soffrire. – Quello è il compito di Nostro Signore, non il mio. Non hai mai creduto nelle cose giuste, adesso vuoi insegnare a me quelle sbagliate?*" (Murgia, 2009, p. 66).

37 "*– Forse tu puoi sopportare l'idea di avermi indietro come un verme, ma io preferirei morire dieci volte da vivo che vivere anche solo dieci anni come uno che è morto. Se mi succede una cosa simile, faccio come Barranca e mi sparo.*" (Murgia, 2009, p. 84).

unaware of the old woman's movements the previous night, finds her in the morning "bound up in her black shawl like a spider trapped in her own web" (*ibid.*, p. 101)[38].

It is important here to highlight how, when Bonaria finally agrees to help Nicola, she does so in good faith, in other words thinking of answering a plea for peace. Murgia leaves very little doubt about the fact that Bonaria is aware and attentive when navigating the murky waters separating an act of mercy from violence. Besides the internal turmoil she experiences after Nicola's death, readers are aware of a previous episode in which a local family called the *accabadora* to ease *Tziu* Jusepi Vargiu's transition to death. But we know that, upon visiting him, Bonaria exits his bedroom cursing all bystanders for calling upon her when the man was not dying at all and was rather being starved to death by his own family[39].

Back to the moment Maria finds her in the morning, this image of the spider reflects Bonaria's heavy heart, grief, and harrowing doubts about her own actions. From the episode mentioned above and from the preceding passage in the novel, we know that she views her duty as that of helping those who are due to cross into death. If we think of the scene in terms of Cavarero's framework, her duty, as *accabadora*, is that of responding to a request for mercy: the *accabadora* bends over the sick or elder, another personification of the helpless, to answer his or her plea for mercy. It is a plea to cut the hair strand which keeps the sufferer attached to life. To this end, the *accabadora* performs a ritual which includes clearing the supplicant's room of all holy objects, religious images, and well-wishing gifts responsible for locking the supplicant into the world of suffering, as this is what the world of the living has turned into for these souls.

Yet, in the opening of chapter 12, we see Bonaria troubled by what just happened with Nicola:

> The *accabadora* shed only a few tears as she left the Bastíu's house, burdened though she was by Nicola's breathing, but each tear cut a new furrow in her already well-lined face. (*Ibid.*, p. 99-100).

In the following lines, we learn that she was barely fifteen when she "first responded to a deathbed plea for peace" and "from then on she

38 "*[R]aggomitolata nello scialle nero come un ragno intrappolato nella sua stessa tela.*" (Murgia, 2009, p. 93).

39 The episode is narrated in chapter 6 (Murgia, 2011a, p. 54-59 and Murgia, 2009, p. 50-55).

had never had any problem distinguishing between compassion and crime." (*Ibid.*)[40]. In stark contrast, she is now heavily burdened by what she saw in Nicola's eyes in his last moments, "not a determination to find peace, but determination to find an accomplice." (*Ibid.*, p. 100)[41].

In these two pages, we witness a dramatic transformation: in a symbolic punishment for overstepping the line separating compassion from murder, in other words for transgressing the boundaries within which the *accabadora* answers a plea for mercy, Bonaria/Athena realises she is rather Arachne. Arachne's vanity and disregard for the gods, a sentiment exemplified by the design on the cloth she wove, condemned her to this metamorphosis famously narrated in Ovid's eponymous work[42]. The chapter opens with a reference to Athena through the image of an owl, an animal closely associated to the goddess that in the theriomorphic tradition represents her wisdom. Athena Glaukopis can see through the darkness[43], when common mortals are almost blind:

> Like owl's eyes, some thoughts cannot tolerate the full light of day. Such thoughts can only be born at night, when they work like the moon, moving

40 "*Non aveva pianto molto mentre veniva via da casa dei Bastíu portandosi il peso del respiro di Nicola, ma ognuna di quelle lacrime aveva lasciato un solco nuovo sul volto dell'accabadora già segnato dal tempo*", (Murgia, 2009, p. 92). "*[…] Aveva visto acconsentire per la prima volta a una richiesta di pace fatta in letto di morte.*" (Murgia, 2009, p. 92). "*[M]ai da allora le era venuto il dubbio di non essere capace di distinguere tra la pietà e il delitto.*" (Murgia, 2009, p. 93). Here again I would like to make a point about the English text: Mazzarella's translation leads the reader to understand that Bonaria performed this ritual for the first time when she was not yet fifteen. However, on this occasion, Bonaria witnessed other women responding to this deathbed plea, essentially becoming part of the ritual. Bonaria's actual role is nevertheless important, as a young girl would have not been thrusted solo into this position.

41 "*Mai prima di quella sera, quando negli occhi di Nicola aveva letto la determinazione di chi cerca disperatamente non la pace, ma un complice.*" (Murgia, 2009, p. 93).

42 Ovid, *Metamorphoses. Volume I: Books 1-8*, trans. by Frank Justus Miller, Loeb Classical Library, Cambridge MA, Harvard University Press, 1916; Book 6.

43 With regard to the meaning of this epithet, Luzzatto and Pompas explain: "*[…] [L]a problematica dicitura 'glaucopide' riferita ad Atena, in Omero, si è prestata a molte interpretazioni: per alcuni autori è da intendersi come 'occhi azzurri', da glaukós, azzurro, che significava anche 'lucente', 'scintillante', 'bigio', 'verde-azzurro' e 'verdastro'; per altri è da intendersi come 'occhi di civetta' nella loro accezione di 'occhi che vedono tutto, occhi che vedono nell'oscurità.*'" Lia Luzzatto and Ranata Pompas, *Il significato dei colori nelle civiltà antiche*, Milan, Rusconi, 1988, p. 133-134; "In Homer, the problematic term 'Glaukopis' in reference to Athena has been interpreted in various ways: for some authors it is to be understood as 'light blue-eyed', as derived from glaukós, light blue, which also meant 'shiny', 'bright', 'greyish', 'blue-green', and 'greenish'; for other authors, the term is to be understood as 'owl-eyed' in the sense of 'eyes that see everything, eyes that see through darkness.'"

> tides of feeling to some invisible distant part of the soul. Bonaria Urrai had many thoughts of this kind, and over the years had learnt how to control them, patiently choosing on which nights to let them surface. (Murgia, 2011a, p. 99)[44].

Nicola's death and the realisation that his plea was not for her to answer hurl the old woman back into the realm of common mortals and we now see Bonaria the spider, trapped in her own web.

This relatively brief passage is followed by the news of Nicola's death. Andría's revelation to Maria comes precisely on the day of Nicola's funeral while

> in that house an unreal lament was in progress not for one but three deaths: the life of Nicola, the innocence of Andría, and Maria Listru's trust in Bonaria Urrai. (*Ibid.*, p. 112)[45].

Maria's realisation is accompanied by the shock at the part played by her elective mother. The web enveloping Bonaria is thus made even thicker by the loss of Maria's trust and the anger conveyed by the latter in the confrontation between the two women which follows suit:

> "All those times when you came back at night..." she said.
>
> "I would have told you when the right moment came, Maria", Bonaria made no attempt to ease the girl's distress.
>
> "When? When would you have told me? Would you have taken me with you? Would you have asked me to hold your shawl while you did it?" Anger grew on Maria's lips like a bitter foam. "When would you have done that?"
>
> "Not now, certainly. When you were ready for it",
>
> "Ready!" The word echoed in the room like an object flung to the floor. "I would never have been ready to accept the idea that you killed people!"
>
> [...] "Don't start giving names to things you don't understand, Maria Listru. You will be faced by many choices you won't want to make in life,

44 *"Come gli occhi della civetta, ci sono pensieri che non sopportano la luce piena. Non possono nascere che di notte, dove la loro funzione è la stessa della luna, necessaria a smuovere maree di senso in qualche invisibile altrove dell'anima. Di quei pensieri Bonaria Urrai ne aveva diversi, e aveva imparato nel tempo a prendersene cura, scegliendo con pazienza in quali notti farseli sorgere dentro."* (Murgia, 2009, p. 92).

45 *"[I]n quella casa si sta[va] consumando in spazi diversi il pianto funebre non di una, ma di tre perdite: il respiro di Nicola, l'innocenza di Andría, e la fiducia di Maria Listru in Bonaria Urrai."* (Murgia, 2009, p. 104-105). I should add that the traditional funeral customs referred to in this novel, such as the presence of professional wailers by the deceased, *attitadora* in Sardinian (despite this not happening at Nicola's funeral at which women do perform their loud cries but are not hired to do so), does facilitate a reading of this bygone world with that portrayed in ancient Greek literary texts, such as the *Odyssey*.

> and you too, like the rest of us, will make them because they have to be made." (*Ibid.*, p. 123)[46].

Maria's anger continues to grow and at one stage she asks provokingly how Bonaria kills people. Bonaria reproaches that Maria is always too quick in judging others. When the daughter replies that she is not the one to be in a hurry, rather the opposite, Bonaria's answer harks back to Cavarero's discussion of the request for help intrinsically written into the image of the infant:

> "They do happen of themselves," she said with a cheerless smile. "Do you think you were self-generated, Maria? Did you deliver yourself from your mother's belly by your own efforts? Or did you need help from someone else, like all living creatures?" [...] "So others made decisions for you, and will make more decisions when necessary. No-one alive has ever reached the light of day without the help of fathers and mothers at every corner of the road, Maria, and you more than anyone should know that." (*Ibid.*, p. 124)[47]

Similarly, Maria's judgemental stance towards Bonaria, while fuelled by the anger she feels at the recent dénouement, reveals a common attitude identified by Cavarero as a challenge faced by the modern subject who

> imprisoned as it is in its own narcissism, [...] neither exposes itself nor leans out: it aims rather at making itself immune from the other through a gesture of vertical self-foundation that pretends not to need the other's inclination. (Cavarero, 2011b, p. 199-200).

Here we come to three crucial lines in this dialogue when Bonaria affirms: "'I too had a part to play, and I have played it.' 'And what part was that?'

46 "*– Tutte le volte che tornavate di notte... – mormorò. – Te ne avrei parlato a suo tempo, Maria –. Bonaria non provò nemmeno a stemperare il turbamento della figlia. – Quando? Quando me lo avreste detto? Mi avreste portata con voi? Mi avreste chiesto di reggervi lo scialle mentre lo facevate? – la rabbia montava sulle labbra di Maria come schiuma amara. – Quando lo avreste fatto? – Certo non adesso... quano fossi stata pronta... – Pronta! – la parola risuonò nella stanza come un oggetto scagliato per terra. – Per accettare l'idea che voi ammazzate le persone io non sarei mai stata pronta! [...] – Non metterti a dare nomi alle cose che non conosci, Maria Listru. Farai tante scelte nella vita che non ti piacerà fare, e le farai anche tu perché vanno fatte, come tutti.*" (Murgia, 2009, p. 115-116).

47 "*– Accadono da sole... – mormorò, sorridendo senza allegria. – Sei nata tu forse da sola, Maria? Sei uscita con le tue forze dal ventre di tua madre? O non sei nata con l'aiuto di qualcuno, come tutti i vivi? [...] – Altri hanno deciso per te allora, e altri decideranno quando servirà farlo. Non c'è nessun vivo che arrivi al suo giorno senza aver avuto padri e madri a ogni angolo di strada, Maria, e tu dovresti saperlo piú di tutti.*" (Murgia, 2009, p. 116-117).

'The final part. I have been the last mother some people have seen'" (Murgia, 2011a, p. 125)[48]. Needless to say, at this point Maria is in no position to comprehend her elective mother's position and her words. For Maria, the role of the mother cannot possibly encompass the duties performed by the *accabadora*, nor the lies, as she sees Bonaria's secretive rituals that broke the bond of trust, which had lovingly tied her to the old woman.

This fatal rupture brings Maria to the decision to leave her island. With the help of Luciana, her Piedmontese schoolteacher, she leaves Sardinia and her home to move to mainland Italy and relocates to Turin. Here she works as a nanny to the two children of a well-to-do local family. She returns to her island and to her elective mother only three years later, after learning that Bonaria suffered a stroke. When Maria returns to Soreni, the *accabadora*, the woman who eases the sufferers' passing, is in fact the one who lies on a deathbed, and Maria comes home to look after her.

CONCLUSION
On tending to the helpless

When Maria is in Soreni, she is confronted by Bonaria's conditions. The old lady suffered a partial paralysis and can no longer speak. She is also too weak and can only lie in bed but remains aware and alert. After a sojourn at the hospital, Bonaria is sent home with Maria who receives instructions on how to palliate the woman's pain. Many passages in the last two chapters of the novel highlight how Bonaria seems trapped on the threshold between life and death. When Bonaria's pain grows further despite the drugs, "her wide-open eyes searched Maria's face with ravenous desperation" (Murgia, 2011a, p. 161)[49]. Even if silent, Maria recognises the plea of the helpless and is disturbed by it. Now she comes to understand the meaning of Bonaria's words, pronounced

48 "*[...] – Anche io avevo la mia parte da fare e l'ho fatta. – E quale parte era? – L'ultima. Io sono stata l'ultima madre che alcuni hanno visto.*" (Murgia, 2009, p. 117).

49 "*[...] [L]e sue pupille dilatate cercavano il volto di Maria con famelica disperazione.*" (Murgia, 2009, p. 151).

years before on the day Maria confronted her: "Never say: I shall not drink from this water." (*Ibid.*, p. 161)[50].

Tormented by Bonaria's relentless anguishing moans, Maria considers Bonaria's condition from an angle she did not contemplate earlier. Still rejecting the old woman's wordless request, she nevertheless ponders why Bonaria cannot let go of life, a thinking line that brings her to consider old traditional beliefs: "Protection or guilt. At [sic] Soreni these were the only things that could cause a bad death" (*ibid.*, p. 163)[51]. To no avail, she purges Bonaria's room of all holy images, statuettes, trinkets, and amulets, including Bonaria's baptismal necklace still hanging around the old woman's neck. By a process of exclusion, she then muses the option of a potential guilt as the impediment to Bonaria's passing. Despite Bonaria's resistance to the idea, Maria visits her old friend Andría, hoping to induce him to forgive her elective mother.

At the mention of Bonaria's crime, the one perpetrated upon his brother, Andría reacts mocking Maria's 'continental arrogance,' suggesting that the time she has spent in Turin has changed her:

> The continent had done you no good, our Mariedda. You've become so arrogant about other people's sins. Has it never struck you that there may be nothing to forgive? (*Ibid.*, p. 168)[52].

Andría's anger over Nicola's forced demise wore off with the years, leaving him to recast Bonaria's actions as a response to Nicola's request for mercy. Andría later overcomes his distant attitude towards Maria too and visits Bonaria in a symbolic act of blessing meant to ease the old woman's passing. It is after his visit that the daunting thought that had devoured Maria's mind for weeks ensues into a clear decision. With the pillow she finds in her elective mother's bedroom, Maria metamorphoses into the *accabadora*, and in this shape she tends to the helpless Bonaria. As her elective mother warned her, she ends up deciding to drink from the water she swore not to drink from[53]. In the closing lines of the novel,

50 "*Non dire mai: di quest'acqua io non ne bevo.*" (Murgia, 2009, p. 152).

51 "*Protezione o colpa. A Soreni erano questi i soli motivi che facevano penare la morte [...].*"(Murgia, 2009, p. 153).

52 "*Ti ha fatto male il continente, Mariedda nostra. Sei diventata arrogante con i peccati degli altri. Non ti è mai venuto il dubbio che forse non c'è niente da perdonare?*" (Murgia, 2009, p. 157).

53 Aureliana Di Rollo analyses the bond between Maria and Bonaria, ultimately sealed through death, as a rewriting of the "socio-symbolic exclusion of the mother in patriarchal

in a moment that seals their reunion, Maria reveals to Andría that she is here to stay and to do what she knows best how to do: she will be a seamstress, like Bonaria was.

In my analysis I have used the terms 'caring', 'vulnerable', and 'helpless' referring to Cavarero's conceptualisation of maternal inclination as the act of bending over the vulnerable and the helpless in response to their call for help. Bonaria's twofold role of *accabadora* and elective mother is built upon the same premise: I argue that she is framed as a caring figure who tends to the helpless, in its dual manifestation. The first adjective, 'caring', denotes a human being, here a woman, who "look[s] at the condition of being human from the perspective of care." (Cavarero, 2011b, p. 195). The second one, 'vulnerable', is built on the Latin term *vulnus* (injury, wound). Its ultimate form for Cavarero, we know, is the child, in that the vulnerable coincides with the helpless. When Bonaria takes Maria as a soul-child she does so because she recognises in her the vulnerable who is not cared for. Yet, as we have seen, adults can also, in specific circumstances, find themselves in a state of helplessness. This is Bonaria's condition in the final chapters of the novel, after the stroke that plunges her in an agony which knows no effective remedy. In a circular motion, Bonaria pleas her soul-child to incline over her, as she did for Maria when she was younger, thus responding to her silent request for care.

Significantly, the circular trajectory of human life is mirrored by another circular motion, that of Maria's choices: she follows in her elective mother's footstep by returning to her island, becoming a seamstress and, most importantly, transforming into the *accabadora* (for Bonaria at least). In this renewed manifestation, the *accabadora* has significant *exempla* to draw from. Firstly, Bonaria's metamorphosis from Athena into Arachne might have gone amiss in the anger Maria felt at the time, but Andría's act of 'forgiveness' fosters a more nuanced reckoning with these

---

cultures" and grounds her discussion in a theoretical framework drawing from scholars such as Luce Irigaray, Luisa Muraro, Adriana Cavarero, and Julia Kristeva (Aureliana Di Rollo, « The Female Life Secret? Mother, Daughter, and New Family Paradigms in Michela Murgia's Accabadora », *Carte Italiane*, 2019, vol. 12, n° 1, p. 99). Di Rollo convincingly argues that Maria's decision to become an *accabadora* and ease Bonaria into death is in fact an act of recognition of the maternal role. Another interesting element of Di Rollo's discussion, equally relevant and in line with my own reading of Murgia's novel, is the association of death with the mother-daughter dyad, which Di Rollo explicitly links to the ancient Greek tradition through the myth of Demeter and Persephone.

past events. Secondly, sustained by Andría's act of symbolic blessing, his tenderness in kneeling at Bonaria's sickbed to recline his head on her blanket, and his gentle caress on her bony hand, Maria abandons her arrogance and embraces her role[54]. Adoptive mother and adoptive daughter, having both proved their fallibility in their own act of arrogance, are reunited into a shared course, the same empathetic destiny.

Gregoria MANZIN
La Trobe University
Australia

54 Maria's experiences in Turin, which I could not delve into due to practical limitations, certainly play a role in her emotional growth and her ability to finally empathise with Bonaria's position. In fact, continuing with my discussion of the *Odyssey* and the world of Greek epics, Maria's departure echoes the journey of the hero as an allegory for a process leading to maturity and the acquisition of wisdom through peril and hardship. It is also how the gods test the virtues of mortals, while at the same time making them pay their dues for their offences. This part of the novel, I argue, further feeds the parallel with the symbology derived from ancient Greek mythology and literature.

LIST OF REFERENCES

INTRODUCTION

CAMPBELL, Kendall M., BRAXTON, Michaela M., TUMIN, Dmitry, and RODRÍGUEZ, José E., « Reverse Mentoring between Minority Students and Faculty », *Journal of Best Practices in Health Professions Diversity*, 2020, 13, n° 2, p. 184-188.

COSTELLO, Lisa A., « Standing Up and Standing Together: Feminist Teaching and Collaborative Mentoring », *Feminist Teacher*, 2015, vol. 26, n° 1, pp. 1-28.

CURTIN, Nicola, MALLEY, Janet and STEWART, Abigail J., « Mentoring the Next Generation of Faculty: Supporting Academic Career Aspirations Among Doctoral Students », *Research in Higher Education*, 2016, vol. 57, n° 6, p. 714-738.

DUCHÉ, Véronique, JEAY, Madeleine, and TRAN-GERVAT, Yen-Maï, eds, *Maître-disciple: une relation topique*, *Topiques, études satoriennes*, n° 5, 2018. https://www.erudit.org/en/journals/topiques/2018-v4-topiques05785/

FOUNTAIN, Jocelynn and NEWCOMER, Kathryn E., « Developing and Sustaining Effective Faculty Mentoring Programs », *Journal of Public Affairs Education*, 2016, vol. 22, n° 4, p. 483-506.

GASTON GAYLES, Joy and KELLY TURNER, Bridget, « Mentoring for Success across the Academic Spectrum », ed. Lori A. Flores and Jocelyn H. Olcott, *The Academic's Handbook, Fourth Edition. Revised and Expanded*, Durham NC, Duke University Press, p. 232-329.

GROGAN, Paul, EVINER, Valerie, and HOBBIE, Sarah, « Keeping up with the Times: Equity Issue is Now Added to Our Self-Reflection Worksheet for Improving Scientific Mentoring », *Bulletin of the Ecological Society of America* (ESA), 2021, vol. 102, n° 2, p. 1-3.

HOMER, *Odyssey*, 2, 220-221, trans. Thomas Hobbes, Clarendon Editions of Works of Thomas Hobbes: Translations of Homer, Volume XXV, Clarendon Press, 2008.

KEARNEY, Melissa S. and LEVINE, Phillip B., « Role Models, Mentors, and Media Influences », *The Future of Children*, 2020, vol. 30, n° 1, p. 83-106.

KOCIUBIŃSKA, Edyta and NIEDOKOS, Judyta, eds, *Maître(s) et disciple(s)*, *Quêtes littéraires*, n° 9, 2019.

LOUE, Sana and LOFF, Bebe, « Mentoring International Research Ethics Trainees: Identifying Best Practices »,*Journal of Empirical Research on Human Research Ethics: An International Journal*, 2013, vol. 8, n° 5, p. 52-58.

NÉVOT, Aurélie, ed., *De l'un à l'autre. Maîtres et disciples*, Paris, CNRS éditions, 2013.

NOACCO, Cristina, BONNET, Corinne, MAROT, Patrick, *et al.*, eds, *Figures du maître. De l'autorité à l'autonomie*, Rennes, Presses Universitaires de Rennes, coll. « Interférence », 2013.

PHRUKSACHART, Melissa, « On Mentoring Future Faculty of Color », *Feminist Teacher*, 2017, vol. 27, n° 2-3, p. 117-132.

POLIKOFF, Morgan S., DESIMONE, Laura M., PORTER, Andrew C., HOCHBERG, Eric D., « Mentor Policy and the Quality of Mentoring », *The Elementary School Journal*, 2015, vol. 116, n° 1, p. 76-102.

STEINER, George, *Lessons of the Masters*, Cambridge MA, Harvard University Press, 2003.

VAN DAM, L., SMIT, D., WILDSCHUT, B., BRANJE, S. J. T., RHODES, J. E., ASSINK, M., and STAMS, G. J. J. M., « Does Natural Mentoring Matter? A Multilevel Meta-analysis on the Association Between Natural Mentoring and Youth Outcomes », *American Journal of Community Psychology*, 2018, vol. 62, n° 1-2, p. 203-220.

WAQUET, Françoise, *Les enfants de Socrate. Filiation intellectuelle et transmission du savoir* XVIIe-XXIe *siècle*, Paris, Albin Michel, 2008.

FIRST PART
Medieval and Early Modern Mentors

ALBANESE, Ralph, « Molière and the teaching of Frenchness: *Les Femmes savantes* as a case study », *The Cambridge Companion to Molière*, ed. David Bradby and Andrew Calder, New York, Cambridge University Press, 2006, p. 151-163.

ALBERT, June, « Playwright Justin Fleming on Helpmann, Moliere and the joy of theatre », *The Australian*, May 28, 2017. https://www.theaustralian.com.au/arts/review/playwright-justin-fleming-on-helpmann-moliere-and-the-joy-of-theatre/news-story/a9f22b3485a436b8ee6a0f87a3f81f43

BEASLEY, Faith, *Salons, History and the Creation of 17th Century France*, Aldershot, Ashgate Publishing, 2007.

BELLI, Silvio, *Libro del misurar con la uista [...]*, Venice, Domenico de' Nicolini, 1565.

BEMBO, Pietro, *Della historia vinitiana di m. Pietro Bembo card. volgarmente scritta. Libri 12*, Venice, Gualtero Scotto, 1552.

BEMBO, Pietro, *Lettere*, IV vols., Bologna, Commissione per i testi di lingua, 1987-1993.

BEMBO, Pietro, *Petri Bembi De Aetna ad Angelum Chabrielem liber*, Venice, Aldus Manutius, 1495.

BEMBO, Pietro, *Prose di. m. Pietro Bembo nelle quali si ragiona della volgar lingua scritte al cardinale de Medici che poi e stato creato a Sommo Pontefice et detto papa Clemente Settimo diuise in tre libri*, Venice, Giovanni Tacuino, 1525.

BERLINGHIERI, Francesco, *In questo uolume si contengono septe giornate della geographia di Francesco Berlingeri fiorentino allo illustrissimo Federigo duca durbino*, Florence, Niccolò di Lorenzo della Magna, n.d. [published before September 1482].

BESSARION, *Bessarionis cardinalis Sabini & patriarche Constantinopolitani capitula libri primi aduersus calumniatorem Platonis incipiunt feliciter*, Rome, C. Sweynheym & A. Pannartz, 1469.

BIERLAIRE, Franz, *Les Colloques d'Érasme: réforme des études, réforme des mœurs et réforme de l'Eglise au XVIe siècle*, Belles Lettres, 1978.

BLAKE, J., « *The Literati* review: Justin Fleming's Linguistic flair brings comedy up to date », *The Syndey Morning Herald*, June 2, 2016. https://www.smh.com.au/entertainment/theatre/the-literati-review-justin-flemings-linguistic-flair-brings-comedy-up-to-date-20160602-gpac8i.html

BOUCHET, Florence, postface to the translation of the *Wandering Knight* in modern French: Thomas D'Aleran, *Le chevalier errant*, ed. Daniel Chaubet, Moncalieri, Centro interuniversitario di ricerche sul viaggio in Italia, 2001, p. 389-398.

BOUWSMA, William J., « Three Types of Historiography in Post-Renaissance Italy », *History and Theory*, 1965, vol. 4, n° 3, p. 303-314.

BOWEN, William R., « Ficino's Analysis of Musical *Harmonia* », *Ficino and Renaissance Neoplatonism*, ed. Konrad Eisenbichler and Olga Zorzi Pugliese, Ottawa, Dovehouse Editions Canada, 1986, p. 17-27.

BROWN, Alison, « Platonism in Fifteenth-Century Florence and Its Contribution to Early Modern Political Thought », *The Journal of Modern History*, 1986, vol. 58, n° 2 (June), p. 383-413.

CABRINI, Anna Maria, « Le Historiae del Bruni: Risultati e ipotesi di una ricerca sulle fonti », *Leonardo Bruni, Cancelliere della Repubblica di Firenze*, ed. Paolo Viti, Florence, Olschki, 1990, p. 247-319.

CÉARD, Jean, « Marot, traducteur d'Érasme », *Clément Marot, « Prince des poètes françois » 1496-1996*, ed. G. Defaux and M. Simonin, Champion, 1997, p. 107-120.

CICERO, Marcus Tullius and POWELL, J. G. F., *Cicero: Laelius, on Friendship (Laelius De Amicitia), & The Dream of Scipio (Somnium Scipionis)*, Warminster, Aris & Phillips, 1990.

CONTARINI, Gasparo, *De magistratibus & republica Venetorum libri quinque, authore Gaspare Contareno patricio Veneto*, Paris, Michel Vascosan, 1593.

COPENHAVER, Brian P., « Scholastic Philosophy and Renaissance Magic in the *De vita* of Marsilio Ficino », *Renaissance Quarterly*, 1984, vol. 37, n° 4 (Winter), p. 523-554.

CORRIAS, Anna, « Imagination and Memory in Marsilio Ficino's Theory of the Vehicles of the Soul », *The International Journal of the Platonic Tradition*, 2012, vol. 6, p. 81-114.

CORRIGAN, T., « Defining Adaptation », *The Oxford Handbook of Adaptation Studies*, ed. Thomas Leitch, New York, Oxford University Press, 2017, p. 23-35.

COSGROVE, Denis, « Globalism and Tolerance in Early Modern Geography », *Annals of the Association of American Geographers*, 2003, vol. 93, n° 4 (December), p. 852-870.

COSGROVE, Denis, « Mapping New Worlds: Culture and Cartography in Sixteenth-Century Venice », *Imago Mundi*, 1992, vol. 44, p. 65-89.

CRYSTAL, David, *The Fight for English*, Oxford and New York, Oxford University Press, 2006.

DANTE, *The Inferno*, trans. Robert Pinsky, A New Verse Translation, Bilingual Edition, New York, Farrar, Straus and Giroux, 2014.

D'ASCIA, Luca, « Tra Platonismo e Riforma: Curione, Zwingli e Francesco Zorzi », *Bibliothèque d'Humanisme et Renaissance*, 1999, vol. 61, n° 3, p. 673-699.

DAVIES, Jonathan, « Marsilio Ficino: Lecturer at the Studio fiorentino », *Renaissance Quarterly*, 1992, vol. 45, n° 4 (Winter), p. 785-790.

DE JEAN, Jean, « The Salons and Preciosity », *A New History of French Literature*, ed. Dennis Hollier, Cambridge MA, Harvard University Press, 1994, p. 297-302.

DE VIGNEUL-MARVILLE, M. (Argonne), *Mélanges d'histoire de la littérature*, 3 vols (I), Rotterdam, 1702.

DE XEREZ, Francisco, *Verdadera relacion de la conqvista del Perv*, Seville, Bartholome Perez, 1534.

DELLA MIRANDOLA, Giovanni Pico, *On the dignity of man*, Indianapolis, Bobbs-Merrill, 1965.

DI SALUZZO, Tommaso III, *Il Libro del Cavaliere Errante* (BnF ms. fr. 12559), ed. Marco Piccat and Laura Ramello, Boves, Araba Fenice, 2008.

DONATTINI, Massimo, « Giovanni Battista Ramusio e le sue 'Navigationi'. Appunti per una biografia », *Critica Storica*, 1980, vol. *17*, n°1, p. 56-100.

EISENBICHLER, Konrad and ZORZI PUGLIESE, Olga, eds, *Ficino and Renaissance Neoplatonism*, Ottawa, Dovehouse Editions Canada, 1986.

EQUICOLA, Mario, *Libro de natura de amore di Mario Equicola secretario del illustrissimo S. Federico 2. Gonzaga marchese di Mantua*, Venice, Lorenzo Lorio da Portes, 1525.

ERASMUS, *Collected Works of Erasmus. Colloquies*, trans. and annotated by Craig R. Thompson, University of Toronto Press, 1997.

FICINO, Marsilio and NICCOLI, Sandra, *El libro dell'amore*, Florence, L. S. Olschki, 1987.

FICINO, Marsilio and SEARS, Jayne, *Commentary on Plato's Symposium on love*, Dallas Texas, Spring Publications, 1985.

FINN, Thomas, « Bookish Women: Female Readers and Women's Education in Molière », *Women in French Studies*, Special Issue, 2012, p. 36-55

FRACASTORO, Girolamo, *Hieronymi Fracastorii Homocentrica Eiusdem De causis criticorum dierum per ea quae in nobis sunt*, Venice, Bartolomeo Zanetti, 1538.

FRACASTORO, Girolamo, *Operum Hieronymi Fracastorii Veronensis quaedam fragmenta ex codice autographo nunc primum vulgata*, Padova, Josephus Cominus, 1738.

GAINES, James, ed., *The Molière Encyclopedia*, Westport, Greenwood, 2002.

GIORGIO, Francesco, *Francisci Georgii Veneti [...] De harmonia mundi totius cantica tria*, Venice, Bernard de Vitalibus, 1525.

GUEUDEVILLE, Nicolas, *Les Colloques d'Érasme. Ouvrage très interessant par la diversité des Sujets, par l'Enjoûment, et pour l'Utilité Morale. Avec des Notes et des Figures très ingénieuses*, 6 Tomes, Leiden, Vander Aa, 1720.

HANKINS, James, « The Myth of the Platonic Academy of Florence », *Renaissance Quarterly*, 1991, vol. 44, n° 3 (Autumn), p. 429-475.

HEADLEY, John M., « The Sixteenth-Century Venetian Celebration of the Earth's Total Habitability: The Issue of the Fully Habitable World for Renaissance Europe », *Journal of World History*, 1997, vol. 8, n°1 (Spring), p. 1-27.

HORODOWICH, Liz, « Armchair Travelers and the Venetian Discovery of the New World », *The Sixteenth Century Journal*, 2005, vol. 36, n° 4 (Winter), p. 1039-1062.

HUCHON, Mireille, *Histoire de la langue française*, Paris, Livre de Poche, 2002.

HUTCHEON, Linda, *A Theory of Adaptation*, New York, Routledge, 2006.

IANZITI, Gary, « Bruni on Writing History », *Renaissance Quarterly*, 1998, vol. 51, n° 2 (Summer), p. 367-391.

JEAY, Madeleine, « L'emprise du narrateur: la manipulation des discours et des récits enchâssés dans le *Chevalier errant* de Thomas de Saluces », in *Nouvelles en mouvement* (XIIIe-XVIe *siècles*) / *Novelle in movimento* (XIII-XVI *secolo*), ed. Margherita Lecco and Jean-Claude Mühlethaler, Alessandria, Edizioni dell'Orso, 2021, p. 81-108, http://journals.openedition.org/memini/1842.

JEAY, Madeleine, « Le narrateur "désinvolte" ou l'écriture en trompe l'œil », *Memini, Construire le sens par la disparité: lectures croisées du* Chevalier Errant *de Thomas de Saluces (1394-1396)*, 2021.

JOHNS, Adrian, « Identity, Practice, and Trust in Early Modern Natural Philosophy », *The Historical Journal*, 1999, vol. 42, n° 4 (December), p. 1125-1145.

JURDJEVIC, Mark, « Prophets and Politicians: Marsilio Ficino, Savonarola and the Valori Family », *Past & Present*, 2004, vol. 183 (May), p. 41-77.

KRISTELLER, Paul Oskar, « Florentine Platonism and Its Relations with Humanism and Scholasticism », *Church History*, 1939, vol. 8, n° 3 (September), p. 201-211.

KRISTELLER, Paul Oskar, *The Philosophy of Marsilio Ficino*, trans. Conant Virginia, Gloucester MA, Peter Smith, 1964.

LABOWSKY, Carlotta, *Bessarion's library and the Biblioteca Marciana: six early inventories*, Sussidi eruditi 31, Rome, Edizioni di storia e letteratura, 1979.

LEONICO TOMEO, Nicolò, *Nicolai Leonici Thomaei Dialogi nunc primum in lucem editi quorum nomina proxima pagina habentur*, Venice, Gregorii de Gregoriis, 1524.

LLEWELLYN, Jonathan, « An interview with Australian Playwright, Justin Fleming about *The Literati* », *Riverside*, December 2015, https://riversideparramatta.com.au/2015/12/an-interview-with-australian-playwright-justin-fleming-about-the-literati/

LONG, Elizabeth, *Book Clubs: Women and the Uses of Reading in Everyday Life*, Chicago, University of Chicago Press, 2003.

MAIER-KAPOOR, Cecilia, « Marsilio Ficino's Medico-philosophical Language of Love: its Genesis and its Reception amongst Sixteenth-century Italian Love Treatises », Johns Hopkins University, 2010.

MANN, Margaret, « Louis de Berquin traducteur d'Érasme », *Revue du Seizième siècle*, tome 18, 1931, p. 308-323.

MAROT, Clément, *Œuvres complètes*, critical edition C. A. Mayer, Slatkine, 1980.

MAUROLICO, Francesco, *Cosmographia Francisci Maurolyci Messanensis Siculi, in tres dialogos distincta: in quibus de forma, situ, numeroque tam coelorum quam elementorum, alijsque rebus ad astronomica rudimenta spectantibus satis disseritur*, Venice, Luca Antonio, 1543.

MCGINN, Bernard, « Cosmic and Sexual Love in Renaissance Thought: Reflections on Marsilio Ficino, Giovanni Pico della Mirandola, and Leone

Ebreo », *The Devil, Heresy, and Witchcraft in the Middle Ages: essays in Honor of Jeffrey B. Russell*, ed. Alberto Ferreiro and Jeffrey Burton Russell, *Cultures, beliefs, and traditions*, Leiden/Boston, Brill, 1998, p. 191-209.

MÉNAGER, Daniel, « Ironie », Érasme, *Éloge de la folie*, ed. Claude Blum, André Godin, Jean-Claude Margolin, Daniel Ménager, Laffont, 1992, p. CXLI-CXLII.

MOLIÈRE Jean-Baptiste Poquelin dit, *La Critique de l'École des Femmes*, 1663.

MOLIÈRE, Jean-Baptiste Poquelin dit, *Le Bourgeois gentilhomme*, *Les Femmes savantes* and *Le Malade imaginaire*, ed. Georges Couton, Paris, Gallimard, 1973.

MONFASANI, John, « Aristotelians, Platonists, and the Missing Ockhamists: Philosophical Liberty in Pre-Reformation Italy », *Renaissance Quarterly*, 1993, vol. 46, n° 2 (Summer), p. 247-276.

MOSCONI, Nicole, « La Femme Savante: Figure de l'idéologie sexiste dans l'histoire de l'éducation », *Revue française de Pédagogie*, 1990, vol. 93, p. 27-39.

MÜHLETHALER, Jean-Claude, « Entre la France et l'Italie: Jules César chez Thomas III de Saluces et Eustache Deschamps », *Cahiers de recherches médiévales et humanistes*, 14 spécial: *La Figure de Jules César au Moyen Âge et à la Renaissance (II)*, 2007, p. 191-205.

MUIR, Edward, « The 2001 Josephine Waters Bennett Lecture: The Idea of Community in Renaissance Italy », *Renaissance Quarterly*, 2002, vol. 55, n°1 (Spring), p. 1-18.

ORTELIUS, Abraham, *Theatrum orbis terrarium*, Antuerpiae: auctoris ære & cura impressum absolutumque apud Ægid. Coppenium Diesth, 1570.

PALLOTTA, Augustus, « The New World and Italian Readers of the Spanish Historie in the Sixteenth Century », *Italica*, 1992, vol. 69, n°3 (Autumn), p. 345-358.

PELLEGRINI, Angelo, « Libertà e dignità dell'uomo in Giovanni Pico della Mirandola: con particolare riferimento alla 'Oratio de Hominis Dignitate' », *Revista Portuguesa de Filosofia*, 2002, vol. 58, n° 4 *Filosofia No Renascimento: Autores e Problemas* (October-December), p. 801-828.

PERRAULT, Charles, *Les Hommes Illustres*, Paris, Antoine Dezallier, 1696.

PERUZZI, Enrico, *La nave di Ermete: la cosmologia di Girolamo Fracastoro*, Florence, Olschki, 1995.

PLATO, *Hapanta ta tou Platonos. Omnia Platonis opera*, Venice, Aldi et Andreae Soceri, 1513.

RAMUSIO, Giovanni Battista, *Navigazioni e viaggi*, ed. Marica Milanesi, VI vols, Turin, Einaudi, 1978-1988.

RAMUSIO, Giovanni Battista, *Primo volume delle nauigationi et viaggi nel qual si contiene la descrittione dell'Africa, et del paese del Prete Ianni, con uarii uiaggi, ... Li nomi de gli auttori, et le nauigationi, et i viaggi piu particolarmente si mostrano nel foglio seguente*, Venice, heredi di Lucantonio Giunti, 1550.

RICCI, Giovanni, *Ossessione turca: in una retrovia cristiana dell'Europa moderna*, Bologna, Il mulino, 2002.

ROBB, Nesca Adeline, *Neoplatonism of the Italian Renaissance*, New York, Octagon Books, 1968.

ROMANINI, Fabio, *Se fussero più ordinate, e meglio scritte...: Giovanni Battista Ramusio correttore ed editore delle Navigationi et viaggi*, Frontiere della modernità, Rome, Viella, 2007.

ROSENBERG, Aubrey, *Nicolas Gueudeville and his work (1562-172?)*. Martinus Nijhoff Publishers, 1982.

ROSS, J. B., « Gasparo Contarini and His Friends », *Studies in the Renaissance*, 1970, vol. 17, p. 192-232.

RUSCELLI, Girolamo, *Le imprese illustri con espositioni, et discorsi del s.or Ieronimo Ruscelli. [...] Con la giunta di altre imprese tutto riordinato et corretto*, In Venetia: presso a Francesco de' Franceschi, senese, 1580.

SHAW, David, « *Les Femmes savantes* and Feminism », *Journal of European Studies*, 1984, vol. 14, p. 24-38

SPERONI, Sperone, *I dialogi di Messer Speron Sperone*, Venice, in casa de' figliuoli di Aldo, 1542.

Statuts et Règlements de L'Académie Française, XXIV, 1635.

STONE PETERS, Julie, *Theatre of the book, 1480-1880: print, text, and performance in Europe*, Oxford, Oxford University Press, 2003.

TARTAGLIA, Niccolò, *La prima [-sesta] parte del general trattato di numeri, et misure [...]*. VI vols, Venice, Curtio Troiano de i Nauò, 1556-1560.

TRACHSLER, Richard, *Disjointures – Conjointures. Étude sur l'interférence des matières narratives dans la littérature française du Moyen Âge*, Tübingen and Basel, A. Francke, 2000.

TRECCANI, *Dizionario Biografico degli Italiani*, 2008, vol. 72.

VENERI, Toni, « Giovanni Battista Ramusio, molto più di uno spettatore. Le quinte delle 'Navigationi et viaggi' », *Italica*, 2012, vol. 89, n° 2 (Summer), p. 162-201.

VINCENT, Jean-Luc, « Vie littéraire: Théâtre et société à l'époque Classique », *Molière, Les Précieuses Ridicules*, Paris, Gallimard, 1998, p. 67-76.

WIEGAND, Wayne A. and DAVIS, Donald G., *Encyclopedia of Library History*, New York, Routledge, 2013.

WINTROUB, Michael, « Taking a Bow in the Theater of Things », *Isis*, 2010, vol. 101, n° 4 (December), p. 779-793.

YORAN, Hanan, « Florentine Civic Humanism and the Emergence of Modern Ideology », *History and Theory*, 2007, vol. 46, n° 3 (October), p. 326-344.

ZAERCHER-KECK, Véronique, « Traduire pour éclaircir: Marot, Aneau et quelques colloques d'Érasme », *Esculape et Dionysos. Mélanges en l'honneur de Jean Céard*, Droz, 2008, p. 1111-1123.

SECOND PART
Mentoring in the 19th and 20th century

ALEXANDER, F. Matthias, *Constructive Conscious Control of the Individual*, ed. Jean M.O. Fischer, 8th ed., London, Mouritz, 2004.

ALEXANDER, F. Matthias, *The Universal Constant in Living*, 3rd ed., London, Chaterson, 1986.

BARSTOW, Marjorie L., « A Letter from Marjorie Barstow », *The Alexander Review*, 1986, vol. 1, n° 1, p. 42-45.

BARSTOW, Marjorie L., *Correspondence with Frank Pierce Jones*, The F. M. Alexander-Frank Pierce Jones Archive, Dimon Institute, New York.

BENOIS, Alexandre, *Reminiscences of the Russian Ballet*, trans. Mary Britnieva, London, Putnam, 1945.

BUCKLE, Richard, *Diaghilev*, London, Weidenfeld, 1993.

CANTÙ, Cesare, *Storia della letteratura italiana*, Florence, Sansoni, 1865.

CARDUCCI, Giosue, *Ceneri e faville. Serie terza e ultima, 1877-1901*. Bologna, Nicola Zanichelli Editore, 1923.

CARRINGTON, Walter, *A Time to Remember: A Personal Diary of Teaching the F.M. Alexander Technique in 1946*, London, Sheldrake Press, 1996.

CHANCE, Jeremy, « Editorial », *Direction Journal*, 1991, vol. 1, n° 8, p. 4.

CIAMPINI, Raffaele, *Vita di Niccolò Tommaseo*, Florence, Sansoni Editore, 1945.

COHEN, Joshua, « Giacomo Leopardi's *Zibaldone*: On the first full translation of a masterwork by Giacomo Leopardi (1798–1837) », *Harper's Magazines*, November 27, 2013. https://harpers.org/blog/2013/11/giacomo-leopardis-zibaldone/

COLE, Amanda, *Marjorie Barstow and the Alexander Technique: Critical Thinking in Performing Arts Pedagogy*, Palgrave Macmillan, 2022.

CONABLE, Barbara, ed., (Festschrift) *Marjorie Barstow: Her Teaching and Training. A 90th Birthday Offering*, Columbus, Andover Road Press, 1989.

CONABLE, William, (ed. by Barbara Conable), « Marjorie Barstow », (Festschrift)

Marjorie Barstow: Her Teaching and Training. A 90th Birthday Offering, Columbus, Andover Road Press, 1989, p. 21-26.

CROCE, Benedetto, *Poesia e non poesia*, Bari, G. Laterza & Figli, 1955.

DENSMORE, Curtis C., « Sappho and the 'Leucadian Leap' », *American Journal of Archaeology*, 1920, vol. 24, n° 2. (April-June), p. 146-150.

DEWEY, John, *Context and Thought*, ed. Jo Ann Boydston, *The Later Works, Volume 6: 1931-1932*, Carbondale, Southern Illinois University Press, 2008, p. 3-21.

DEWEY, John, *Democracy and Education*, Radford VA, Wilder publications, 2008.

EKSTEINS, Modris, *Rites of Spring: The Great War and the Birth of the Modern Age*, Reading, Black Swan, 1990.

FERTMAN, Bruce, (ed. by Barbara Conable), « Earn it Anew », (Festschrift) *Marjorie Barstow: Her Teaching and Training. A 90th Birthday Offering*, Columbus, Andover Road Press, 1989, p. 66-68.

FOKINE, Michel, *Fokine: Memoirs of a Ballet Master*, ed. Anatole Chujoy, trans. Vitale Fokine, London, Constable and Company, 1961.

FREDERICK, Michael, (ed. by Barbara Conable), « Interview with Michael Frederick by Barbara and Bill Conable », (Festschrift) *Marjorie Barstow: Her Teaching and Training. A 90th Birthday Offering*, Columbus, Andover Road Press, 1989, p. 46-53.

GIORDANI, Pietro, *Epistolario. Edito per Antonio Gussalli*, vol. V. Milan, Borroni e Scotti, 1854.

GIORDANI, Pietro, *Opere*, vol. II, Florence, Felice Le Monnier, 1846.

GIORDANI, Pietro, *Pagine scelte*, ed. Giovanni Forlini, Piacenza, Cassa di Risparmio di Piacenza, 1984.

GIORDANI, Pietro, *Scritti*, Milan, Istituto Editoriale Italiano, 1930.

GRIGORIEV, Sergei, *The Diaghilev Ballet 1909-1929*, Hampshire, Dance Books, 2009.

GUARRACINO, Vincenzo, *Guida alla lettura di Leopardi*, Milan, Mondadori, 1992.

GUGLIELMI, Guido, *L'infinito terreno. Saggio su Leopardi*, Lecce, Piero Manni, 2010.

ITALIA, Paola, *Il metodo di Leopardi*, Rome, Carocci editore, 2016.

JONES, Frank Pierce, *Body Awareness in Action: A Study of the Alexander Technique. Introduction by J. McVicker Hunt*, New York NY, Schocken Books, 1979.

JONES, Frank Pierce, *Correspondence with John Dewey*, The F. M. Alexander-Frank Pierce Jones Archive, Dimon Institute, New York.

KARSAVINA, Tamara, *Theatre Street: The Reminiscences of Tamara Karsavina*, London, Columbus Books, 1948.

LEOPARDI, Giacomo, *Canti*, ed. Niccolò Gallo and Cesare Gàrboli, Turin, Einaudi, 1962.

LEOPARDI, Giacomo, *Canti*, ed. Franco Fortini, trans. Paul Lawton, Dublin, UCD Foundation for Italian Studies, 1996.

LEOPARDI, Giacomo, *Epistolario di Giacomo Leopardi. Nuova edizione ampliata con lettere dei corrispondenti e con note illustrative*, ed. Francesco Moroncini, vol. I (1810-1819), Florence, Felice Le Monnier, 1934.

LEOPARDI, Giacomo, *Epistolario di Giacomo Leopardi. Nuova edizione ampliata con lettere dei corrispondenti e con note illustrative*, ed. Francesco Moroncini, vol. VI (1830-1837), Florence, Felice Le Monnier, 1940.

LEOPARDI, Giacomo, *Opere*, ed. Mario Fubini, Turin, UTET, 1977.

LEOPARDI, Giacomo, *Operette morali. Essays and Dialogues*, trans. Giovanni Cecchetti, Berkeley, Los Angeles, London, University of California Press, 1982.

LEOPARDI, Giacomo, *Prose e poesie*, ed. Rolando Damiani and Mario Andrea Rigoni, vol. II, Milan, Mondadori, 2003.

LEOPARDI, Giacomo, *The Canti, With a Selection of His Prose*, trans. J.C. Nichols, Manchester, Carcanet, 1994.

LEOPARDI, Giacomo, *Tutti gli scritti inediti, rari e editi 1809-1810*, ed. Maria Corti, Milan, Bompiani, 1972.

LEOPARDI, Giacomo, *Zibaldone di pensieri*, 2 vols, ed. Giuseppe Pacella, Turin, Einaudi, 1991.

LEOPARDI, Giacomo, *Zibaldone*, ed. Michael Caesar and Franco D'Intino, trans. Kathleen Baldwin, Richard Dixon, David Gibbons, Ann Goldstein, Gerard Slowey, Martin Thom, Pamela Williams, New York, Farrar, Straus and Giroux, 2013.

LUPORINI, Cesare, *Leopardi progressivo*, Florence, Sansoni, 1947.

MACDONALD, Patrick, « In the 80's: Alexander Technique Lesson by Patrick Macdonald – Part 1 of 2 », YouTube, Edo Svorai and Noam Renen (Hadassim2), 1980s, https://www.youtube.com/watch?v=QPPxyHCWPu8

MADDEN, Cathy, *Teaching the Alexander Technique: Active Pathways to Integrative Practice*, London and Philadelphia, Singing Dragon, 2018, Kindle e-book edition.

MAISEL, Edward, ed., *The Resurrection of the Body: The Essential Writings of F. Matthias Alexander. Introduction by Edward Maisel*, Boston, Shambala, 1986.

MALAGOLI, Luigi, *Il grande Leopardi*, Florence, "La Nuova Italia" Editrice, 1937.

MARTONE, Mario, *Il giovane favoloso*, Rai Cinema, 2014.

MASSINE, Leonide, *My Life in Ballet*, ed. Phyllis Hartnoll and Robert Rubens, London, Macmillan, St. Martin's Press, 1968.

MOORE, Lucy, *Nijinsky*, London, Profile Books, 2013.

MURRAY, Alexander D., « The Role of Women in the Growth of the Alexander Community », *American Society of Alexander Teachers* AGM, 2002.

NICHOLLS, Mark, « Brush up Your Shakespeare: Performance Anxieties in *Shakespeare in Love* », *Journal of Film and Video*, 2003, vol. 54, n°4, p. 3-15.

NICHOLLS, Mark, « Scythian Rhapsody: *The Red Shoes*, *Le Sacre du Printemps*, Creative Youth and Regenerative Rage », *Quarterly Review of Film and Video*, 2017, vol. 34, n° 5, p. 425-444.

NICHOLLS, Mark, « Crazy Days at Culver City: Reflections on Hollywood Histories and the Popular Documentary », *Ormond Papers*, vol. 14, 1997, p. 175-182.

NICHOLLS, Mark, « *The French Lieutenant's Woman*: Charles Smithson beyond the Pale and Mike beyond the Run », *Lost Objects of Desire: The Performances of Jeremy Irons*, Oxford, Berghahn Books, 2012, p. 82-101.

NIJINKSY, Vaslav, *The Diaries of Vaslav Nijinsky*, ed. Romola Nijinsky, Berkeley and Los Angeles, University of California Press, 1968.

NIJINSKA, Bronislava, *Bronislava Nijinska: Early Memoirs*, trans. and ed. Irena Nijinska & Jean Rawlinson, Durham and London, Duke University Press, 1992.

OTTIWELL, Frank, (ed. by Barbara Conable), « Let Us Now Praise Marjorie Barstow », (Festschrift) *Marjorie Barstow: Her Teaching and Training. A 90th Birthday Offering*, Columbus, Andover Road Press, 1989, p. 1-4.

PANZINI, Alfredo, *Casa Leopardi*, Florence, Le Monnier, 1948.

PANZINI, Alfredo, *Il libro dei morti, Romanzi d'ambo i sessi*, Milan, Mondadori, 1941.

RAMBERT, Marie, *Quicksilver*, London, Macmillan, 1972.

RICKOVER, Robert, « The Teaching of Frank Pierce Jones: Robert Rickover Talks to Tommy Thompson », *Body Learning*, 2014, MP3 file.

SCHEIJEN, Sjeng, *Diaghilev: A Life*, trans. Jane Hedley-Prole and S.J. Leinbach, Oxford & New York, Oxford University Press, 2009.

STILLWELL, Janet O'Brien, « Marjorie Barstow: An Interview », *Somatics*, 1981, n°3 (Autumn/Winter), p. 15-21.

STRAVINSKY, Igor and CRAFT, Robert, *Memories and Commentaries*, London, Faber and Faber, 2002.

STRAVINSKY, Igor, *Chronicle of My Life*, London, V. Gollancz, 1936.

TASKER, Irene, *Connecting Links*, London, The Sheldrake Press, 1978.

TOMMASEO, Niccolò, and BELLINI, Bernardo, 1865, *Dizionario della lingua italiana*, vol. XV, Milan, Rizzoli, 1865.

TONELLI, Luigi, *Leopardi*, Milan, Dall'Oglio Editore, 1987.

VOSSLER, Karl, *Leopardi*, Munich, Musarion Verlag, 1923.

WEED, Donald L., « Our Debt to A.R. Alexander », *Interactive Teaching Method: A revolutionary approach to the Alexander Technique*, 2012, web, 19 July 2012.

WHITE, Eric Walter, *Stravinsky: The Composer and His Music*, London and Berkeley, 1966.

WHITTAKER, Erika, « The FM Alexander Memorial Lecture », delivered before the Society of Teachers of the Alexander Technique (STAT) on October 26, pamphlet, 1985.

WYNHAUSEN, John, (ed. by Barbara Conable), « From Portland to Lincoln: From Chiropractic College to the World of the Alexander Technique », (Festschrift) *Marjorie Barstow: Her Teaching and Training. A 90th Birthday Offering*, Columbus, Andover Road Press, 1989, p. 132-133.

THIRD PART
Modern and Contemporary Novels

ARENDT, Hannah, *Responsibility and Judgement*, New York, Schocken Books, 2003.

ARENDT, Hannah, *The Human Condition*, Chicago, The University of Chicago Press, 1958.

BAJANI, Andrea, MURGIA, Michela, NORI, Paolo, and VASTA, Giorgio, *Presente*, Turin, Einaudi, 2012.

BEER, Rosia, « Gesturing to an empty theatre? Author, Text and Audience in the Fiction of Fatou Diome and Aïssatou Diamanka-Besland », *RELIEF*, vol. 5, n° 5, 2011, p. 44-61.

CAVARERO, Adriana, *Horrorism: Naming Contemporary Violence*, trans. William McCuaig, New York, Columbia University Press, 2011a.

CAVARERO, Adriana, « Inclining the subject: Ethics, alterity and natality », ed. Jane Elliott and Derek Attridge, *Theory after 'Theory'*, London and New York, Routledge, 2011b.

CAVARERO, Adriana, *Inclinations: A Critique of Rectitude*, trans. Amanda Minervini and Adam Sitze, Stanford CA, Stanford University Press, 2016.

DIOME, Fatou, *The Belly of the Atlantic*, trans. Lulu Norman and Ros Schwartz, London, Serpent's Tail, 2006.

DIOME, Fatou, *Celles qui attendent*, Paris, Flammarion, 2010.

DIOME, Fatou, *Impossible de grandir*, Paris, Flammarion, 2013.

DIOME, Fatou, *Inassouvies nos vies*, Paris, Flammarion, 2008.

DIOME, Fatou, *Le Ventre de l'Atlantique*, Paris, Éditions Anne Carrière, 2003.

DI ROLLO, Aureliana, « The Female Life Secret? Mother, Daughter, and New Family Paradigms in Michela Murgia's *Accabadora* », *Carte Italiane*, 2019, vol. 12, n° 1, p. 89-104.

FÉNELON, François de Salignac de la Mothe, *Les Aventures de Télémaque suivies des aventures d'Aritonoüs*, La Haye, Adrian Metjens, 1701 [1699].

HASKELL, Rosemary, « Plotting *Migritude*: Variations of the *Bildungsroman* in Fatou Diome's *Les ventre de l'Atlantique* and *Celles qui attendant* », *South Atlantic Review*, 2016, vol. 81, n° 1, p. 136-156.

HOMER, *Odyssey*, trans. James Huddleston, The Chicago Homer.

IPPOLITO, Christophe, « *Trois contes, Trois femmes puissantes*: le puzzle et l'oiseau migrateur », ed. Daniel Bengsch and Cornelia Ruhe, *Une femme puissante: l'œuvre de Marie Ndiaye*, Amsterdam and New York, Rodopi, 2013, p. 305-318.

JORDAN, Shirley, « La puissance de Khady Demba », ed. Daniel Bengsch and Cornelia Ruhe, *Une femme puissante: l'œuvre de Marie NDiaye*, Amsterdam and New York, Rodopi, 2013, p. 263-283

KLOTZ, Judith B., « Meetings with Mentor », *Science, New Series*, 2005, vol. 308, p. 1112.

LAZAR, David, « On Mentorship », *The Ohio Review*, 1994, n° 51, p. 25-33.

LUZZATTO, Lia, and POMPAS, Renata, *Il significato dei colori nelle civiltà antiche*, Milan, Rusconi, 1988.

MOBERG, Dennis J. and VELASQUEZ, Manuel, « The Ethics of Mentoring », *Business Ethics Quarterly*, 2004, vol. 14, n° 1, p. 95-122.

MURGIA, Michela, *Accabadora*, Turin, Einaudi, 2009.

MURGIA, Michela, *Accabadora*, trans. Silvester Mazzarella, Berkeley CA, Counterpoint, 2011a.

MURGIA, Michela, *Ave Mary. E la chiesa inventò la donna*, Turin, Einaudi, 2011b.

MURGIA, Michela, *Chirú*, Turin, Einaudi, 2015.

MURGIA, Michela, « Elena », *Le nuove Eroidi*, Milan, Harper Collins, 2019a.

MURGIA, Michela, *Futuro interiore*, Turin, Einaudi, 2016.

MURGIA, Michela, *Istruzioni per diventare fascisti*, Turin, Einaudi, 2018a.

MURGIA, Michela, *Il mondo deve sapere. Romanzo tragicomico di una telefonista precaria*, Milan, ISBN, 2006.

MURGIA, Michela, « L'aragosta », *Piciocas. Storie di ex bambine dell'isola che c'è*, Bologna and Naples, Caracò, 2012a.

MURGIA, Michela, « L'eredità », *Sei per la Sardegna*, Turin, Einaudi, 2014.

MURGIA, Michela, *L'incontro*, Turin, Einaudi, 2012b.

MURGIA, Michela, *L'inferno è una buona memoria. Visioni da* Le nebbie di Avalon *di Marion Zimmer Bradley*, Venice, Marsilio, 2018b.

MURGIA, Michela and LIPPERINI, Loredana, *L'ho uccisa perché l'amavo (falso!)*, Rome and Bari, Laterza, 2013.

MURGIA, Michela, *Noi siamo tempesta*, Milan, Salani, 2019b.

MURGIA, Michela, *Persone che devi conoscere*, Padua, Messaggero di Sant'Antonio, 2018c.

MURGIA, Michela, *Stai Zitta, e altre nove frasi che non vogliamo sentire più*, Turin, Einaudi, 2021.

MURGIA, Michela, *Viaggio in Sardegna. Undici percorsi nell'isola che non si vede*, Turin, Einaudi, 2008.

NDIAYE, Marie, *Mon cœur à l'étroit*, Paris, Gallimard, 2007.

NDIAYE, Marie, *Trois femmes puissantes*, Paris, Gallimard, 2009.

NNAEMEKA, Obioma, « Introduction: Imag(in)ing Knowledge, Power, and Subversion in the Margins », *The Politics of (M)othering: Womanhood, Identity, and Resistance in African Literature*, London, Routledge, p. 1-26.

OVID, *Metamorphoses. Volume I: Books 1-8*, trans. Frank Justus Miller, Loeb Classical Library, Cambridge MA, Harvard University Press, 1916.

SHERINGHAM, Michael, « Mon cœur à l'étroit: espace et éthique », ed. Andrew Asibong and Shirley Jordan, *Marie NDiaye: l'étrangeté à l'œuvre*, Villeneuve d'Ascq, Presses Universitaires du Septentrion, 2009, p. 182.

STABILE, Alberto, *I buoni maestri: chi sono, che cosa ci hanno insegnato sedici protagonisti della nostra cultura*, Milan, Mondadori, 1988.

TOIVANEN, Anna-Leena, « Retour au local: *Celles qui attendent* et l'engagement diasporique de Fatou Diome », *RELIEF*, 2011, n° 1, p. 62-77.

WAQUET, Françoise, *Les enfants de Socrate. Filiation intellectuelle et transmission du savoir* XVIIe-XXIe *siècle*, Paris, Albin Michel, 2008.

INDEX NOMINUM

ABSTRACTS

Charles FORSDICK, "Preface" / Charles FORSDICK, « Préface »

Mentoring is part of the set of professional responsibilities expected across a wide variety of sectors in our contemporary world. Literary texts can assist in the interrogation of mentoring as a practice and can also illuminate its intersections with other relational and developmental practices. The core activities of the Humanities – reading literature, analysing history, studying human interactions in their multiple forms – are themselves an invaluable form of mentorship in their own right.

Le mentorat fait aujourd'hui partie des missions professionnelles attendues dans de très nombreux secteurs. Les textes littéraires peuvent aider à questionner la pratique du mentorat et mettre en lumière ses intersections avec d'autres pratiques relationnelles et de développement. Les activités de base des sciences humaines – lire la littérature, analyser l'histoire, étudier les interactions humaines sous leurs multiples formes – constituent en elles-mêmes une forme inestimable de mentorat à part entière.

Véronique DUCHÉ and Gregoria MANZIN, "Mentoring partnerships as avenues for growth" / Véronique DUCHÉ et Gregoria MANZIN, « Les partenariats entre mentor et mentoré. Des possibilités de croissance »

Mentoring is nowadays recognised as a key factor of professional and personal growth. This volume encompasses reflections on the relationships forged by mentors and mentees in history, literature, and the performing arts. These essays examine the various shapes of mentoring, its power dynamics, as well as the reciprocal process of change the mentoring relationship can instigate. They do so by unveiling the blurred margins of mentoring, together with the benefits and risks this relationship entails.

Le mentorat est aujourd'hui reconnu comme un facteur clé de croissance professionnelle et personnelle. Cet ouvrage comprend des réflexions sur les relations nouées entre mentors et mentorés dans les domaines de l'histoire, de la littérature et des arts de la scène. Ces essais examinent les diverses formes de mentorat, sa dynamique de pouvoir, ainsi que le processus réciproque de changement que peut susciter la relation de mentorat. Pour ce faire, ils lèvent le voile sur les contours flous du mentorat, ainsi que sur les avantages et les risques intrinsèques à cette relation.

Madeleine JEAY, "A wandering knight's quest for a mentor. Thomas de Saluces's *Le Chevalier errant*" / Madeleine JEAY, « Un chevalier errant en quête de mentor. *Le Chevalier errant* de Thomas de Saluces »

Thomas de Saluces's *Chevalier Errant* is an allegorical prosimeter written in captivity in Turin between 1394 and 1396. It takes the form of a learning journey told in the first person, punctuated by successive encounters that the Knight makes during an itinerary that leads him from the Court of Love to the domain of Fortune, then to a meeting with Knowledge. In this allegorical autobiography, personal allusions are intertwined with didactic aims, political actuality with literary reminiscences.

Le *Chevalier Errant* de Thomas de Saluces est un prosimètre allégorique écrit pendant son emprisonnement à Turin entre 1394 et 1396. Il prend la forme d'un roman d'apprentissage raconté à la première personne, rythmé par les rencontres que fait le Chevalier au cours d'un itinéraire qui le mène de la Cour de l'Amour au domaine de la Fortune, puis à une rencontre avec la Connaissance. Dans cette autobiographie allégorique, les allusions personnelles s'entremêlent avec les objectifs didactiques, et l'actualité politique est intercalée de ressouvenances littéraires.

Anne-Laure METZGER-RAMBACH, "The Relationship between Mentor and Mentee in the French versions of Erasmus' *Colloquia*. Clément Marot and Nicolas Gueudeville" / Anne-Laure METZGER-RAMBACH, « La relation entre mentor et mentoré dans les versions françaises des *Collquia* d'Érasme. Clément Marot et Nicolas Gueudeville »

The *Colloquies* delighted and fascinated its translators because of its sophisticated approach to the shaping of the mind. Marot and Gueudeville retain this turn of mind in their intent never to convey too clear a teaching. The mentor's role is not exclusively the author's, as some characters assume this responsibility. The assessment of meaning becomes all the more challenging as the identity of the mentor keeps shifting, while the essence of mentorship tends to self-annihilation.

Les *Colloquia* ont ravi et fasciné ses traducteurs en raison de la finesse avec laquelle Érasme aborde la formation de l'esprit. Marot et Gueudeville ont conservé cette manière de concevoir l'enseignement dans leur intention de ne jamais dispenser un enseignement excessivement clair. Le rôle du mentor n'est pas exclusivement celui de l'auteur puisque certains personnages assument cette responsabilité. L'évaluation du sens devient d'autant plus difficile que l'identité du mentor ne cesse de changer, tandis que l'essence du mentorat a tendance à s'auto-détruire.

Gianluca CAPUTO, "Staging past and present mentors on the global theatre of printed knowledge. Neoplatonic cosmography and ethos in Giovan Battista Ramusio's *Navigations and Travels* (1550-1559)" / Gianluca CAPUTO, « Mettre en scène des mentors d'hier et d'aujourd'hui dans le paysage mondial du savoir imprimé. cosmographie néoplatonicienne et éthos dans les *Navigations et voyages* de Giovan Battista Ramusio (1550-1559) »

The present study seeks to explore the diplomacy of culture that Giovan Battista Ramusio employed in his collection of European travel literature entitled *Navigations and Travels*. The Secretary of the Republic of Venice exhibited his Neoplatonic interpretation of European discoveries in commendations and dedications, evaluating the literary and visual means through which the gratitude ascribed to intellectual filiations contributed to create a new, global relation between mentors and mentees.

La présente étude vise à étudier la diplomatie de la culture que Giovan Battista Ramusio a déployée dans sa collection d'écrits sur ses voyages européens intitulée *Navigations et Voyages*. Le secrétaire de la République de Venise a exposé son interprétation néoplatonicienne des découvertes européennes dans des recommandations et dédicaces, analysant ainsi les moyens littéraires et visuels par lesquels la gratitude attribuée aux filiations intellectuelles a contribué à créer une nouvelle relation globale entre mentors et mentorés.

Kirk WEEDEN, "Molière as a mentor. *Literati* and learned ladies in contemporary Australia" / Kirk WEEDEN, « Molière comme mentor. *Literati* et les femmes savantes dans l'Australie contemporaine »

This paper explores the adaptation of *Les Femmes savantes* as *The Literati*, by Australian playwright Justin Fleming. With a focus on mentoring, it uses Fleming's work as a vehicle to explore the transferal and transformation of the ideas of literary 'greats' to and by contemporary playwrights – between mentor and mentee across time and space. It outlines how Fleming successfully though problematically maintains Molière's irreverent tone and disdain for apparent cultural upstarts for a 21st century Australian audience.

Cet article étudie l'adaptation des *Femmes savantes* dans la pièce *The Literati*, par le dramaturge australien Justin Fleming. En mettant l'accent sur le mentorat, il se sert du travail de Fleming pour explorer le transfert et la transformation des idées des « grands » auteurs, vers et par les dramaturges contemporains, c'est-à-dire entre mentors et mentorés à travers le temps et l'espace. Il décrit comment Fleming conserve avec succès le ton irrévérencieux et le dédain de Molière pour les parvenus culturels, pour un public australien du XXIe siècle.

Luigi GUSSAGO, "'I never was, and never will be [...] anyone's master'. Pietro Giordani and the Fabulous Young Man" / Luigi GUSSAGO, « "Je n'ai jamais été et ne serai jamais [...] le maître de qui que ce soit". Pietro Giordani et le Jeune Homme Fabuleux »

This essay explores Leopardi's personal and intellectual connection with Giordani. Hailed by Giordani as the restorer of Italy's past dignity, the young poet joins his mentor in the battle against the Northern European romantic vogue; a rebellion which leads to Leopardi's very personal translation of romantic ideals. By analysing poems and other sources, we demonstrate how Giordani's classicist lesson, far from being forgotten, re-emerges in the fragmented style of Leopardi's last anti-idylls.

Cet essai se penche sur le lien personnel et intellectuel de Leopardi avec Giordani. Salué par Giordani, qui lui attribue d'avoir rendu sa dignité à l'Italie, le jeune poète Leopardi rejoint son mentor dans la bataille contre le courant romantique nord-européen; cette rébellion conduit à la traduction très personnelle de Leopardi des idéaux romantiques. En analysant des poèmes et d'autres sources, nous démontrons que l'enseignement classique de Giordani, loin d'être oublié, ressurgit dans le style fragmenté des dernières anti-idylles de Leopardi.

Mark NICHOLLS, "Private passions and company priority. The love and work story of Sergei Diaghilev and Vaslav Nijinsky" / Mark NICHOLLS, « Passions privées et priorité à la compagnie. Histoire d'amour et collaboration entre Sergei Diaghilev et Vaslav Nijinsky »

This essay presents a creative practice history of the relationship between the fine art curator and opera/ballet impresario Sergei Diaghilev and his most famous dancer, Vaslav Nijinsky, in the context of mentoring partnership. Through close-readings of primary accounts, Herbert Ross' fictional film, *Nijinsky*, and Emile Ardolino's screen version of the ballet *Petrushka*, I look at what this mythic story tells about key relationships as commonly occur within the creative and performing arts.

Cet essai présente l'histoire, faite de pratique créative, de la relation entre le commissaire des beaux-arts et imprésario d'opéra/ballet Sergei Diaghilev et son danseur le plus célèbre, Vaslav Nijinsky, dans le contexte d'une relation de mentorat. À travers des lectures approfondies de récits de première main; du long-métrage de fiction d'Herbert Ross, Nijinsky; ainsi que de la version télévisée du ballet Petrouchka réalisée par Émile Ardolino, j'étudie cette histoire mythique et ce qu'elle nous dit des relations clés qui se nouent couramment dans les arts de la scène et arts créatifs.

Amanda COLE, "Constellation mentorship" / Amanda COLE, « Mentorat-constellation »

This chapter examines the mentorship of Marjorie Barstow, the first American teacher of the F.M. Alexander Technique (AT), a method of improving awareness of one's underlying coordination in activity. The factors that led to Barstow's own, very particular, model of teaching are many. I call her training a 'constellation-mentorship' and show how, in turn, she mentored the most influential American writer on the technique, Frank Pierce Jones, and supported the first American research into the AT.

Ce chapitre étudie les activités de mentorat de Marjorie Barstow, la première enseignante américaine de la technique F.M. Alexander, une méthode permettant à une personne de mieux prendre conscience de sa coordination sous-jacente au cours d'une activité. Les facteurs qui ont conduit au modèle d'enseignement très particulier de Barstow sont nombreux. Je qualifie ses enseignements de « mentorat-constellation » et je montre comment, à son tour, elle a mentoré l'écrivain américain Frank Pierce Jones, le plus influent dans le domaine de la Technique, et a soutenu la première étude américaine sur la « Technique Alexander ».

Pauline EATON, "Mentoring subversions. An exploration of success and failure in two mentoring relationships in Marie NDiaye's *Mon cœur à l'étroit* and *Trois femmes puissantes*" / Pauline EATON, « Les subversions du mentorat: un examen du succès et de l'échec de deux relations de mentorat dans *Mon cœur à l'étroit* et *Trois femmes puissantes* de Marie NDiaye »

Mentoring in the corporate or academic world is informed by an ethical code to which mentor and mentee subscribe. This essay explores two fictional mentoring relationships, which, judged in terms of the mentee's increase in self-awareness, are successful. Yet their ethical foundation, read against good practice in non-fictional mentoring, is dubious in many respects. These fictional relationships invite us to question the motivations that lie at the base of real-world mentoring relationships.

Le mentorat dans le monde de l'entreprise ou de l'université est encadré par un code éthique auquel souscrivent mentors et mentorés. Cet essai étudie deux relations de mentorat fictives qui, à en juger par la plus grande conscience de soi acquise par le mentoré, semblent avoir réussi. Pourtant, leur fondement éthique, qui va à l'encontre des bonnes pratiques dans le mentorat non fictif, est douteux à bien des égards. Ces relations fictives nous invitent à questionner les motivations qui sous-tendent les relations de mentorat dans le monde réel.

Charlotte MACKAY, "Informal female mentorship in Fatou Diome's *Celles qui attendant*" / Charlotte MACKAY, « Mentorat féminin informel dans *Celles qui attendent* de Fatou Diome »

This chapter explores informal female mentorship in Fatou Diome's 2010 novel *Celles qui attendent* (*Women Who Wait*). The novel's protagonists attempt to better their circumstances by developing their own codes of female mentorship in a context far removed from orthodox mentoring settings. Informal mentor-mentee partnerships between friends and family members ultimately redefine intellectual and emotional growth whilst underscoring the important role that context plays in mentorship expression.

Ce chapitre étudie le mentorat féminin informel dans le roman *Celles qui attendent* de Fatou Diome paru en 2010. Les protagonistes du roman tentent d'améliorer leur situation en élaborant leurs propres codes de mentorat féminin, dans un contexte très éloigné des cadres de mentorat orthodoxes. Les partenariats informels mentor-mentoré entre amis et membres de la famille redéfinissent finalement la croissance intellectuelle et émotionnelle, tout en soulignant le rôle important que joue le contexte dans l'expression du mentorat.

Gregoria MANZIN, "The ethics of care in a traditional rural society: Adopting a soul-child in Michela Murgia's Sardinian novel *Accabadora* (2009)" / Gregoria MANZIN, « L'éthique du soin dans une société rurale traditionnelle: l'adoption d'une fille d'âme dans le roman sarde *Accabadora* de Michela Murgia (2009) »

Michela Murgia's *Accabadora* focuses on the relationship between Bonaria and Maria, the female protagonists. Bonaria takes on Maria as a soul-child when the girl is six years old. The novel focuses on the theme of 'the mother' in its two symbolic manifestations embodied by Bonaria, elective (adoptive) mother and angel of mercy to the dying. While reading Bonaria as a new Mentor/Athena (*Odyssey*), I unravel the dynamics of this relationship with the help of Adriana Cavarero's ethics of care.

Accabadora de Michela Murgia traite de la relation entre les protagonistes féminines Bonaria et Maria. Bonaria adopte Maria comme sa fille d'âme quand la fillette a six ans. Le roman se concentre sur le thème de « la Mère » dans ses deux manifestations symboliques incarnées par Bonaria, mère de choix (adoptive) et ange de la miséricorde pour les mourants. En interprétant le personnage de Bonaria comme un nouveau Mentor/Athéna (*l'Odyssée*), je démêle la dynamique de cette relation vue par le prisme de « l'éthique du soin » d'Adriana Cavarero.

TABLE DES MATIÈRES

SECOND PART

MENTORING IN THE 19TH AND 20TH CENTURY

THIRD PART

MENTORS IN CONTEMPORARY NOVELS

Achevé d'imprimer par Corlet,
Condé-en-Normandie (Calvados),
en Juin 2022
N° d'impression : 176570 - dépôt légal : Juin 2022
Imprimé en France